TOURIST TRAP

Other books in the Virgin True Crime series

TOURIST TRAP

When Holiday Turns to Nightmare

Patrick Blackden

First published in 2003 by

Virgin Books
Thames Wharf Studios
Rainville Road
London W6 9HA

ISBN 0 7535 0845 1

Typesetting by TW Typesetting, Plymouth, Devon

Printed and bound by Mackays of Chatham PLC

CONTENTS

ACKNOWLEDGMENTS

Many thanks for all those who shared stories with me, particularly W. Lee, Joel Quenby, Chris McBride, the editors of Farang Online (www.farangonline.com) and the Khao San Road website (www.khaosanroad.com), and everyone I've met on my travels. Thanks also to the staff at the British Library, to Random House for permission to quote from *Platform*, and to my editor Kerri Sharp, without whom . . . A very special thanks is reserved for Simon Whitechapel and Simon Fowler for indispensable information and feedback. And finally, thanks to my family for their continued support.

If you would like to comment on any of the issues raised in this book, or if you have stories related to those told here, please contact me, either by writing to me c/o Virgin Books, or by emailing me at pblackden@hotmail.com

INTRODUCTION

Picture this. You're a long way from home: let's say India. Perhaps you're taking a year off after leaving school. A gap year – it's what almost everyone else does nowadays. Travel broadens the mind. You've been in India for a couple of weeks now. At first you were a little overwhelmed – the smells, the colours, the sounds, the poverty – but now you're starting to take it in your stride. You love travelling on Indian trains – that's the way to see the real country. You've sat on the top of a carriage, drinking sweet chai from clay mugs that are thrown away after one use, the ochre shards littering the embankment. You've seen an entire village lined up by the railway at dawn, brushing their teeth. Today you're inside a carriage; you've decided to treat yourself a little, pay a bit more for a first-class ticket. Luxury is still relatively cheap here, and you need a reward after the hassle of queuing to buy your ticket.

You're sharing the carriage with a well-to-do Indian businessman. It's a long journey and, at midday, when you start to feel hungry, your new companion pours scorn on the wares of the pakora and samosa vendors who run alongside the train as it slows to a crawl. He insists that you eat with him instead. You're flattered, and feel that this will be an authentic, real experience, a world away from the mediated, glossy brochure holiday of the package tourist. Excited, and grateful, you begin to eat.

You wake up to a blinding headache. You feel queasy and groggy. It's often disorientating waking up in a foreign country, but this time you know something's seriously wrong. It looks like you're in a cell. An Indian prison cell. You call for the guard and begin to piece your life back together. You've been out cold for 48 hours. All of your belongings have gone – rucksack, wallet, passport. You attacked the policeman who tried to wake you up at the train's destination;

this is why you're in a cell. You work out later on that your food was probably spiked with datura – few other substances would have had the same impact – and vow never to accept food from a stranger again.

Doesn't sound too bad? How about this? Let's say you're a young Western man in a bar in Rio de Janeiro, coming to the end of your holiday. You've had a good time; you're even feeling a little smug, thinking about how your tan and tales of conquest will go down with the boys at home. A beautiful girl sidles up to you and sits on the next stool along. It's so perfect it's almost tacky. You buy her a drink and start talking. She seems receptive, smiling and nodding in all the right places. When she asks if you have a girlfriend at home you smile and lie. Her English is good but not perfect, which only adds to the appeal.

You go to the Gents to preen and prepare yourself for the rest of the evening. When you return the girl has bought you another drink. You're impressed, and when she suggests going back to hers a little later you can't believe your luck. It never works this way at home. You're starting to feel a little unsteady, though. You try very hard to stay on top of the situation – you can handle your drink. She mustn't think you're weak. But by the time you arrive at her apartment block you're leaning on her for support. Should be the other way around. Funny thing is, it doesn't seem to bother her. By the time you're in her room, sex is the last thing on your mind. Now she seems like an angel, letting you lie down on the bed, taking your shoes off. Bliss.

Waking up with a jolt doesn't do it justice. It's more like your every nerve is wired to a klaxon, as though you've stubbed your entire body. You're in a bath. It's filled almost to the brim with water, the surface covered with ice cubes. If it wasn't for these you might think you were burning. Your skin has gone blue. To one side you can see a note, and you will your arm to pick it up. It tells you not to get out of the bath. Both of your kidneys have been removed. You need to call the hospital – the number is written on the bottom of the note – and tell them what has happened. The realisation hits you like a brick wall.

Still not impressed? Just another urban myth? At least you're not dead. One last scenario. You don't really like big culture shocks, and nor do you get a kick out of putting yourself in dangerous situations. Goa's probably the only place you'd go to in India. Africa's out of the question: too many diseases and animals that want to eat you. But you've been travelling before, in Thailand and across southern Europe. This time you're in Australia. It's big but it's a safe country where they speak your language. Still, there's almost too little adventure here; even the backpackers are following the tour-bus itinerary. You want to work outside for a while, do some fruit-picking, somewhere like Childers in Queensland.

People have told you that hitching here is great, the best way to get around and meet people. You decide to give it a go. But your first day's a disaster – you spend six hours sitting by the side of the road, reading a paperback and leaping up every time you hear something coming. You're covered in dust and choked by exhaust fumes and just about ready to give up, when someone stops. You're delighted – a comfortable ride in a 4WD. The driver's fairly talkative at first, so you tell him about where you've been and where you're going. Then his questions become a little more intrusive: Does anyone know where you are? Is anyone expecting you at your destination? You blurt out the truth – nobody knows where you are – before you have time to think it through. The driver falls silent.

When he next speaks his tone has changed. Where before he was affable and open, he is now surly and belligerent. You don't like the way the conversation's going, either. Your driver's a racist, and venting his rage doesn't seem to help him much. You don't want to look at him directly for fear you might catch his eye, but his face has darkened and you can see flecks of spittle on his lower lip. You've been non-committal in your replies so far; you vehemently disagree with what he's been saying, but something tells you it's a bad idea to argue with him, and in any case he's given you a lift. Beggars can't be choosers.

He falls silent again, which should be a relief, but it isn't. The situation's starting to take on a nightmarish aspect. After a while he pulls over, muttering about getting something from the back. You don't know what to do. Should you get out? Run? But you're in the middle of nowhere, your rucksack's in the back and you don't have any food or water. Even if you could get away from him you wouldn't be able to survive for long in the bush. The thought seems absurd – you think of survival programmes you've seen on TV, US militias, Ray Mears, and can barely suppress a giggle. The whole thing's ridiculous: of course nothing's going to happen to you. But now he's back, and he's holding a couple of lengths of dirty rope. It takes a few seconds to register that he's telling you this is a robbery. But you don't have much to steal: you're a backpacker who's trying to save money by hitch-hiking. He ignores your protestations and ties you up. It's only then that you catch a glimpse into the open bag at his feet. You can see flashes of short blades and the dull reflection of gunmetal. There's something larger in there too. You can see a wide hilt – a double-hander – and a scabbard disappearing into the darkness. But why would he be carrying a sword?

Every year hundreds of millions of wide-eyed tourists embark on the adventure of a lifetime. From English girls fresh out of public school and tittering their way across Asia to New York bankers taking a sabbatical to walk around Tierra del Fuego, tourists seek an escape from the daily round, a break from the rigours of work or study.

But tourism is not without its own rigours, its own dangers. Most holidaymakers will come back with nothing worse than a touch of sunburn and an enduring hangover. Some will fall victim to theft, having their rucksacks stolen or being relieved of camera and wallet at knifepoint. A few will fall terribly ill, jaundiced and raving in a foreign hospital bed, or watching in fascinated horror as worms crawl under their skin. And some will never make it home at all, their minds fried by bad drugs or their bodies washed up on a beach, throats sliced from ear to ear for a handful of dollars.

Such tragic ends are not met only in the developing world. Some of the most heavily publicised tourist crimes of the last decade have occurred in the USA and Australia – safe countries, where people 'like us' live. The slaughter of a string of European tourists in Florida during the mid-1990s, or the recent murder of Caroline Stuttle, a British backpacker thrown to her death from an Australian bridge early in 2002, following other tourist murders in a country generally considered an easy travelling option, have made us realise that nowhere is safe.

There are many reasons why tourists become the victims of crime. They often carry large amounts of cash and valuables – such as cameras – with a high resale value. They are instantly recognisable as ready sources of income, marking themselves out by language, behaviour and appearance. They follow recognisable patterns of movement – around hotels, transport hubs and amusement centres – and can be ambushed easily; and they don't know their way around, often frequenting dangerous places unwittingly.

Some, overwhelmed by the glamour and excitement of being in a foreign country, will take risks they wouldn't take at home, following strangers down alleyways, trusting other tourists when they shouldn't and flirting with danger by buying drugs or visiting prostitutes. And crimes against tourists are rarely punished: most holidaymakers are only in the host country for a short time and are unlikely to follow any legal process against an assailant who has been caught if it involves returning to the country to attend a trial.

Tourists do not belong to the local community and may therefore be seen as justifiable targets for crime. It may be thought that they can afford to be robbed, that they are insured, that the thief needs the money more, or perhaps that the tourist's flagrantly non-essential use of income and brash behaviour deserve to be punished. Coming from an alien culture, tourists are depersonalised, representing richness and privilege in the eyes of many locals; some may even be attacked as a form of protest against the inequitable distribution of tourism proceeds, much of which will often return to multinational corporations rather than filtering down to local inhabitants.

And some attacks may stem from a resentment over the detrimental effects of tourism. What is sold to the tourist as paradise is somebody else's home. Traditional ways of life vanish quickly when tourist development moves in, and where a local may have been a farmer he will now be obliged either to sell his land cheaply or have it taken from him because of his imprecise property rights. Unless he can craft souvenirs, or take a job as a taxi driver or hotel porter, he is now unemployed. If he stays, he can watch in horror as the environment is degraded by hotel building and speculative land development, the scarce water resources redistributed to the highest bidder, and his people reduced to penury and prostitution. Amazement at the behaviour of the foreign visitors turns to resentment as the tourists are blamed for this new servility, this brash colonisation of paradise; their apparently endless leisure and wealth, their lack of respect for local custom and religious belief, all mark them out as the enemy.

Tourism, even within developed countries, breeds crime. For every obsequious waiter and diligent chambermaid attending to guests at the latest luxury beachfront hotel there is a hustler and a prostitute, a mugger and a vagrant, all keen for their slice of the tourist pie. Many are attracted to an area for precisely the same reason as tourists – the promise of sun, sex, sand and endless leisure. The marketing of a tourist enclave as a hedonist's paradise often has damaging consequences – Australia's Gold Coast has been described as the country's rape capital, in a development linked to the imagery of bikini-clad women and the promotion of their easy availability used by the local tourist industry to sell the area.

Tourist growth leads to social upheaval, as itinerant workers flock to an area seeking jobs, which not all of them will find, and some, their goals frustrated, will turn to crime. Others will be drawn from the outset by the promise of easy criminal pickings, and it is not long before organised crime follows the pickpockets and hustlers.

And it's easy to forget that tourists are not just victims of crime but often criminals themselves. The growth of entertainment industries based on pubs and nightclubs in tourist areas leads in turn to an increase in antisocial or criminal behaviour – drunkenness, drug use, punch-ups, robbery and rape. Some tourists, in no hurry to go home, will stop at nothing to make more money, often hustling their own countrymen or spiking tourists' drinks before robbing them blind. Sometimes the worst dangers come when you least expect them.

Tourism is big business. It is the world's largest peacetime industry and provides many of the world's developing nations with their principal source of foreign income. Despite recent setbacks to the industry through incidents such as the terrorist attacks of 11 September 2001 or the Bali bomb of October 2002, it looks set to grow even larger, with long-term trends such as the liberalisation of international airspace, an increase in global wealth, cheaper flights and the growing use of the Internet as a travel tool all contributing towards its expansion. In 2001 there were 693 million tourist arrivals between nations and the World Tourism Organisation predicts that this will grow to over one billion by 2010.

It should come as no surprise, then, that most countries seek to play down fears of serious tourist crime. Local tourist industries will often mention incidents of low-level tourist crime, in order to persuade tourists to use officially sanctioned guides and to pay for activities they might otherwise indulge in for free – maintaining low levels of fear to keep tourists in their place – but serious tourist crime goes underreported, with tourist boards characteristically at pains to point out that their countries are friendly and safe. The damage that can be done by the press, which has no such qualms about reporting tourist crime and indeed finds something uniquely compelling in the trajectory of the holiday gone horribly wrong, is easy to see from the cases of Florida, where the numbers of European visitors dropped by 20 per cent in 1994 following well-publicised tourist crimes in 1993, and South Africa, still struggling to play down its reputation as the rape capital of the world. And the popularity in the news media of the story of tourist terror has bled from fact into fiction – the story of the lone female hitch-hiker kidnapped and sexually assaulted is one of the leitmotifs of the late twentieth-century crime-writing genre.

But if the tourist industry is keen to have us ignore contemporary crime, some sectors of it feed off its historical counterpart. There are a number of companies in London that offer 'Jack the Ripper' walking tours; Waco, Texas, reported a massive upsurge in visitor numbers after the Branch Davidian complex fire; prisons such as Tasmania's Port Arthur, latterly the site of a killing spree that left 35 tourists dead, or San Francisco's Alcatraz are among the most popular regional tourist attractions; and at Waxahachie, Texas, Bonnie and Clyde bank hold-ups are re-enacted during the town's annual Gingerbread Festival. The examples of such 'dark tourism' are legion, from JFK assassination re-enactments – be your own man on the grassy knoll – to the tourist industries surrounding Dachau and Auschwitz. For some sectors of tourism, corpses sell tickets.

Tourist Trap does not deal with natural disasters, accidental death, attacks by wild animals, or illnesses, which together account for the vast majority of tourist deaths. Neither does it deal with explicitly political crime – kidnappings, bombings and terrorist murders; the subject is too large to be contained in a chapter of this book, and I hope to cover it in a forthcoming work. What it does cover is tourist crime, with tourists as both the victims and perpetrators of crime. To make this book an exhaustive account of such crimes would reduce some chapters to a series of lists; it has seemed more worthwhile to cover a few of the more interesting cases in detail.

The first two chapters introduce the key ways in which tourism relates to crime. 'If You Go Down to the Woods Today' deals with the way danger has become a yardstick of authenticity for many tourists, and goes on to explore what happens when people take things too far on holiday, with a special focus on air rage, football hooliganism and the Jerusalem Syndrome. The second chapter, 'The Naked Eye', deals with the way tourists objectify the people and places they visit, and are objectified in turn. These two-way assumptions are at the root of a wide spectrum of crimes, from tourist rape to gem scams. They have also led to the most appallingly grisly murders, as we will see in the next two chapters.

'Concrete Blonde' tells the story of Lucie Blackman, a young British woman working as a hostess in Tokyo, whose body was found dismembered in a cave after a disastrous encounter with a rapist obsessed with the West. 'Never Get Out of the Bus' explores the events leading up to the lynching of a Japanese tourist and the driver of his bus by Guatemalans convinced their victims were child-abducting Satanists.

'Staying On' looks at the lives of tourists who don't come home – because they have vanished voluntarily, joined cults, been jailed or simply disappeared – and the nightmare quests of those who search for them. 'The Hippie Hippie Shakedown' explores the life and crimes of Charles Sobhraj, who terrorised the Asian tourist trail during the 1970s and is suspected of having stolen the lives and identities of fifteen young tourists. This chapter is the longest in the book and is in many ways its centre, as Sobhraj's story encompasses many of the themes dealt with elsewhere – the lure of toying with one's identity abroad, the dangers of trusting fellow tourists or expatriates, and the apathy of certain countries' police forces in solving tourist murders.

'Road Kill' deals with a more recent serial murderer that preyed on tourists, Australian Ivan Milat, and the contemporary killers who keep his monstrous legacy alive. Many of these cases were dealt with in more detail in my last book, *Danger Down Under*. Finally, in 'Love You Long Time', we explore the sleazy world of sex tourism – its roots, its enduring appeal and the people and circumstances that keep it alive.

1. IF YOU GO DOWN TO THE WOODS TODAY

TRAVEL AND THE CULTURE OF DANGER

Bad things happen when you travel. Or so, at least, we are led to believe by the myths and fairy tales that are the corner-stones of Western culture. Hansel and Gretel wander into the woods to ease the financial burden on their parents, only to be met by a cannibal hag intent on making them her next meal. Theseus, before slaying the Minotaur, first has to deal with Procrustes, a murderer who waylays passing travellers with false hospitality, offering them a bed for the night. His bed fits everyone – if they are too short they are stretched to fit, if too tall their head or feet are lopped off. Virtually all mythical journeys – from Classical to Arthurian – feature dangers that must be met and overcome.

These journeys represent rites of passage, transitional phases during which the mettle of man must be tested in the fire of danger. The association of travel with rites of passage is not only mythical: cultures from Africa to Aboriginal Australia have traditionally sent young men on journeys during which they are forced to endure hardships and brave dangers before being accepted back into the tribe.

This sense of travel as dangerous initiation belongs also to the industrialised West. To travel has always been hard, dangerous work: the English word 'travel' derives from the French 'travail', or work, which in turn originates in the Latin noun 'tripalium', a three-staked instrument used for torture.

Modern tourism can be said to have its roots in the 'Grand Tour' embarked upon by privileged young European men in the seventeenth and eighteenth centuries. Part of the appeal of this Continental circuit would have been the frisson of excitement at the thought of meeting foreign highwaymen, or the risk of some unusual natural disaster, the survival of which would provide material to keep drawing-room company amused for years to come on their return. A contemporary English-Italian phrasebook prepared the disaster-struck voyager with the correct translation of 'Good heavens! The postilion has been struck by lightning!'

Many travellers were waylaid by *banditti*, and Germany was particularly dangerous in the seventeenth century: cannibalism was said to be rife in Brandenburg county, and one traveller, riding to Hamburg in 1652, counted in one day 34 piles of faggots marking spots where previous travellers had been murdered. Eighteenth-century English society was scandalised by stories of three Englishmen killed just outside Paris in 1723, after having been watched changing money in Calais, and the 1725 murder of William Yates, a young traveller on his way to Italy. Ironically, many injuries suffered by the English abroad were said to be brought about by their own behaviour, as they would routinely ride around drunk, abusing and whipping locals in a xenophobic frenzy.

Today, danger is a key element in the marketing of certain forms of tourism. An advertisement placed in several guidebooks by the online portal Yahoo! for their travel service, Yahoo! Travel, encapsulates the appeal well. In it, a young man, sweating heavily and with an expression somewhere between terror and exhilaration – complete adrenaline-fuelled focus – is being chased by a charging bull. The slogan reads: 'Will you have enough stories to tell your grandchildren?' The target audience is clear: young, independent budget travellers, the kind who make a clear distinction between the journeys *they* undertake and package tourism, feeling the latter describes a sanitised, more mediated and altogether safer experience. Even the modern traveller myths, contemporary tales of initiation through hardship such as *Deliverance* or *The Beach*, place themselves firmly in the independent travel camp. In student circles and in the language of the seasoned tourist, 'going travelling' carries far more kudos than 'taking a holiday'.

Package tourism began with the departure of the first Thomas Cook-conducted excursion train from Leicester Station in the English Midlands on 5 July 1841. One of the appeals to the rapidly growing middle class of newly industrialised Britain of such organised holidays was that they could enjoy the romance of travel without the hardships; few missed the hassles of foreign exchange and the dangers of swarthy thuggery. Yet, while package tourism was hugely successful during the twentieth century, the watchword today is authenticity, a concept many regard as antithetical to the Eurostyle high-rise hotels of package holidays.

And authenticity means danger, or at least a flirtation with it. Adventure tourism is one of the fastest-growing sectors in this rapidly expanding industry. From whitewater rafting to shark feeding, the adrenaline rush brought on by a generally illusory brush with danger is enough to convince most office workers that their true calling lies elsewhere; like Indiana Jones, they might at any point disappear from a staid job to adventure their way around the globe. Tales of danger encountered – and conquered – lead to an informal hierarchy among the tourist community, each hardy voyager jockeying for position to tell the best tale of the worst illness, the most hair-raising robbery, the narrowest escape from a crocodile's jaws.

Even part of the attraction of stately safari tours is the proximity to man-eaters such as the lion or crocodile; somehow the fact that the herbivorous hippopotamus accounts for more human deaths in Africa each year than either of these great carnivores has still not made the animal a major tourist attraction. And here lies something of a paradox: it is only the illusion of danger, danger with a secure safety net, that is usually sought. Nobody goes on disease tours, hoping to expose themselves to dengue or ebola, although it should be noted that some tourists do visit war zones, thereby deliberately exposing themselves to high levels of personal risk.

Robert Young Pelton's book *The World's Most Dangerous Places*, its associated website (www.comebackalive.com) and television series have made an institution of this kind of tourism, although Pelton's aim seems less excitement for its own sake than a mistrust of the mass media and a desire to see what places are like for himself. Pelton and his fans, however, represent the exception to the rule; most tourists like their danger with the exit clearly marked.

Even so, as the authentic whiff of danger sought by many tourists drives them further and further from the beaten track, so too do the dangers increase. Blithely treating the developing world as an arena in which they can 'find' themselves, armed with nothing but an expensive camera and a fat money-belt, many tourists are shocked by the hostility and envy they encounter – hostility and envy that can easily translate into action. The hostility often derives from an irony of which many tourists are unaware: while well-heeled Western tourists seek to escape their pampered bubble through such adventures, to prove their mettle away from their cosseted environments, many locals will be engaged in a literal struggle to survive.

A brush with danger is far from the only motivating force in contemporary tourism. Holidays have long acted as an escape valve for the pressures of modern life – a way to 'let off steam'. The Industrial Revolution created both a need for and an ability to buy periods of escape for the purposes of relaxation. It was recognised that people could not work all the time: to be productive, they needed holidays, an escape from daily drudgery. Such escape was often validated as educational – a cross-cultural experience – and sold as yet another product to be consumed, to take its place in defining the consumer among his peers. Advances in jet travel technology, an increasingly wealthy Western middle class and the active pursuit of tourism as a development strategy for poor countries all came together to form tourism as it is today.

Yet while lip service has been paid to the idea of holidays being 'educational', the function actually served is usually quite different. Holidays provide a socially sanctioned form of escape through fantasy, play and sexual adventure, which contains the impulses towards these as potential forms of rebellion and sells them back to the consumer. Mild taboo-busting is encouraged, whether through eating and drinking to excess, keeping odd hours, wearing garish clothes, enjoying a range of sexual partners or spending money recklessly – all are part of the holiday experience, particularly in the popular sun, sex and sangria resorts such as Tenerife or Ibiza. Crossing boundaries is the tourist's occupation, and a flirtation with behavioural extremes is here the norm.

Tourist enclaves tend to be zones in which the usual rules do not apply. They are often sited in areas which act as boundaries, such as the beach, which straddles land and sea, tame civilisation and wild nature. Such enclaves seem constructed to facilitate a sense of play and abandon, spatially isolated both from home and from the culture of the country in which they are situated. Once a tourist is taken away from his familiar environment of work, family and friends, and placed in an area both unregulated and unfamiliar, unusual behaviour may follow, especially if the alcohol is cheap. The following tourist was interviewed about the behaviour of his fellow holidaymakers in 1995 in Ibiza:

> They're abroad, they're a bit wrecked and they start doing things that they wouldn't normally do at home. Mainly because your own inhibitions go down. You're in an area which may or may not be new to you, but the [people] are. Because people don't know you, you certainly feel as if you can behave in a way that is different to the way you normally behave. And I know quite a few people that are at home and they're normally really uptight and prudish, you see them on holiday and you think 'that's not the same person'. I mean they're screaming round the bars, they're throwing drugs down their necks like they're going out of fashion, they're drinking like fish, they're sleeping with anything they can get.

That this appeal is key to modern tourism has long been realised by those involved in running holiday resorts. Gerard Blitz, who founded Club Med, had worked previously with concentration camp victims, and came to believe that a diet of sport and sun could help them and others forget the horrors of war – that these sun-bleached retreats could provide a return to prelapsarian innocence, to an Edenic state of perpetual play. The director of development for Club Med in 1996 explained that: 'The Club's philosophy is that everyone must find a way to be free in his mind, in his body and with other people. One can be natural and do things one would not want to do in everyday life.' In this sense it doesn't really matter which physical destination a tourist goes to on holiday: the key is to find somewhere that fits his psychological make-up and needs.

Some commentators have described modern holidays as the last vestiges of carnival culture, which was suppressed through the seventeenth and eighteenth centuries as being dangerously anarchic. Carnival would involve traditional social and political hierarchies being turned on their head, normal codes of conduct and dress abandoned, and disorderly, improvident and excessive behaviour encouraged. But if holidays stand for today's carnival, they represent it in a far reduced form – a holiday is seen as a reward for diligent work, rather than a prospective lifestyle in itself, and is hardly likely to disrupt the established order. When people begin to question the necessity for work at all, and embrace the holiday lifestyle as a permanent situation – as did some of the hippies – they are regarded as extremely dangerous to the status quo.

While mild taboo-breaking is encouraged on holiday, some people take it too far. The behaviour of British tourists on the Balearic and Canary Islands, among other resort-rich areas, has led to a string of arrests for rape, assault and drunk and disorderly behaviour; lacking any commitment to the future of the area, attachments to local people or conventional involvement in the rules, informal social control of tourists is virtually impossible.

The phenomenon has classical antecedents in the myth of Dionysus and his followers, the Maenads. The Greek god, otherwise known as Bacchus, was raised by nymphs and satyrs, and spread the knowledge of wine everywhere he went in a celebration of hedonism. His followers would travel from city to country to worship the god during his festivals, leaving responsibility behind to embrace the freedom and spontaneity of a deliverance from social prohibition and order. But they would always return to the world of rationality and order after the festivals, aware that Dionysian ecstasy could not be productive unless it interacted with the world of Apollonian law and order – much as holidays are a temporary escape from the mundanity of working life.

Dionysian cults were notorious for tearing animals limb from limb at the height of the festivities; this frenzied dismemberment recalled the mythical death of King Pentheus, rent apart by Maenads when he persisted in persecuting the god. While most tourists won't take their Bacchanalian revelry this far, some stop not far short of it, as we'll see in the following notorious instances.

I'M MILLY, FLY ME

Long-haul flying can be trying at the best of times, and the behaviour of your neighbour can make a big difference to your trip. A squalling infant can destroy any hope of sleep, and even a snoring passenger can be a pain. So what do you do when your neighbour gets belligerently drunk and defecates on the food trolley?

As jet travel has become ever cheaper and planes ever more crowded, the incidence of the phenomenon known as air rage has increased. The food trolley incident above actually happened, in October 1995, and assaults involving urine, scalding hot coffee and even plastic cutlery are becoming increasingly common. The following recent cases are among the most extreme.

July 1997. On a flight from Houston, Texas, a couple became agitated after being denied an upgrade to first class from their coach-class seats. When they were told to return to their seats the man grabbed two coffee pots and scalded a pair of flight attendants with the boiling liquid, then attempted to open the forward aircraft door, while telling his partner to enter the cockpit. She kicked the cockpit door until a blowout panel shattered, but an off-duty pilot in the cockpit kept the door closed. Cabin crew and passengers struggled to restrain the incensed couple until the plane was landed and the couple were taken into custody.

December 1997. While flying from Baltimore to Los Angeles, Dean Trammell, a well-built college American football player, began to wander up and down the aisles blessing the other passengers and proclaiming that he was Jesus Christ. He then tried to enter the cockpit, intent on making a proclamation over the PA, but after a brief altercation was led back towards his seat by flight attendant Renee Sheffer. He never made it. After grabbing Sheffer's breasts he became enraged and threw her across three rows of seats. Other passengers and off-duty pilots attempted to restrain him but suffered from extensive bites, cuts and bruises; Sheffer suffered kidney and bladder trauma, spinal trauma and internal bleeding as well as numerous minor injuries. The plane landed with the jock messiah, who later admitted he'd taken LSD before the flight, tied by the wrists and ankles and further restrained by two men sitting on him.

October 1998. When Steve Handy, a drunk British passenger, was asked to stop smoking by a flight attendant, he hit her on the head with a large vodka bottle, leaving her with a wound requiring eighteen stitches.

January 1999. Another drunk Briton, halfway through a fourteen-hour flight, harassed the woman sitting next to him, ripping off then biting through her headphones, then punched the door window, breaking through the inner layer and threatening to cause a decompression. It took four flight attendants and four passengers to restrain him.

Occasionally the incidents have resulted in death. In December 1998 a Finnish national became abusive on a Hungarian flight from Bangkok to Budapest. After punching a pilot and attempting to strangle a flight attendant the man was restrained, and an onboard doctor administered a tranquilliser. The plane made an emergency landing in Istanbul where the man was found to have died from the combination of the tranquilliser with other drugs in his system. A similar incident occurred in May 1999 when a Senegalese man died on being sedated after a violent episode on a flight from Paris to Dakar, the sedative having mixed fatally with drugs already in his system.

In August 2000 Jonathan Burton, a young American flying from Las Vegas to Salt Lake City, became violent shortly before landing, screaming obscenities, attacking passengers and crew and punching a hole in the cockpit door. Burton was restrained by passengers and eventually killed. An autopsy showed that he had been strangled, but the US Attorney's office said that it would not press criminal charges against those involved in restraining him, as his death had resulted from an act of self-defence by panicked passengers. Some passengers, however, criticised the cabin crew for making a PA announcement allegedly antagonising Burton, and for not intervening when a passenger continued to jump up and down on the apparently unconscious man's chest.

In July 1999 a 28-year-old man from Tokyo smuggled an eight-inch knife on to a Japanese flight with the intention of overpowering the cockpit crew and flying the plane himself. He stabbed the captain in the neck and shoulder, forced the crew to leave the cockpit and took control of the aircraft while his victim bled to death. The plane plummeted to within 300 metres of the ground before the controls were wrested away from the novice pilot, who later explained to police that he loved playing flight simulation games and wanted to test his skills in a more realistic environment.

Air rage is nothing new; there are records of cases going back as far as the birth of commercial aviation. But the frequency of incidents has increased exponentially over the years, with the explosion in cut-rate fares and attendant flight overcrowding leading to a 400 per cent increase in disruptive incidents between 1993 and 1998.

There are many factors that make contemporary air travel a stressful experience, especially at the budget end of the industry. Passenger density is higher than it has ever been before, as more and more rows of seats are placed in already overcrowded planes; passengers are discouraged from walking around the plane, even on long-haul flights that can now last up to fifteen hours; flight attendants can be rude and uncooperative, with the rise in air rage incidents mirrored by a massive rise in complaints against attendants; and delays, misinformation, poor baggage handling, long check-in queues and chronic overbooking make many fliers stressed before they even board the plane.

Up to one in five passengers on the average plane is said to share a fear of flying, and no-smoking restrictions remove one stress reliever on which some are dependent. Many drink to relieve stress, but the effect of alcohol is heightened at altitude; mixed with medication for anxiety or depression it can lead to severely impaired judgement and chronically antisocial behaviour. Airlines that have discontinued free alcohol have seen a sharp drop in air rage incidents.

Airline advertising has been blamed for creating unrealistic expectations about the reality of contemporary air travel, selling an image of relaxation and ease in harsh contrast to the elbow-jostling battle for space that characterises many modern flights. Adverts have also been linked to the sexual harassment of some flight attendants, by featuring suggestions of their easy sexual availability, a trend that peaked with the provocative stewardesses of the 1970s ad captioned 'I'm American Airlines – fly me'. This may also have helped to popularise the idea of the 'mile high' club, and occasionally passengers have been arrested after participating in full sex in public, mid-flight.

There's also a sense in which air rage has become a self-fulfilling prophecy. Some passengers might feel that such behaviour is justified by precedents, making it relatively acceptable, and the media's treatment of air rage incidents might suggest activities that would not otherwise occur to the passenger. Moreover, giving the phenomenon a name and treating it as a syndrome will for some lessen the sense of responsibility for their actions. Flights are, after all, boundary zones, and for some the sense of holiday licence to behave badly starts as soon as they arrive at the airport.

HOOLIGAN HOLIDAY

What makes me laugh is when the missus says, 'You must be football mad, you, going all over the place to watch the Arsenal and England.' But they don't understand, do they? It's not just the football, is it? It's all the other. The boozing and the fighting and the good laughs you have when you're away. They don't know anything about all that. They just think it's the football.

'Kel', Arsenal fan, 1981

Tell any man in the football-loving nations of Central or South America that you're English, and their eyes will light up. '*Eres hooligan?*' they will ask. Are you a hooligan? The image of an overweight, topless, sunburnt man wearing Union Jack shorts and wallowing like a punch-drunk walrus in a Continental fountain while shouting 'I'd rather be a Paki than a Turk' is enduring if not endearing, and defines for many the Brits abroad. This peculiar brand of tourism also incorporates a wide range of criminal behaviour – theft, vandalism, racial abuse, assault and murder – and is one of the most notorious examples of holiday deviance on record.

English football hooliganism was a local phenomenon until 1974, when Spurs fans were reported to have 'gone on the rampage' in Rotterdam, and Manchester United fans brawled with locals in Ostend city centre. The association of hooliganism with followers of the national team's away matches followed in the late 1970s, and persists – albeit in a less severe form – today. The notoriety of English supporters on the Continent probably peaked in 1985 at Heysel Stadium, Brussels, when, less than an hour before the scheduled kick-off, Liverpool fans charged across a terrace to attack Juventus fans, many of whom fled in panic; a crumbling wall collapsed, killing 39 people, most of them Italians. In the wake of the incident English teams were banned from playing in Continental Europe for five years, and many saw this as marking the end of the worst excesses of English hooliganism abroad.

There is a long tradition among English fans abroad of spending as little money as possible en route to matches – or even making a profit. Trains can be bunked, tills looted and shops robbed of their produce, fans entering en masse and leaving with their pockets stuffed full of food and alcohol; the sheer weight of numbers leaves shop owners powerless to stop them. A similar ruse is employed in cafés, with many establishments on the Continent requesting payment of the bill only after goods have been consumed. This is seen by many fans as evidence of the stupidity of the foreigners, and the attendant ingenuity of the English in hoodwinking their hosts.

But some proprietors refuse to put up with such behaviour. In Brussels during the mid-1980s a café owner, incensed by watching a group of Tottenham fans eat his food, drink his beer and break his furniture then walk out without paying, pulled out a shotgun from behind the bar and shot a fan dead. It turned out later that he'd picked one of the few honest punters – the victim had paid his bill.

Looting occurs sporadically during riots, and organised shoplifting is not unknown, light-fingered fans exporting their talents to capital cities around the world. Sometimes the connections to organised crime are stronger: a Manchester-based operation during the 1980s printed fake American dollars for sale to football fans who would then travel to remote areas relatively unused to tourists to exchange the counterfeit funds.

Racial abuse is typical, ranging from Heil Hitler salutes given to any foreigner by skinheads affiliated to the BNP, or its forerunner the National Front, to insults chanted at uncomprehending locals. In this the hooligan contingent is not so far different from other Brits abroad, whose xenophobia manifests itself in an unwillingness to behave according to local custom or to learn phrases in the local language. The attitude of Frank, a Nottingham-based England supporter interviewed in Spain, is typical: 'Well, we've been here three days now, and if they haven't learned English yet, that's their problem.' The 1982 arrest of four English football fans on the balcony of their hostel, naked and cleaning their genitals with the Spanish flag, is indistinguishable from the kind of behaviour that has brought more recent notoriety to British holidaymakers in Ibiza and Ayia Napa.

The level of vandalism and assault associated with England supporters is not what it once was – police strong-arm tactics and the rising cost of football support mean that the days of cars being torched, concrete blocks put through bus windows and opponents kicked into long stays in intensive care are gone. Nowadays English fans are more likely to be on the receiving end of violence, whether from overzealous truncheon-wielding policemen keen to practise their kidney blows, or fans from other countries: two Leeds United supporters, Kevin Speight and Christopher Loftus, were killed by Turkish Galatasaray fans in Istanbul in 1999, leading to protracted street battles between English and Turkish fans.

This incident demonstrates that hooliganism is no longer a peculiarly English disease. Like many other forms of English youth culture it has been successfully exported to countries ranging from Germany to Argentina, as shown by incidents such as the German fan beating a French policeman into a coma during France 98.

But the notoriety of England supporters as the most accomplished hooligans persists, and is in a sense self-perpetuating. Media predictions such as the following, made in the *Observer* on 4 June 2000, just before England's Euro 2000 match against Germany at Charleroi, Belgium, are common:

> *Charleroi is set to be turned into a battlefield with visiting thugs, local Turks and Neo-Nazi troublemakers based in the towns staging bloody confrontations. The authorities privately admit mayhem is almost guaranteed because huge numbers of mainly ticket-less fans will crowd into Charleroi's narrow streets.*

Such coverage is likely to drive away family supporters and encourage 'visiting thugs' to attend – which is probably, in a sense, what the papers want. Bad behaviour makes for good copy, and nobody wants to read about a tournament in which nothing went wrong. The very presence of the world's media, cameras and journalists out in force and waiting for something to happen, will encourage violent confrontation, and their reporting of any confrontation will invariably distort the event. The infamous use of a water cannon to pacify beetroot-faced England fans hurling plastic chairs at their German counterparts in Charleroi apparently lasted no longer than ten minutes but made the headlines in all the British papers the next day, while the 15,000 England fans enjoying peaceful drinks with German fans in bars around the town were not deemed worthy of coverage.

But such media distortion was not taken into account by the British Government, which rushed through emergency legislation to restrict the movements of suspected hooligans after the embarrassing Charleroi incident, or by the Belgian police, who indiscriminately beat and deported hundreds of fans simply on the grounds that they were English. Or rather that they were presumed to be: among the fans rounded up and deported to Manchester were an American and a Geneva businessman who'd won a five-star trip to Euro 2000 in a magazine competition.

The Belgians were taking no chances, as explained by Alain Courtois, in charge of the tournament organisation, in a Sabena in-flight magazine:

Belgium will be ruthless in implementing a special law allowing police to detain for up to twelve hours anyone whose appearance gives cause for concern. For example, by showing tattoos, wearing overly patriotic shorts or having a crew cut.

It seems that the simple expedient of wearing a wig and long trousers could have saved many England fans from a ruined holiday.

For all the British Government's hand-wringing about hooliganism, the phenomenon is rooted in the political climate of many European countries, in which the major political parties seek to outdo each other in nationalism and anti-immigrant sentiment. International football tournaments themselves encourage this kind of nationalism, and the media's portrayal of each match as a mini-battle does nothing to improve the situation. The escalation of English hooliganism during the Thatcher years, with her xenophobic rhetoric and populist harking back to times of empire and triumph in war, illustrated the connection between politics and the behaviour of England fans all too clearly.

The decline of England as an economic and world power, as well as a confused sense of national identity – celebrations of Englishness tend to be frowned upon in the country's contemporary multi-ethnic society, St George's Day is still not a national holiday, and the George Cross has at times been a byword for racism – all contribute to a misguided expression of patriotism through lager-fuelled boorishness. Hang-ups about masculinity, along with racist, sexist and xenophobic attitudes, only serve to fuel the fire.

But patriotism isn't the only appeal. Away from bosses, family, partners and other institutional checks and balances, the trips abroad are for many supporters like a prolonged Saturday night out, only better – the fact of being in a foreign country means that they can get away with a lot more. The sense of being away from responsibility, exacerbated by alcohol and often other drugs, can make for a great party atmosphere, but it also means that events can spiral very quickly out of control. And for some this is exactly what is craved. Football hooliganism – the riotous behaviour, the drunken merriment and sense of anarchy – fits into the true tradition of carnival, with its threat of social breakdown and mockery of social mores. As the authorities, particularly in Europe, have sought to sanitise and control the contemporary descendants of carnival, so the participants have become more and more militant in their chaotic behaviour.

Perhaps, finally, the crowd violence fills a need satisfied in few other ways. Bill Buford, the editor of the literary magazine *Granta*, immersed himself in the culture of British football hooligans while researching his book *Among the Thugs*. He found a sense of excitement in 'being in a crowd in an act of violence' he'd rarely experienced before, a transcendent loss of individuality and total immersion in the moment that proved compulsive. Although an unlikely hooligan himself – Buford is bearded, American and editor of one of the most well-respected British literary magazines – he spent almost ten years researching his topic, travelling with hooligan crews and eventually enduring a savage beating at the hands of Italian police, which finally dampened his enthusiasm.

WE ALL GO A LITTLE MAD SOMETIMES

While tourists who commit assaults on aeroplanes or indulge in football hooliganism can be said to make a conscious decision on some level to behave in this way, other tourists' embrace of the irrational or psychopathological is somewhat less voluntary.

On average, between three and four tourists are every year diagnosed as having Jerusalem Syndrome; in 1999 more than 50 diagnoses were made, probably due to the advent of the millennium. The term 'Jerusalem Syndrome' was coined by Dr Yair Bar-El, ex-director of the Kfar Shaul Psychiatric Hospital in Jerusalem and at the time of writing district psychiatrist for the Ministry of Health, after studying 470 tourists who had been referred to Kfar Shaul for treatment for temporary insanity between 1979 and 1993.

He found that the tourists fell into three distinct groups: those who arrived already mentally ill; those who came as pilgrims, with deep religious convictions, often belonging to fringe religious groups and believing that they must carry out specific acts to bring about Armageddon or the second coming of Christ; and those Bar-El considers to exhibit the true Jerusalem Syndrome. This last group is characterised by having no history of mental illness, and arriving in Jerusalem as normal tourists, often on package tours of the Holy Land.

A remarkably similar picture of disintegration emerged from Bar-El's studies. On the tourist's second day in Jerusalem he or she would be overcome by a sense of anxiety and a desire to be away from family, friends or tour group. They would often indulge in rituals of cleansing and purification, shaving off all their body hair and showering obsessively, and would then don white robes, often fashioned from the sheets of their hotel bed. So dressed, they would visit the holy places, most often those associated with the life of Jesus, and begin to deliver loud sermons in public, bemoaning humanity's materialistic concerns and preaching a return to spiritual values.

This in itself would not warrant hospitalisation, but when the afflicted tourists began to harass other visitors or obstruct the holy places they would be obliged to receive treatment. Some had specific religious or political goals, such as the Californian who came seeking a red heifer for purification purposes, as indicated in Numbers 19, or Dennis Rohan, the young Australian Christian tourist who in 1969 set the El Aksa Mosque on fire, to the horror of the Muslim world.

For the tourists of Bar-El's third group, the symptoms of the condition are extremely specific: they can remember everything about their lives, including their true identities, and the reaction passes within a week, or sometimes as soon as they are taken away from Jerusalem.

The role of choice for Christian men is John the Baptist; for women it is the Virgin Mary. Jews of both sexes tend to identify with Jesus. Local residents are affected by the syndrome in its broader manifestations, and the religious breakdown of the tourists studied by Bar-El revealed that 66 per cent were Jewish, 33 per cent Christian and the remaining 1 per cent had no known religious affiliation.

However, the 'true' sufferers of the Jerusalem Syndrome, Bar-El's third group, were 97 per cent Protestant, with most of these tourists having been raised in ultra-orthodox homes which were organised around the Bible as the key source of domestic authority. This is thought to have led to an internalised and highly idealised view of Jerusalem; perhaps the shock of visiting the contemporary city with its secular and economic concerns can catalyse a psychotic reaction.

Bar-El indicated that in his opinion the preponderance of Protestants afflicted by the syndrome could be put down to the lack of spiritual ecstasy in the church's rituals; ecstasy may be an essential part of the religious experience, and it is better provided for in Catholicism, Judaism, Islam and the Eastern religions. This may also account for the recent surge in popularity of ecstatic Protestant churches, in some of which glossolalia, or speaking in tongues, is enthusiastically practised.

Another possible explanation of the syndrome is that the psychogeography of Jerusalem itself catalyses messianic experiences – delusional behaviour by another name. The logical extreme of this interpretation sees the syndrome at the root of Christianity, Judaism and Islam, many of the monotheistic religions' key prophets having had revelatory experiences there.

The psychogeographical interpretation of the Jerusalem Syndrome recalls another, rarer syndrome that also afflicts tourists – the Florence Syndrome, otherwise known as the Stendhal Syndrome, after the French writer who found himself overwhelmed by the beauty of works of art in Florence in 1817. An Italian psychiatrist, Graziella Margherini, observed while working at the Santa Maria Nuova hospital an unusual condition among patients who had undergone severe emotional disturbances while looking at works of art; she collated her findings and presented them in a book, *La Sindrome di Stendhal*. Among the cases considered is that of Franz, a Bavarian tourist who, while visiting the Uffizi Gallery in Florence, became confused and suffered some sort of visual impairment. He was obliged to leave the gallery after spotting Caravaggio's *The Young Bacchus*; Margherini's Freudian explanation for the event focuses on the tourist's repressed homosexuality, brought to the fore by Caravaggio's homoerotic imagery.

More common than these flirtations with insanity is 'going troppo'. The phrase, which is originally Australian, refers to a peculiar form of temporary insanity afflicting people of European descent in tropical climates. During this writer's time working as an English teacher in eastern Bolivia, one of the other teachers, also a Briton, fell victim to this curious affliction. The headmaster of the school was alerted one morning by another colleague to the fact that this British teacher was wallowing naked in a roadside canal that carried raw sewage. The headmaster duly found the faeces-smeared teacher and drove him home to put him in the shower; checking on him shortly afterwards, the headmaster found the demented staff member attempting to put out one of his eyes. This warranted a more heavy-handed approach, and the teacher was taken to the local psychiatric hospital, where he received several powerful injections of Valium before becoming sedated. After a brief stay in the hospital the teacher returned to the UK, convinced that his breakdown had occurred as a direct result of meddling with occult practices, as proscribed by the Bible – he was an enthusiastic Tarot reader – and he found solace in the consensual and socially permitted 'insanity' of Christianity.

In Australia the phrase applies to natives as much as to tourists, and 'going troppo', or 'mango madness' as it is also known, is a recognised syndrome from November to February in the Northern Territory, characterised by excessive violence, acute depression and suicidal tendencies. The phrase is also used to refer to living in primitive conditions in the bush, and in typically Australian fashion has been appropriated by tour operators keen to stress the 'craziness' of their parties. Brisbane-based 'Go Troppo Showboat Cruises' boasts that 'Our primary function is to party', and the Australian Big Picture Travel Co. warns potential clients for their 'Troppo Zone' parties that they should be in prime condition to endure the 'all night (and all day) parties'.

The condition, which tends to affect expatriates more than tourists, and can thus generally be assumed to take some time to develop, may originate from nothing more complex than chronic dehydration – some experts advise drinking fifteen litres of water daily in the tropics – and overexposure to a pitilessly hot sun. Britons in particular tend to ignore local customs regarding avoidance of the midday sun, hence the song 'Mad Dogs and Englishmen . . .'

* * *

In the next chapter we'll look at the way tourists objectify the people and places they visit, and are objectified in turn, leading to rip-offs, scams, rapes – and murder.

2. THE NAKED EYE

BURSTING THE TOURIST BUBBLE

In the last chapter we covered flirtations with danger and madness as motivations for travel. But why else do we travel? To see a little of the world. To take stock of our lives. For an adventure, a stop-gap before entering a new phase. To defer the workaday existence of office life. The vector of tourism is overwhelmingly city to country, rich to poor, north to south. Some of the more obvious reasons for this are easy to explain – it's warmer in the south, and even a poorly paid worker from the West can live like a king in the developing world – but other, subtler factors are also at play.

People from the developed world often travel to the developing world in search of a sense of authenticity missing at home, and in an attempt to define their identity in the face of a clearly differentiated 'other'. This identity is usually characterised by a concept of themselves as neutral, if adventurous, observers. In the back of many tourists' minds is the thought of how they will articulate their experiences back home; the photographs, the stories, are all aimed at reinforcing particular ideas of who they are among their peers.

Travel is also an attempt by Western tourists to assure themselves that the eternal and unchanging exist outside their own rapidly changing culture. Seeing a dance performed in traditional dress reassures them that some cultures stay the same, even as they suspect that the display is put on for their benefit, and they capture the moment with cameras, instinctively hoping to freeze time.

For this reason tourists are often dismayed to see indigenous people adopting Western lifestyles and clothes. Traditional behaviour and costume reassure them that Western culture has not adversely affected the rest of the world, and keeps a subject/object, us/them differentiation clear, fitting the idealised image of the happy, carefree, indigenous person so familiar from tourist brochures and guidebooks. With the adoption of Western lifestyles the distinction becomes more vague and indistinct, the objectification of people and landscape more difficult to maintain.

Tourists travel seeking pristine wilderness environments, their minds shaped by pastoral assumptions entirely alien to local inhabitants, and are disappointed to see poor people chopping down trees for fuel; they forget, glorifying the life of the subsistence farmer, that in many developing countries the city is an escape from the rigours and poverty of country life. They demand environmental solutions imposed from without, glossing over the fact that these people are simply doing what the inhabitants of the developed world did centuries ago, and the fact that the US and Europe continue to consume and pollute far more than any developing country.

Tourists objectify local people as part of the landscape, something to be consumed visually. Western fantasies of what constitutes authenticity are projected on to indigenous people, who are often forced by the economy of tourism to act out these roles. Drug and sex tourists take such objectification still further, viewing a country and culture as interesting only for the narcotics available, or a people solely as sex objects or their merchants. But this objectification does not work only in one direction. As we'll soon see, tourists are often objectified themselves – sometimes with horrific consequences.

SHOULDER TO SHOULDER ON THE LONELY PLANET

If you lose your guidebook . . . well, you might as well go home.

German tourist, Omoa, Honduras,
September 2002

A map is not the territory. A menu is not the meal. And a guidebook is not the country. Yet many tourists rely on guidebooks to filter, objectify and help them understand their experiences; a friendly voice telling them what to do and how to feel. Of course it is often problematic to travel without a guidebook at all – routes can be difficult to work out and sites of interest are easily missed – but an over-reliance on them has led to the peculiar phenomenon of tourist or 'backpacker' trails.

Here specific hotels and restaurants will be given over almost exclusively to the tourist trade while other, virtually identical establishments will be frequented only by locals and business travellers. The trails have become in some cases extremely specialised; tourists from Israel are able to travel around Asia or South America staying in hotels and eating in restaurants populated exclusively by other Israelis, and tourist hubs such as the town of Antigua in Guatemala boast other, rarer specialisations such as guesthouses catering specifically for Japanese tourists.

On a more mundane level, English or Irish-themed pubs around the world provide a peculiarly ersatz impression of never having left home, and areas popular with British package tourists proudly display British flags along with 'We speak English' signs, and serve imported Walls sausages in their full English breakfasts. Some Spanish islands are so heavily populated by German holidaymakers that they are considered by many to be *de facto* German colonies; visiting tourists will be greeted in German and often made to feel distinctly unwelcome if they reply in Spanish or English. The authorities in Mallorca were obliged recently to pass a law preventing shops from displaying information only in German to encourage German shoppers and discourage the poorer locals.

The tourist trail provides a safety net for those unwilling or unable to mix with locals for linguistic or cultural reasons; some would say that it also provides an alternative source of company from locals who may see tourists exclusively in economic terms, as potential clients. Yet the low-budget tourist trail – the backpacker trail – is virtually identical in any country which has one, dreadlocked youths in shoddily made 'ethnic' clothes exchanging drug stories and email addresses as they flit from cheap guesthouse to jungle trek and back.

The irony of backpacker trails is that they are constructed in a fairly arbitrary manner. A guidebook researcher may spend one night in a town in which he or she eats a good meal at a restaurant chosen almost at random; the restaurant will then receive a good write-up in the next edition of the guidebook and be swamped by tourists, and standards at the restaurant will often slip as the owners realise they have a secure source of clientele, whatever their food is like.

Some restaurant owners take even greater advantage of tourists' reliance on guidebooks. In Saigon a restaurant called the Bodhi Tree, which donated profits to a programme designed to help street children, received enthusiastic write-ups in early Vietnam guidebooks and became extremely successful, so much so that the owner of the building in which the restaurant was situated evicted the restaurateur and set up his own restaurant in its place, the Original Bodhi Tree, offering an exact replica of the original restaurant's menu but keeping all the profits to itself. The original owner, meanwhile, leased the next-door property and again set up a restaurant called the Bodhi Tree, making for many furrowed brows and fruitless guidebook referencing among visiting tourists.

As well as carving out well-defined routes and itineraries, the backpacker trail is also subject to a paradoxical desire to cover fresh, 'unspoilt' territory; as though the inclusion of a description of a beach or mountain village in a Lonely Planet book as 'unspoilt' were not enough to ensure its rapid touristification. First the backpackers will arrive, and vegan cafés and rustic dormitories will spring up to satisfy their predictable needs; then, as the area becomes more 'touristy', with the development of resorts catering to package tourists, the backpackers will move on in search of new ground to cover.

It's worth bearing in mind that this is often exactly what many locals, and the governments of the countries concerned, want: the tourist trade is enormously important economically, and for many poor countries it is their principal source of foreign exchange. Package tourists, moreover, tend to spend

far more than low-budget backpackers, and the touristification of previously remote areas brings with it huge economic
benefits.

For this reason strenuous efforts are made by countries'
tourist boards to objectify the countries themselves, enthusiastically embarking on branding exercises designed to sell a
manufactured, pre-packaged image of the country in question. Some tourist boards make no bones about doing this; a
recent Australian drive to lure tourists was named 'Brand
Australia'. But for some natives, those who do not stand to
benefit financially from the tourist trade and who often suffer
as costs rise and standards of living drop in their area, the
transformation of their country and its culture into an
exhibition for wealthy foreigners provides a potent source of
resentment.

STOP, AIM, SHOOT

Tourism has been described as the new colonialism, and there
is clearly a similar power differential at play. Rich tourists
come to poor countries, or visit poor areas of their own
countries, so that they can live in relative luxury. The ability
to travel for enjoyment at all is a rare privilege; most people
in the world travel only for economic reasons, to gather wood
or to take goods to market. Even the ability and desire to 'go
for a walk' reveals assumptions of privilege.

As well as power differentials, patterns of representation are
also common to both tourism and colonialism. The suprem-
acy of vision in both has been clear from the time of the great
Western European exhibitions of the nineteenth and early
twentieth centuries, which objectified and exoticised artefacts
from colonised countries and encouraged a detached style of
viewing that persists today. The world is here an exhibition,
an endless parade of objects laid on solely for our viewing
pleasure; as observers, subjects of what we might call the
tourist gaze, we are wry, uninvolved and invisible to the
players in the events unfolding before us. Of course, many
contemporary tourists recognise, coming from image-
saturated cultures, that authenticity should be sought by other

means; this is part of the appeal of the experience of danger and adventure explored in the previous chapter. But vision is still paramount; it is extremely rare, for example, to encounter a tourist without a camera.

The camera not only objectifies its subject but also confers power on the user. It can be used aggressively – the first recorded use of the word 'snapshot' is in the context of hunting, to denote quick shots taken without precise aim – and provides a further barrier and distinction between subject and object. Cameras also act as tourist status symbols, as visitors use expensive state-of-the-art technology to record moments in the lives of people subsisting on a diet of rice and beans.

The history of the use of the camera in the developing world offers interesting insights into its use by tourists today. It is well known that in many 'primitive' cultures the camera has traditionally been viewed with distrust, as an artefact which can steal one's soul; similar ideas were current in Europe at the birth of the new technology, the French photographer Nadar reporting that the celebrated novelist Balzac was convinced that with each photograph taken the person depicted lost a layer of skin. New technologies will always portend doom to some.

One of the earliest uses of photography in Europe was to provide portraits of criminals and the insane, in an attempt to classify them and prove that their appearances determined their criminal natures. The new medium was used similarly in the colonies to classify, type and dominate the indigenous people. Some Europeans would even use cameras as magical objects, to terrify the natives into submission. This use was soon adopted by indigenous peoples themselves, many of whom came to believe that photographs were magically charged objects conferring power over the person photographed. In rural Kenya in the 1950s, for instance, photographs were held behind mirrors by witch doctors, then pierced or slashed, the harm translating itself to the subject of the photograph.

In such a climate the unauthorised taking of a photograph was obviously viewed with profound distrust and fear.

Nowadays the taking of unauthorised or inappropriate photographs is more likely to be met with anger, which is often expressed through violence. The 2001 *Rough Guide to the Maya World* describes 'two gringos being severely beaten up for photographing the interior of the church at San Juan Chamula' in Mexico, and the consular offices of the UK and USA warn prospective visitors to ask for permission before taking photographs in Guatemala, as tourists have been attacked there for taking inappropriate photographs before.

For some tourists, asking permission to take photographs is a cautionary step too far; a posed photo is, it is argued, a far cry from the pure ideal of people photography. The problem is compounded by a recognition that giving money to the people photographed encourages a begging mentality and an even stronger concentration on the economic aspect of the relationship between tourist and local.

But events such as the San Juan Chamula attack prove that the idea held by some tourists, that they are in a sense 'invisible' observers, is untenable. It is impossible to see what a scene would be like without one's presence; the fact that the observer is there changes everything. The attack also points to the fact that the objects of the tourist gaze are self-aware subjects, who objectify the tourists as much as they are themselves objectified. The tourist gaze is now held and returned. Any sense of the object of the tourist gaze as the 'other' – any clear differentiation between 'us' and 'them' – is weakened. The differentiation becomes still murkier with the increased mobility of formerly marginal peoples to developed world centres, even as tourists from the developed world are increasingly drawn to the peripheries of the developing world. When the tourists go home they are increasingly likely to find the 'other' there, whether as refugee, guest worker or student.

Tourists are, moreover, increasingly often burlesqued and ridiculed by those they visit; among other developments have been the insertion of masked caricatures of tourists from 'NY' or 'LA' into dance performances at a Zuñi pueblo in south-western USA. Zuñi folklore, in common with other folklores, has characteristically absorbed foreign stories which are then recontextualised for use by the pueblo's people; in order to survive, cultural forms must be fluid enough to incorporate contemporary developments such as tourism. But the way such incorporation takes place shows us that when tourists are objectified by indigenous locals, the results are not particularly flattering.

The objectification of tourists has broad ramifications. It happens in Western culture too: take the stereotype of snap-happy coachloads of Japanese tourists, for instance, which is occasionally used as a metaphor for Asian imperialism or invasion. One such instance occurs at the end of the Australian film *Romper Stomper*, as a coachload of Asian tourists takes photos of the film's two lead characters, both Australian skinheads, fighting on a beach. The inference is clear: the Australian characters' infighting has allowed the Asian immigrants to dominate their country and culture. Here, power comes from the lens of a camera.

WHITE GIRLS ARE EASY

The principal way in which tourists are objectified is, of course, that they are walking wallets, nothing more than reliable sources of money which can be extracted, if needs be, by force. Yet other forms of objectification are both subtler and more dangerous. To objectify someone is to depersonalise them, to make them less human. Objectified images of Western women, through media such as cinema, TV and advertising, have been seen as contributing to the rape of Western tourists in the developing world by encouraging the assumption that Western women are 'easy', sexually promiscuous.

Even where local law prohibits female display in advertising and operates a strict censorship policy on the sexual content of cinema films and TV, such as in many Middle Eastern countries, cosmopolitan young men will return from permissive Paris or LA with news of the sexual delights on offer. In many countries with such censorship there is also a booming trade in illegal pornographic videos, which only serve to reinforce and sharpen the stereotypes.

For the unsophisticated, untravelled and uneducated, such decontextualised images of Western women often provoke a queasy attraction: a fascination with the easy sex apparently on offer paired with a horror at the monstrous culture that could promote such treatment of women. The rape of Western tourists sometimes reflects this dichotomy, representing both attraction to and punishment of a woman who is perceived to be sexually available. The crime is therefore easy for the rapist to justify to himself.

Even the authorities in some countries less permissive than the West hold this view and use it to justify or excuse tourist rape. The number of increasingly brutal rapes of tourists in Goa, Southern India's notorious beach party mecca, have led Western tourists to publish a pamphlet entitled *Rape Alert*, which is distributed among the area's restaurants and guesthouses: 'No girls should feel safe! Stick to the main roads, avoid dirt tracks, and when in your house, make sure that all windows and doors are locked. [The police] have no idea of the amount of rapes [of foreign tourists] in Goa.'

Police awareness of the issue was bolstered by the 1997 gang rape of two young Swedish women by eight men in Anjuna, while returning to their guesthouse after a late-night beach party; their male companion was forced to watch the rape at knifepoint, and all of the tourists were also robbed of their money and possessions. But even in the wake of such crimes, one local constable saw fit to comment that: 'They're leading [licentious lives] all the time . . . then some complain of rape. Police who effected the arrests won't even get monetary rewards, but just a favourable comment in their service records.'

While not seeking to justify tourist rape at all, it's worth pointing out that some tourist behaviour does nothing to dispel stereotypes about promiscuous Western women. In countries in which women are well-nigh invisible in public life, the sexual freedom expressed explicitly by some Western female tourists will not go unnoticed. Moreover, tourist dress sense rarely takes into account prevailing local social mores, and many tourists, giddy with the freedom and heat of their sojourn in an exotic, sultry land, stop wearing bras and put on more revealing clothes than would often be acceptable in their own home countries. Such behaviour is in certain cultures a systemic violation of the codes that govern male/female relationships, and often invites unwelcome proposals if not outright hostility.

Of course the objectification of Western women is not the sole cause of tourist rape. Many tourists are reluctant to press charges when raped, fearful of being caught up in tortuously slow foreign legal systems, and can thus be seen as 'safe' victims; they are just passing through, and may find it difficult to identify their assailants; and they are not a part of the local community, a member of which would find it easier to identify assailants and the rape of whom might cause more local consternation. Moreover, in some countries, even when charges are brought the crime is considered of so little import that a conviction will carry nothing more than a light fine or short sentence.

The case of Briton Yvonne Carter, who was drugged and raped by a Bolivian tour guide who has yet to face justice for the crime, despite being suspected of having carried out at least three other sexual assaults on tourists, is revealing in this respect. The 28-year-old north London physiotherapist travelled to Bolivia in 1999, having heard about a herbal medicine project situated in the jungle near Rurrenabaque in the Amazon Basin to the north-east of the country; the project was run by a North American professor. No stranger to budget travel, Carter had visited South America before, in 1995, and spoke good Spanish.

She and two friends selected Israel Janco Caceres to lead them on a seven-day jungle trek; his name was listed in a Lonely Planet travel guide as being reliable and knowledgeable, and he seemed to espouse exactly the kind of eco-tourism on which Carter and her companions were keen. This first trek was a success, and Carter's group asked to be taken on a second trip into the jungle, this time focusing more on the local botany. Caceres agreed.

As before, the group slept out in the jungle, and suffered heavily from mosquito bites. After two days Caceres offered his charges herbal medicine to alleviate the itching, telling them that the tree sap he'd used was so bitter that he'd decided to wrap it in dough balls. Carter, keen to try at first hand the local herbal medicine, accepted the offer. Late that night she awoke, dizzy and in pain. She knew immediately that something was wrong, and could feel a sticky substance around her crotch. She woke her friends, one of whom suspected that she'd been raped, and they decided to leave. As they packed their belongings Caceres pretended to sleep on, but the group took his machete in case he planned to follow them. They also found a bag of dough balls, which they took for analysis. A La Paz chemist later found that some contained antihistamine and others diazepam, otherwise known as Valium; Carter feared that she had been dosed with the latter.

As they waited by the river for a boat, the first to arrive was one owned by Caceres's brother, who recognised the group as that travelling with Israel. He saw that Carter was crying and asked her what was wrong; but before long it dawned on him that his brother had raped yet another tourist. It transpired later that Caceres's family – and indeed the wider community – were well aware of the guide's predilection for tourist rape.

Back in Rurrenabaque Carter was taken to a hospital, where doctors confirmed her suspicions. She went to the local police to report the rape, but they laughed at her and carried on playing a game of football. Appeals to the town mayor and other high-ranking local officials were similarly fruitless, although Carter did find out that Caceres had definitely done this before. The American professor running the herbal medicine project told her about another girl who had suffered a similar assault, and explained that little was likely to happen to Caceres: rape was part and parcel of the local culture of machismo.

Undaunted, Carter and her friends put up posters around town to warn other tourists. Caceres had by now been seen back in town, but police seemed reluctant to arrest him, perhaps fearing that the publicity of a rape trial would have a negative impact on the booming local tourist trade.

Carter returned to La Paz and contacted the British Embassy, which helped her to organise a press conference, although they maintained that they had no authority to interfere in the Bolivian judicial system – they couldn't have the serial rapist arrested. While in La Paz she read an article in the English-language *Bolivian Times* from 18 June 2000. It was written by 'Micah', another female tourist who had been raped by Caceres, eighteen months before, after having been given 'herbal pills' for a swollen hand:

> *I know now that they were Valium and Caceres gave them to me so that he could do whatever he wanted to and hope I would be sleeping too deeply to know about it. But I did wake up to find my trousers ripped and Caceres sexually assaulting me . . . Back in Rurrenabaque I discovered that Caceres had raped another traveller last year. It was a big town scandal . . . A few weeks later Caceres was back working as a guide.*

Following Carter's press conference she made further radio and press appearances, after one of which a female lawyer contacted her and promised to take on her case for free. Caceres finally received a conviction for rape after a trial in which he was accused of several sexual assaults; but the conviction was meaningless without a sentence, which the courts failed to pass. This reluctance to jail Caceres was seen to result partly from the lack of importance attached to such crimes in Bolivia (when custodial sentences are passed for rape they last on average between two and four years) and partly from the delay in pursuing the prosecution (the British Foreign Office wrote to Carter telling her that a custodial sentence had been deferred due to the length of time taken to bring Caceres to justice).

In April 2002 Carter finally heard some good news: Caceres had been jailed. But the case had nothing to do with his repeated tourist rapes: this time he had been found guilty of the evidently more serious crime of stealing a motorcycle.

BITTER TEARS IN THE LAND OF SMILES

The friendly, smiling nature of the Thai people is one of the country's biggest selling points, and is reiterated endlessly in travel brochures and guidebooks. Many will leave the country with a positive image of its people, having had their trust in the friendliness of locals reinforced. But there is a marked contrast in Thai culture between public 'front' and private 'back', an emphasis on image over content and a marked skill in role-playing, which lend themselves well to con games. For some the Thai people's friendliness and trustworthiness is a cruel illusion rudely shattered by such crimes. The first of these popular con games covered below involves gems, and the second involves sex tourists.

Perhaps more chilling than any of the Thai jewel scams detailed below is the following, allegedly pulled on British charity worker Phil McLean in the Gambia in 1992. McLean claimed that a Gambian witchdoctor, Pateh Bowaro, had offered to sell him two gems he claimed were diamonds; when McLean declined the offer, Bowaro asked him to take the gems to the UK to have them valued. He did so, and returned to the Gambia with the message that they were topaz; he was then arrested and charged with having sold the diamonds in the UK and lying to Bowaro about them being topaz. McLean is said to have fallen ill before the trial after having been threatened with a voodoo curse, inflicted by a witchdoctor whom McLean's girlfriend described as spending 'all his time chanting in the village and dancing round cow horns'. McLean was sentenced to jail in the Gambia for between two and six years.

In Thailand the MO is standard and rather less exotic. The guide dresses well and appears respectable; rather than describing himself as a guide (the con almost invariably involves a man), he will pass himself off as a teacher, a businessman or some other professional, and will approach tourists – couples or lone holidaymakers – near hotels. The guide will be fluent in English and will ask the tourists where they come from. If the reply is the US, UK or Canada, he will tell them that he has been to their country and was so well treated that he would like to return the favour – free, of course. Hospitality for hospitality.

To many new arrivals in Thailand, this confirms their most cherished hopes about the Land of Smiles, and his offer is difficult to refuse. Even those who are at first suspicious warm to his good manners and are impressed when he tells them, with some embarrassment, that not all his countrymen are trustworthy. He warns them about guides who will take them only to establishments at which they get kickbacks, and about false labelling on consumer goods. While reminiscing about their home country, he offers to take them to a good restaurant.

The tourists are glad to be shown a good place to eat, and usually offer to pay for the meal. Their guide will then take them to a temple or for a ride on the river; he is full of interesting facts, and the tourists arrange to meet him again the following day to learn more about this fascinating country.

Before they part company he casually drops into the conversation that he is an amateur gemologist and wants to take them to a jeweller who is honest – one of the few in Thailand. The shop is some distance from the main shopping areas, which the guide tells them keeps prices low – low rent, low profit. Sometimes he will tell them that he wants to buy a gem for his mother, or another member of his family, and is taking advantage of a special cheap offer which is about to end. The shop is trustworthy – he knows the owner, or, if not, it is run by the government. If the tourists express a concern that they know nothing about gems, he will tell them not to worry because the government-run shop will explain everything to them.

In the shop a salesgirl takes over, reiterating what the guide has told the tourists: this is a government-run shop and there is a special discount on gems for one day only. The tourists are assured that their credit card is acceptable, and that they will be able to resell any gems they buy for at least twice the price in their home countries. Often printed guarantees are given to the tourists when they buy gems, which appear to confer a further measure of authenticity while in fact guaranteeing nothing.

Their guide tells them he has his own work to get back to and leaves, reassuring the tourists that they will see him tomorrow. After making a substantial purchase the tourists leave; and in time they go home, and have the gems valued. To their horror and immense disappointment, they are told that the stones are worth only a fraction of what they paid.

When the tourists discover that their gems are virtually worthless, they are often unable to return to the shop, either because their time is too short, they are worried about becoming embroiled in a complicated legal struggle, or because they have taken advantage of the jeweller's offer to send the gems back to their home address. If they do go back to the shop, they are usually not able to secure any kind of refund and are sometimes threatened. Receipts are often stamped 'non-refundable', and if no receipts are presented the shop owner will usually deny that the gems were bought at that shop.

In 1992 one Chinese tourist bought 'rubies' in Mae Sai on the Burmese border for $300 each, only to discover on his return to Hong Kong that they were in fact cubic zircons worth around $7.50. He had been given a written guarantee that he could return the stones, and had taken a photo of the stall girl who'd sold them to him, so he took the opportunity of another trip to Thailand to seek a refund, carrying the stones, the guarantee, the photo and the report on the value of the stones he'd been given by a Hong Kong jeweller.

The salesgirl denied that she'd sold him the gems; she insisted that the photo was not of her (despite the fact that she was even wearing the same top as in the photo), the guarantee was forged, and the Hong Kong report was a fake. Eventually the tourist moved off, exasperated, and sat at a nearby bar having a drink. When he saw some other tourists arrive at the girl's stall, he watched them for five minutes, then approached and showed them his stones and the Hong Kong letter.

The salesgirl screamed, swore at the Chinese tourist and tried to grab the letter; she then called over to another stall, and shouts went around the stallholders. A policeman soon arrived, and snatched the guarantee, the photo and the Hong Kong report from him; the tourist tried to explain, to no avail. The stones were forced into his shirt pocket and he was dragged into an alleyway, where the papers were torn up in front of him. He was then punched and shouted at, although he couldn't understand what the policeman was saying; when he tried once more to explain what had happened, the policeman drew a gun and pushed the barrel into his chest. This had the desired effect of quietening him down, and the policeman escorted him on to a bus out of town. In Chiang Mai he went to the police to complain, but he could see that his story was falling on deaf ears.

Even if tourists do manage to get the Tourist Police to take up their claim, they are usually able to receive a refund of only around 50 per cent of what they paid for the gems. If they try to take the case further they are told that it is difficult to prove that a crime has actually taken place – there is no set price for gems and, therefore, even such gross overpricing as is carried out by these jewellers is not criminal. Efforts to control the scam have led the Tourism Authority of Thailand (TAT) to award their stamp to approved shops, but even this seems to have had a detrimental effect, as some shops forge the stamp while others, which have been awarded the genuine stamp, begin sharp practices in the full awareness that they have an assured customer base.

Ironically, some foreigners have now allegedly begun to scam the scammers. According to the president of Thailand's Jewellery Association, some foreign tourists cooperate with tour guides to buy gems, then after the guide is given his commission the tourist will return to the jewellery shop with a policeman, complaining that the quality is no good and demanding his money back. After this the guide and tourist share the commission.

Pattaya was a sleepy fishing village on Thailand's eastern coast, 147 kilometres south-east of Bangkok, until the Vietnam War. Then GIs stationed at Nakorn Ratchasima base began to spend their R&R (rest and relaxation) periods there, renting huts on the beach. They liked what they saw, and told their friends, until the village's main industry was catering for the needs of American marines. Today Pattaya town stretches for fifteen kilometres along the coast, foreign-owned factories and go-go bars defining its new status in equal measure.

It is one of the world's premier destinations for sex tourism and, while we'll deal with this phenomenon in more detail in 'Love You Long Time', the sex industry in Pattaya offers some other characteristic examples of how crime stems from objectification; in this case, tourists' objectification of Thai women as easily available sex objects and Thai objectification of Western tourists as easy sources of cash. Many tourists who visit Pattaya, lured by its silken-limbed promise, fall victim to a number of scams.

Some come looking not just for easy sex but for a wife, having perhaps had bad experiences with partners in their native countries and giddy with lust at the fantasy of truly submissive women. But as Thai commentator Siriporn Skrobanek has pointed out, 'In no other country do people expect to make long-term relationships with sex workers, let alone think of marrying them. So what is going on in their minds when they meet the women in the bars and clubs?' Mistaking sunshine for benevolence, they are often kept in sexual thrall until they have outlived their usefulness, then relieved of their money and unceremoniously dumped. Successful and enduring matches are made – but they are the exception rather than the rule.

A Thai-published book entitled *Handbook of English Love Letters* gives examples – in Thai and English – of form letters that may be used to extract money from lovestruck Western beaus or to ensure a ticket to the tourist's country. It's worth quoting a couple of these at length to convey the professionalism of this phenomenon, as well as the degree to which it has become institutionalised. A letter-writing campaign would begin with something like the first letter, but before long the financial demands – for water buffalo, hospital care, or a new roof – mount:

Dear . . .

How are you? I hope you're getting on well. I think you'll be very surprised to see my letter as it is my very first letter to you.

Since you have left Thailand, I feel very lonely, I have no close friend like you. I still remember the day on which both of us went to have a drink together. I think you are a very nice man indeed. I think of you day and night and I don't know why I have this strange feeling. I have never felt like this about anyone else before. To be very frank, I can't even keep myself from thinking of you for a minute. Actually, according to Thai custom, it is not good for a woman to express such a feeling towards a man, especially a foreign man, but I can't keep any secret now I have met you and I feel happy to reveal it to you. I only hope that some day you will have another chance to visit Thailand and I'll be so happy if you get the chance.

I hope to read your sweet letters soon.

Yours always,

My dearest . . .

How is life over there? I think you will be very surprised to receive my letter at this time as I have never written to you before. I hope it won't waste much of your time but I have urgent news to tell you; mother suddenly fell ill and is now in Suan Dok Hospital in Chiang Mai Province. I will probably visit her this coming Saturday. Can you come along? Of course, she will be very happy to see you. She always ask about you whenever I go home. Darling! Will it be alright if I ask you for more money? I am reluctant to tell you about this, but you are very generous and gentle, I have no one to help at this time, so I decided to send you this letter before going there and I don't know if your money will reach me in time as I'm leaving for Chiang Mai this Saturday.

Darling! Could you let me know by Express Telegram? If you can come along with me I'll postpone my trip. Alright? Indeed, I need you as companion very much and if we have

time I'll take you to see my relatives in Chiang Mai as well.
Let me say goodbye for now.
Looking forward to hearing from you very soon.
Yours passionately,

The ultimate objective of this approach is usually to persuade tourists to buy land and property locally, in the misguided belief that they are purchasing a love nest in which to live out their years in a heady daze of constant arousal. Thai law, however, forbids foreigners from owning more than 49 per cent of a Thai property; so often, once a property is bought in the name of a Thai woman, she will cut off relations with her distraught lover, sometimes revealing that she is already married to a Thai man.

The frequency with which this occurs can be attributed to two key factors in Thai culture – its growing materialism, in which tourists are seen by many as fair game, to be squeezed as dry as possible, and its focus on the importance of family. However doting a relationship appears to be between a Western tourist and a Thai woman, her first duty will always be to her parents. Many of these property-buying scams are designed to help the girl's family leave the economically deprived countryside for a better life closer to the city.

But most sex tourists don't come looking for a permanent partner. To relieve them of their funds less elaborate scams are employed, principal among them 'drug and rob' attacks. Sedative drugs – the notorious Swiss 'date rape' drug Rohypnol is thought to be the current drug of choice – are administered to unwitting punters by spiking a drink, offering an 'aphrodisiac' or, increasingly, by an invitation to lick a girl's breasts, which will have been coated in a narcotic substance. This last trick is not confined to use on tourists; Thai nationals, often unable to resist such an offer, have often been relieved of wallet and watch this way, waking up disorientated in a hotel room the following morning. Nor is the scam exclusively used in Thailand; recent reports from Colombia suggest that it is becoming popular there too.

Those who wake up are the lucky ones. For many tourists robbery shades into the darker realm of murder. Objectification leads to depersonalisation, and when somebody is depersonalised they become far easier to kill. We can see this in wartime propaganda – enemies are not only depersonalised but also dehumanised, to prevent them from being seen as similar to us. Serial killers also often depersonalise their victims before taking their lives: as we'll see later, Ivan Milat tied cloth around the head of one of his victims then used it for target practice. It might be argued that the depersonalisation inherent in prostitution is one of the factors making prostitutes the preferred victims for many serial killers; that and their propensity to step into a stranger's car without letting anyone know where they are going – just like a hitch-hiking backpacker.

In the Philippines the Ativan gang – so named for the brand of sleeping pill they use to spike unwary victims' drinks – are thought to be responsible for a string of tourist disappearances and deaths, often sending its female members to lure tourists into drinking Mickey Finns. It is unclear in many of these cases whether the death of the victim results from poorly judged dosing or a deliberate pragmatism that concludes that the risk of capture after a particularly large haul lessens with a dead victim.

In 1996 the Thai police began to investigate the mysterious heart attack deaths of 45 foreign male tourists in Pattaya hotel rooms during the previous year. The pattern was always the same: the victim would die of a heart attack resulting from a massive drug overdose and be found by a hotel cleaning lady, with saliva foaming from his open mouth, his face a ghastly rictus of pain. The men, usually between 30 and 35 years old, had come from all over the world, from Europe and the USA to Malaysia and the Middle East. Many had last been seen alive at a notorious bar called the Marine, and local police worked in concert with Interpol, which supplied undercover European agents, to solve the crimes. Thai and European police had worked together before: a paedophile ring had been busted by Dutch and Scandinavian police in Thailand a few years previously.

Police staked out the bar, following drunk tourists as they were drugged and robbed but biding their time before moving in, needing more evidence to make a murder charge stick. After two months they were ready. An undercover agent, flashing his money at the bar, was surrounded by girls; two of the most beautiful in the bar were sent over to him and suggested moving to a hotel room. The agent accepted the offer and signalled to his colleagues to follow. Once the trio were in the hotel room the girls undressed and offered the agent an 'aphrodisiac'; at this point police raided the room, arresting the two prostitutes, a gang of four waiting outside in a car and the gang's accomplices inside the bar itself. One of the arrested prostitutes, a sixteen-year-old girl, confessed that the gang had killed a number of tourists, and told police of the variety of methods used to drug the unlucky punters then rob them. If the haul was large the victim would usually be killed with a drug overdose, which would be administered by the girls' accomplices in the gang.

Local newspaper reports around the time of the raid described one of the gangsters behind the robberies as a German national with a Thai wife known as 'Vassana'. He was thought to groom and train girls specifically to act as bait for foreign male tourists, taking them to designated hotel rooms to be drugged and robbed. The gang was also held responsible for bullying foreign tourists into paying protection money during their stay in Pattaya.

The recent increase in drug and rob incidents in Pattaya may well stem from exposés of Thailand's sex industry in the world media during the mid-1990s, an anti-sex-tourism initiative that resulted in a 28 per cent drop in tourist arrivals in Thailand. Some of those involved in the sex tourism industry, unhappy with the drastic reduction in the market and unwilling to alter lifestyles to which they had grown accustomed during the industry's boom years, turned to robbery and murder to supplement their incomes.

And there's no doubt that these robberies are characteristically extremely lucrative. Credit cards are not widely accepted in the sex trade, and many punters carry large amounts of cash as well as valuables. *Sereechai Weekly*, a Thai newspaper in the US, reported a number of stories of which the following are typical: 40-year-old US tourist Cheklerkulai Josephine lost his gold necklace, Rolex watch and cash, a loss totalling around $20,000 in value, after licking the breasts of a young Thai woman in her hotel room; and 51-year-old German tourist Juhanee Koshonen lost around $17,000 of valuables after falling victim to a similar set-up.

Drug and rob incidents are among the most common means whereby tourists are robbed, and sex tourists are far from being the only victims. Charles Sobhraj is probably the most notorious practitioner of 'drug and rob' crimes, and is covered in 'The Hippie Hippie Shakedown'. Coaches belonging to the Cristobal Colon line in Mexico advertise a warning to passengers not to receive food or drink from any strangers, and crimes such as the following are common in India:

Josh and I must have looked a sight. After six months of travel we were both utterly emaciated, long-haired and wearing shabby Indian clothes that I certainly hadn't changed out of for many a month. Josh was in even more of a state than me – half dead really. I had insisted on travelling 2nd or 3rd class on trains throughout the trip – partly for economic reasons, partly some kind of proper traveller vibe I had going. But Josh insisted on travelling first class to Bombay and I couldn't really argue given his state.

In first class you get a little room with two bunk beds either side and a table in the middle. We were sharing with a 30-something Indian couple from Bombay. The wife was quite pretty, and they seemed quite wealthy in a showy kind of way – bright, really tacky Indian clothes – like bad Bollywood movie stars. The wife said very little. We were both instantly suspicious of the husband, as he kept trying to engage us in conversation in a pushy way. He bragged about his Rolex and his business in Bombay, and kept attempting to ask us questions about our wealth. He was obnoxious, obsequious – downright dodgy. I think we even had a conversation when they went out of the room about being careful with this guy. We popped some Valium and ordered our breakfast for the next day.

Our travel companions woke us up in the morning announcing the arrival of breakfast. Josh thought later the man added some powder to the orange juice, having poured some in his own glass first, explaining that it was vitamins, or something like that. I don't remember that, and find it hard to believe – particularly given the conversation we'd had about him. I was sharper than Josh in the morning because I had done less Valium. I ate all my food and downed my juice. Josh only ate a little, and had a couple of sips of juice.

Many hours passed. We were woken in Bombay station by the guard. The train was empty and had been for some time. It's difficult to remember exactly how I felt at the time. I knew I had been robbed immediately. I lost my camera, all my cash (about £50), but still had my plane ticket and travellers' cheques. Josh lost his camera, Walkman, some tapes, all his money and all his travellers' cheques. I think he must have been much ruder to the guy on the journey than me! I went mad at the guard and started shouting at him and pushing him around. Josh tried to calm me down but it didn't work and the police turned up. I think the police quickly cottoned on to what had happened; they led us into their office, took statements and gave us tea etc. I, however, grabbed a pole and dived over the table, knocking the main policeman backwards off his chair. I landed on him and pinned him down with the stick on his neck. I then proceeded to shout and scream obscenities at him. That's pretty much all I remember. Apparently they drove us to the Bombay Salvation Army hotel.

I was mad for three days before becoming sane again – Josh looked after me. A doctor at the Salvation Army told me they had drugged us with datura. I have since found out that it is a powdered root that basically puts you to sleep but has the unpleasant side effect of inducing near-psychotic behaviour in small doses, and permanent madness and often death in larger doses.

The following two chapters cover cases in which the objectification of foreign visitors, both in very different ways, led to their deaths. The first deals with the Japanese hostessing scene and the death of Briton Lucie Blackman; the second deals with the Guatemalan lynching of Japanese tourist Tetsuo Yamahiro.

3. CONCRETE BLONDE

TOKYO HOSTESSES AND THE DEATH OF LUCIE BLACKMAN

It was a friend's older sister who first put the idea into her head. Tokyo chic was growing then, even as the economy of the Rising Sun shrank. Rumours spread around the girls' schools of the English Home Counties, whispered tales of the ridiculous sums of money to be made there; girls who'd left to 'teach English' in Tokyo during their gap years returned smugly confident at their new financial health. Hostessing wasn't even like prostitution. All you had to do was be a companion to drunk businessmen: light their cigarettes, pour their drinks, feign interest in their jokes and compliment them on their karaoke skills. Of course, some girls might choose to take it further – that was up to them and, if they did, they didn't like to talk about it.

To 21-year-old Lucie Blackman it sounded like a dream job. She fitted all the criteria for success in the hostessing market, being young, good-looking, Caucasian and blonde. Moreover, she was looking for something different, a change from her job as an airline stewardess with British Airways. The job netted her only £15,000 a year working the long-haul routes to Africa and the Americas, and left her feeling permanently jetlagged. She could make that much in two good months as a hostess, and would be able to save money. If she didn't like it, she could always leave when she wanted to: this wasn't a career. Perhaps she could travel around Asia on the money she saved, or use it to become financially independent in the UK.

Lucie entered Tokyo with a tourist visa on 4 May 2000, and shared a room in a Yoyogi *gaijin* (foreigner) house with Louise Phillips, a friend who'd accompanied her from England to look for work. It didn't take long to find hostessing jobs: there were no signs of economic slump, of slashed expense accounts, in the Roppongi district, Tokyo's neon-lit after-hours playground. Suited salarymen still swilled sake in the hostess bars, while *gaijin* traders and US soldiers mixed with the city's youthful elite in drug-soaked nightclubs. Plenty of room for a young blonde Englishwoman to fit in.

Lucie started working at Casablanca, one of the area's more popular hostessing bars. At first she hated it. She was lonely and contacted her family by email or telephone daily – despite her experience of long-haul flights she'd rarely been away from the family home in Sevenoaks, Kent, for longer than four days before. She was also having trouble adjusting to the hours.

Work started at around 9 p.m. and finished at around 2 a.m., after which most of the girls would visit the area's nightclubs to unwind, many spending their newly earned cash on readily available drugs. Lucie felt jetlagged and she wasn't even flying.

At first she resented the pressure to go on *dohans* – paid dates with some of the clubs' clients, who would take the girls out to dinner before the start of their working day then drop them off at the clubs. The clubs earned a cut from each *dohan* and used a quota system to ensure that their hostesses made money for them even outside the premises. But the lavish gifts bestowed on the girls were theirs to keep, and Lucie quickly realised that she could make a lot more money this way, as it encouraged repeat customers to treat her as their special favourite.

After a couple of months she'd settled into the scene. She'd started making money, and knew she'd make more as she built up relationships with the clients. She'd even gone on a few dates – rather than *dohans* – with a US serviceman, Scott Fraser, who was stationed on the aircraft carrier USS *Kittyhawk*.

On 1 July Lucie left her flat to go on a *dohan* with a Casablanca customer, who'd promised her a prepaid mobile phone if she had lunch with him. She didn't tell anyone his name and planned to meet up with Scott and Louise later that evening. She called Louise three times during the day: first at 1.30 p.m. to say that she'd met her lunch date, second at

5.00 p.m. to say that she was being taken to the beach, and lastly at 7.00 p.m., when she told Louise that she would be back in half an hour. She then called Scott and left the same message. She was never seen or heard from alive again.

INSIDE THE CASABLANCA

Hostessing is loosely related to the Japanese *geisha* tradition which ensured historically that samurai a long way from home were not deprived of female company. Nowadays it bears more resemblance to the erstwhile Playboy bunny clubs: the club rents the girls out by the hour to accompany the men and act as platonic girlfriends. They may choose to have sex with their clients; that is up to them. More usually they are there to look good, to impress a businessman's client, to help the closing of a deal, or simply to act as a foil to blustery, drunk salarymen, a focal point that cements the ritual bonding key to Japanese business life.

Most hostesses are Japanese, but in the early 1980s Caucasian women became increasingly popular in some of the more upmarket clubs, with young, blonde, English-speaking beauties the most coveted companions. It was always going to happen. The peculiar Japanese fixation on certain Western cultural forms and artefacts – golf, scotch, rock'n'roll – translates to sex as well. But this isn't the only reason for the appeal: exoticism is key here, as elsewhere in the global sex industry. And while many Western hostesses will deny that they are part of such an industry, known in Japan as the *mizushobai* (water trade), there is no doubt in the eyes of Japanese commentators of their social position.

The most upmarket hostess bars are more likely to be found in Ginza or Akasaka than Roppongi. Here expensive designer wear is the norm, clients must be introduced, and bills are sent discreetly to the workplace. A sexual relationship at this end of the spectrum does not just entail money changing hands but often invitations to trips abroad to accompany the client, or new apartments, love nests in which a hostess may live.

At the lowest end of the scale women from Eastern Europe or Southeast Asia are paraded around topless or naked in hostess bars that are little more than brothels. Here the links to organised crime are strongest, with many hostesses entering the country on forged documents or as fake wives to low-ranking yakuza, Japanese gangsters. When these women go missing there is no national outcry – they are rarely missed at home and there are plenty more to take their place. As one Southeast Asian hostess put it in a TV interview during the search for Blackman, 'No one would have been interested if it had been one of us.' But many are reluctant to leave on the rare occasions that aid agencies take up their plight; theirs is a world of few options, and hostessing – for all of the attendant exploitation and danger – pays.

The Casablanca – which has changed its name since the Blackman scandal – operates between the two ends of the scale. It is not in the upper echelon of Roppongi hostess bars, but nor is it a brothel. Japan's elite would shun the bar, while yakuza are known to frequent it; its location, above a strip club and sandwiched between a videogame arcade and a 'sexual harassment' bar, gives an idea of its level of class.

The specialist nature of many Japanese sex establishments is often surprising to Western observers more used to go-go bars and lapdancing clubs. At 'sexual harassment' bars the hostesses are dressed as secretaries and the men may fondle and pet them at whim; at 'no-pan' bars waitresses wear no panties, and drinks are kept on high shelves – to serve customers they must reach up, displaying themselves in the process; and at yobai clubs, named after the folkloric practice of men taking brides in their sleep, prostitutes feign sleep during their clients' drunken fumblings.

It is not only young Western women who flock to Japan to make money doing things they wouldn't be seen doing at home; there is a long tradition of Hollywood stars who shun the advertising industry in the West but happily make adverts in Japan. And until recently, hostessing wasn't seen as dangerous for the fresh-faced middle-class blondes who still flock to Tokyo looking for easy money.

But as the Japanese economic bubble has burst, more is expected of the hostesses for less money. Pressure to have sex on *dohans* is greater, and many clients have predilections – as demonstrated by the popularity of bondage and SM practices in Japan – the hostesses may find, at the very least, painful. Many hostesses get mixed up with yakuza, and there are rumours of links to the sex slave trade in Nigeria. Where once the only danger to Western hostesses seemed to be boredom, the game is now sleazier, nastier and a lot more brutal.

Blackman is not the only Western hostess to have gone missing. The case of Canadian Tiffany Rain Fordham, who went missing in 1997, has still not been solved. 27 at the time of her disappearance, Fordham, who had worked as a hostess in Roppongi before, vanished there in late September after a night out with friends. Her fiancé, Jason Frechette, spent three months scouring the city for leads, but found nothing; local police considered him their prime suspect for a while but eventually cleared him of any involvement. The case is still open – but with every month that passes the chances of finding out what happened to Fordham grow increasingly slim.

SEASIDE *DOHAN*

On the day after Lucie's disappearance her flatmate received a phone call from a man who identified himself as Akira Takagi. He told her that 'Lucie has joined a newly risen cult. She is safe and training in a hut in Chiba.'

Louise promptly called Lucie's mother in England, who in turn called her other daughter, Sophie, and her estranged husband Tim. Sophie, who worked as a cardiac technician at a local hospital, prepared to fly to Tokyo the next day. Tim went to his bank and secured a loan of £20,000, although by the time his investigation was over he would have spent almost five times that, most of the money donated by relatives. After leaving the day-to-day running of his small home-building company to his partners, he flew out to join Sophie.

Together they launched a media blitz, distributing 30,000 posters featuring Lucie's picture in the first two weeks alone, and giving a series of press conferences. But they seemed to be the only people taking Lucie's disappearance seriously. They were dismayed by what they saw as police apathy and a reluctance to follow up leads. The calls Lucie had made on 1 July would surely be the best lead – but the police explained that privacy laws made it illegal to trace them, and that in any case the technology to do so was beyond them. Their enquiries at Casablanca were similarly fruitless: nobody could give them any information regarding Lucie's date. They worried that because Lucie had been working illegally in Japan – she had only had a tourist visa – the authorities had taken the attitude that she deserved whatever fate had befallen her.

Help came from strange quarters. The British tabloid the *Sun* speculated that Lucie might have been kidnapped by an 'evil Japanese cult' for use as a sex slave. More usefully, a friend of Lucie's father had worked as a limo driver for Virgin boss Richard Branson; he called Branson's office and Virgin subsequently offered to help the Blackmans set up a Tokyo office for their investigation.

From the outset the Blackmans had petitioned the British Foreign Office for their help, and the case had been brought to the attention of Prime Minister Tony Blair. Coincidentally Blair was due to visit Japan on 21 July for the Group of Eight economic summit, and he took the opportunity to raise the issue with the Japanese prime minister, Yoshiro Mori.

The diplomatic contact finally had an impact on the investigation: Tim Blackman was told that the legal and technical difficulties with tracing Lucie's last calls had been resolved. The wealth of speculation in both the local and international press added further weight to the investigation. In Japan the issues involved – the treatment of women, Tokyo's moral decadence, and the country's relationship with the West – led to the case being the touchstone for a sense of national crisis. The lurid speculations about sex and drug cults were matched in their feverish intensity only by the bouts of soul-searching which filled editorials – how had it come to this?

Aside from the phone calls, the Blackmans' own investigation yielded many other leads. Some were distracting: a letter purporting to be from Lucie, and stating that she was alive and well and did not want to be found, was sent to the investigation office in Tokyo. Tim Blackman didn't recognise the signature as that of his daughter. In another development, a 52-year-old Japanese man committed suicide in Tokyo three days after having been questioned about Lucie's disappearance by police. Several police posters concerning Lucie's possible abduction were found in the dead man's apartment. The motives for the suicide are unknown to this day.

More fruitful were the calls from other hostesses. Three foreign women came forward with stories of how they had been working as Roppongi hostesses when they were invited on a *dohan* to a seaside restaurant with a well-to-do Japanese businessman, who had identified himself under a different name to each of the women. He had taken them to his apartment, inviting them to watch a film with him or asking for help moving boxes, and had proposed that they should drink a glass of wine with him on their arrival. If the wine tasted strange it was, he explained, because it contained special herbs; it was a rare wine from India or the Philippines, a notable treat they probably hadn't enjoyed before.

Each of the girls woke up 24 to 48 hours later in the man's apartment, feeling nauseous and weak, with no memory of what had happened; he told them either that they had drunk too much the night before, or that there had been a gas leak. The women, none of whom were convinced by his explanation, knew that the police would ignore their complaints – they were working in Japan illegally, after all – and had waited until now to come forward.

'WOMEN ARE ONLY GOOD FOR SEX'

Japanese police, who had more officers assigned to this case than to the notorious sarin nerve gas attack on the Tokyo subway in 1995, finally arrested a failed real-estate speculator, 48-year-old Joji Obara, in connection with Blackman's disappearance. The calls she'd made had been traced back to his prepaid mobile phone, and a search of his seaside apartment uncovered not only blonde hairs matching hers but also an undeveloped roll of film featuring her in pictures taken not far from the apartment. But he denied knowing her, and in the absence of a body police were unable to charge him for any crimes relating to the missing English hostess.

However, police did find, while searching a number of other properties belonging to Obara, not only the frozen body of an alsatian in a freezer – Obara hoped that he could soon 'reanimate my loving pet into a clone dog' – but also around 200 videos depicting him allegedly molesting 'sleeping' women. In some he is said to be wearing only a Zorro mask.

Police scoured the videos for evidence of rapes with which he could be charged, and found that among his victims were the three foreign hostesses who'd contacted the Blackmans. They agreed to help the prosecution, and Obara was duly charged with several rapes.

Obara's reaction to the charges was to release a statement to the press that the women had consented to have sex with him: 'These ladies who are supposed to be victims are all foreign hostesses or sex club girls. Many took cocaine or other drugs in front of me, and all of them agreed to have sex for money.' But the evidence told a different story. Police had found Obara's diaries, in which between 1983 and 1995 he had mentioned the names of 200 women in relation to 'conquer play', which prosecutors later maintained was a euphemism for drug rapes. Code words were written alongside most of the names, many of which were thought to represent the types of drugs given to the girls. Other statements made by Obara in his diaries, and leaked to the press, did nothing to help his case: 'I can not do women who are conscious', a sinister take on the practice of *yobai*, or 'Women are only good for sex. I will lie to them. I will seek revenge. Revenge on the world.'

The videos themselves don't appear to show consensual sex either, with Obara struggling to carry prone bodies to a bed, tie them down and secure gags – known in at least one case to have been soaked with chloroform – over their mouths. He would then penetrate them, often with foreign objects, and sodomise them, usually over a period of twelve hours. He recorded each assault with high-quality video equipment and arranged lights around the bed for maximum exposure. One of his victims, left too close to the lights, suffered from burns, and he told her when she awoke that she'd burned herself while drunk.

CHAINSAWS AND CEMENT

On 9 February 2001, the final day before their search was due to end, police finally found Lucie Blackman's body. They'd searched the beach near Obara's apartment in the Miura district before, but nobody had thought to look under the discarded bathtub lodged in a small cave. This time they lifted the tub and found heavily decomposed human remains in plastic bags. The body had been sawn into eight pieces. They wouldn't have been able to identify Blackman from these, but her head had been encased in cement. When the block was broken open so that her dental records could be checked, police had an instant clue as to the identity of the corpse – the long, natural blonde hair.

Police soon pieced together a chilling account of Obara's activities following Blackman's disappearance. On 2 July he called local hospitals to ask how to treat a victim of a drug overdose; shortly afterwards he called the coastguard to ask about their protocol for dealing with bodies found at sea. The next day he bought a chainsaw, cement mix – which matched the cement used to encase Blackman's head – and other tools from a local hardware shop. That afternoon the manager of the apartment block called police to report that one of his tenants was acting strangely. When police duly called on Obara he had cement on his hands, and became agitated when they asked to see his bathroom, refusing to let them in. Incredibly, they left without pressing the issue.

Obara, a compulsive hoarder rather than a master criminal, not only kept video evidence of his crimes but also recorded all of his phone calls and kept the receipts for the tools with which he is alleged to have dismembered Lucie Blackman's body. Police found other receipts in his apartment linking him to another hostess, Australian Carita Ridgeway. In 1992 he had taken Ridgeway to a hospital, telling staff that she had eaten bad shellfish. She died a few days later, misdiagnosed as having suffered liver failure from food infected with hepatitis. Obara even comforted her parents when they came to collect their daughter's body.

By sheer coincidence Ridgeway's liver had been preserved at the Tokyo Women's Hospital, where her autopsy had been performed, and in the wake of Obara's arrest and the reopening of the Ridgeway case it was tested for chloroform. The test showed toxic levels of the drug, and Obara was charged with fatally drugging and raping Ridgeway.

But police had left it too long to charge Obara with Blackman's murder: her remains were so far decomposed that the cause of death was uncertain, and they had no witnesses to the alleged murder, although they have hinted that they have a video of Obara assaulting her.

It has been suggested that police ineptitude and indifference has allowed Obara to escape justice before. In October 1997 a young British hostess arrived at Club Cadeau, her place of work, seriously ill. She had been on a *dohan* with a client now thought to have been Obara, and believed herself to have been drugged and raped. The club owner took her to hospital, where tests revealed that her liver function was seriously depleted. He then took her to the police in an attempt to help her file rape charges, but they refused to open a case: he was a club owner, and she was a hostess. Whatever had happened, they didn't want to know.

Obara maintains his innocence of all charges, stating when told of the discovery of Blackman's body that the police must have put it there. His trial was delayed for a year when all of his lawyers resigned, and it looks likely to drag on for some time.

'THE ONLY WAY I COULD GET YOU WOULD BE TO DRUG YOU'

Joji Obara was born in 1952 to a poor Korean family in Osaka. His father worked his way up from being a scrap collector to a taxi driver, and by investing his savings he managed to buy a fleet of cars. He diversified into owning a string of pachinko (a popular cross between pinball and slot machines) parlours, which made him a fortune. But for all his financial success, he was aware that being Korean meant that he would always be treated as a second-class citizen, and he instilled in his son a determination to transcend his heritage; the young Obara, asked to write a message in his junior high-school yearbook, stated that 'Upbringing is more important than family name.'

Obara attended Japan's most prestigious high school, his father sending him to live with a maid in a Den'en Chofu mansion he bought specifically for the purpose. When Obara's father died, he left extensive holdings in Tokyo and Osaka to his seventeen-year-old son.

Obara graduated from university with degrees in politics and law in 1981, and became a naturalised Japanese citizen. Like many of his peers, he saw himself at the forefront of the Japanese boom economy, scorning a stable corporate job in favour of disastrous real-estate speculation. His investment company, Plant, which he formed towards the end of the boom years, crashed badly in the early 1990s, and Obara was bailed out by his mother, who still owned the lucrative pachinko chain. After she paid a creditor nearly $33 million in cash the company reportedly became a front for a yakuza money-laundering operation.

Obara continued to live in style, even as the Den'en Chofu mansion began to crumble and the three vintage sports cars he didn't use rusted in the garage. He became a creature of the night, prowling Roppongi in his Ferrari or his red Rolls-Royce Silver Cloud; police records show that almost all of his phone calls were made between sunset and sunrise.

Before his arrest in 2000 he had been in trouble with the police only once, when he was arrested in a women's toilet in 1998 in the beach town of Shirahama. He was in drag and attempting to videotape a woman urinating; he was fined the equivalent of $75 and charged with a misdemeanour.

Like many men of his generation, Obara had a veneration verging on the obsessive for certain Western qualities. He had surgery on his eyes to Westernise them, and at 1.7 metres tall took growth hormones in the misguided belief that they would make him taller, as well as wearing inserts in his shoes. Perhaps mindful of the failure of such efforts, Obara shunned the camera. Staff at his real-estate company were forbidden to take photos of him, and the media had to rely on one grainy photo taken in the 1970s.

Some of his peers, when faced with the evidence indicting Obara as a serial rapist, have had a curious response. Naoko Tomono, a journalist who has written extensively about the Obara case for the Japanese press, explains that: 'They respect him as a man comfortable going to expensive bars and picking up Western girls.' Other commentators point out that his apparent obsession with Caucasian women is typical of Japanese men of his generation. Strange tributes have been paid to the serial rapist, as men began to introduce themselves to Roppongi hostesses as 'Joji Obara'. One hostess at Casablanca was told by a client that 'I know a girl like you would never sleep with me. The only way I could get you would be to drug you.'

The British press predictably made much of this idea of a fiendish Oriental's fixation on blonde Caucasian women; some related it to the obsession with Western women shown by Japanese cannibal Issei Sagawa, who murdered and ate parts of a Dutch student in Paris in 1981. Sagawa attempted to explain his actions by writing: 'I am a very short, ugly, yellow monkey man. I admired the tall, beautiful white girls, and I wanted to taste them. I strongly wanted to eat their meat.'

But the vast majority of Obara's rape victims were Japanese; some, who realised that they had been raped, were allegedly paid off by him to keep quiet. If this serial rapist had been operating for twenty years, word was sure to have spread locally, and Western women may have been attractive victims to Obara for another reason altogether – they were less likely to have been warned about him, and wouldn't recognise the danger signs as readily as Japanese women might. He may also have thought they were less likely to go to the police; if Blackman had not died – and it is unlikely, given the evidence, that he had meant to kill her – Obara might still be drugging and raping women from Roppongi's hostess bars.

That it took the disappearance of a blonde, photogenic and media-friendly English girl to expose Obara has been pointed to by some as typical of the bias and distorting effect of the Western media. Most views are not as extreme as the following, taken from an Internet posting on the site set up to help track down Tiffanny Fordham:

> *I am Japanese woman, and I am sick and tired hearing lucie blackman name she is white woman in Japan and white woman in Japan come to take our man from us – I hope lucie blackman goes to HELL and all you filthy white foreigners in my country – you people are filthy people and I hate all white foreigner so I am happy lucie dead!! fuck you!!*

But it has not gone unnoticed that the deaths or disappearances of other hostesses in Japan – and there have been many – do not receive the same level of media interest or police investigation.

And nor would they in the West. Imagine a woman from Japan, Thailand or Korea working illegally in the sex industry in London, for instance, who went missing. The case would barely merit a single mention in local newspapers, much less the national news. This is not a hypothetical situation: a visit to Soho's Chinatown reveals the faces of many missing women staring out from posters on Japanese and Chinese restaurant windows.

But this is of little comfort or concern to the Blackman family, who were in the news again in January 2003 in a bizarre coda to the Obara saga. A 59-year-old London man was charged with attempting to defraud the family during the investigation by delivering what he claimed was vital information regarding Lucie's whereabouts in exchange for large sums of money. The man was also charged with a further count of deception relating to a Chelmsford family whose son is missing; police reported that the techniques allegedly used in both cases were identical. For some the grief of a family is just one more business opportunity.

4. NEVER GET OUT OF THE BUS

TOURIST LYNCHING IN GUATEMALA

Nobody's really sure exactly where the rumour started. A Satanic cult from abroad was coming to the Guatemalan mountain village of Todos Santos to abduct children. The children were to be killed in sacrificial rituals, their hearts removed, in what was perhaps an atavistic memory of Aztec excesses. Whatever the source, a local newspaper and radio station added form and weight to the story: the cult had hired the football pitch as its base of operations, with the complicity of local officials; the leader of the cult was from LA; and the sacrifice of the villagers' children was to take place during an all-night orgy of bloodletting.

The local government of the Huehuetenango department, in which Todos Santos is located, issued their own statements denying that any Satanic activity was scheduled to take place. But their protestations probably only helped to fuel the fire, especially in a village where Spanish is not the main language and the bulk of whose inhabitants can neither read nor write; in any case, if the rumours were untrue, why were people talking about them on the radio? Bad news spreads like a virus; retractions rarely carry the same weight. Sometimes we want to believe the worst.

On 29 April 2000 a large tour-bus run by Service Travel Service (STS) and containing 23 tourists, the majority of whom were Japanese, descended upon Todos Santos. The village is the most frequently visited area in the Cuchumatanes, the largest non-volcanic peaks in Central America, and the only place to receive a steady flow of tourists. The isolation of the village and its setting, nestled in the lap of immense cloud-wreathed mountain ridges, are part of the attraction; but the real draw is the indigenous culture. The men wear intricately woven shirts, no two the same, and red and white striped trousers which, to the untrained English eye, resemble butchering apparel. The women's clothes are even more remarkable: impossibly complex patterns woven into purple *huipiles* (sleeveless smocks) which are worn over dark blue tops.

The village, sleepy and quiet for most of the week, draws massive crowds for the Saturday market, traders coming from tiny *aldeas* (small settlements) for miles around to trade in food, quack remedies and donated US clothing: it is not unusual to see children wearing full traditional costume over a T-shirt proclaiming the glories of some long-defunct American wrestler.

The Japanese tour bus, grey with tinted windows, had come on a market day, during which the photographic opportunities would be far greater. The children in Todos Santos look especially spectacular, wide-eyed with strong, healthy features and winning smiles, and as some of the tourists filed out of their guest house, ready to record events with forensic determination, many planned to capture the moment with pictures of these exquisitely clad infants.

One tourist leaned over a 22-year-old woman who carried a child wrapped in a shawl on her back. As the child began to cry the tourist reached forward, keen to help; but the mother, convinced that her worst nightmares had come true, screamed out that the Satanists were stealing her child. Her husband joined the fray, and another woman called out to the market traders to help stop the Satanists from harming any children. Rumours quickly spread that the Japanese had already taken some babies on to their bus, and a crowd formed around the tourists, its numbers swelling as villagers flocked to the scene. The tourists moved on, unable to understand the angry faces and dark mutterings that surrounded them. Then a stone was thrown, and all hell broke loose. The tourist who'd reached for the child was set upon, and one of his friends, 39-year-old Tetsuo Yamahiro, tried to help him. The enraged crowd pelted Yamahiro with sticks and stones until he was unconscious; the death blow was said to have been struck by a grandmother wielding a stick more normally used for weaving.

The Guatemalan tour-bus driver, 44-year-old Edgar Castellanos, heard the commotion and tried to help those of his charges who had barricaded themselves inside the tour bus. But the crowd reserved a special wrath for this countryman who had betrayed them – Castellanos was also beaten with sticks and stones and then hacked into pieces with a machete. His body was then drenched with petrol and set on fire. The police finally managed to lead the remaining tourists to protective custody after telling the mob that the Japanese were being arrested; even then two policemen were injured in a scuffle. When the newly elected mayor confronted the crowd and asked with a megaphone for the parents of any child that had been harmed to step forward, none did; the realisation dawned on the mob, many still intent on blood vengeance, that an appalling mistake had been made.

In the days following the attack the bodies were recovered; that of Yamahiro was flown back to Japan, along with most of the Japanese tourists, who had unsurprisingly decided to cut their holiday short. Police were charged with finding the leaders of the mob, and local newspapers were filled with hand-wringing editorials pleading for Guatemala not to fall into anarchy: apart from anything else, the tourist dollar was too important for that to happen.

It was noted that, ironically enough, the department of Huehuetenango had been especially well favoured with Japanese development money, and it was hoped that the event would not muddy the waters between the two countries. STS made a statement advising tourists to ask for permission before taking photographs in future, and stated that they would continue to run services to the village. An editorial in one local paper noted that the company would be obliged to offer an especially irresistible promotion to renew interest in the route.

The police soon found four people who, they contended, had initiated and taken the key part in the lynchings. The four – all men – were charged with murder and jailed, amid complaints that they were being made scapegoats for an act which in effect had no leaders. If the treatment of the men was aimed as a sop to the tourist industry and the Japanese government, however, it worked: tourists still visit Todos Santos, and the Japanese government still funds development programmes in the Cuchumatanes. In June 2000 the four men were acquitted due to lack of evidence.

HERE BE DEMONS

Lynchings are extremely common in Guatemala. The national newspapers for the fortnight following the Todos Santos incident ran stories on two separate, unrelated lynchings, and a quick scan of contemporary papers reveals that the problem has not gone away. Huehuetenango department, an economically deprived area in the far north-west of the country, is the most badly affected, and most lynchings follow the identification – often erroneous – of a thief or a kidnapper; in one incident two men who stole a football during a game were killed. There is little faith in the police in Guatemala; they are considered by most to be rotten to the core, and any thieves who are arrested are said soon to be able to buy their way back on to the streets.

Why were the rumours of Satanic rituals so strong? Rural Guatemalans are a superstitious people; magic and religion are for them inextricably linked. The disapproval of the Catholic Church has done nothing to stop the worship of Maximon, or San Simon, Guatemala's very own Baron Samedi: an amoral divinity, the patron saint of thieves and prostitutes, whose lifesize dummy, clad in Western clothes, is entreated to help worshippers who bring offerings of tobacco, candles and *aguardiente*, which is routinely poured into the dummy's mouth. A Maximon shrine typically features supplicants being 'cleansed' with lashes of a herb, tarot and palm readings on tables at the far end of the room, and a fire just outside, around which women and children work themselves into a sweat by hyperventilating on huge cigars as proof of their devotion. Christianity has strong roots here, but it is of a kind resembling the early Western Christian era, during which even the blackest grimoires adopted a pious tone.

Initially Christianity was introduced into Guatemala by the Catholic Church, which in its modern manifestation at least is reluctant to commit itself on the subject of Satan and his demonic hordes. Following the CIA-sponsored ousting of President Arbenz in 1954, prompted by his government's land reforms, which were considered damaging to US commercial interests, Guatemala's *de facto* military dictatorships suppressed the activities of the Catholic Church. They argued that priests were subversives who routinely allied themselves with the land reform cause, then considered uniquely the province of terrorists.

Into the vacuum stepped a host of evangelical organisations, which were welcomed by dictators for being politically more conservative, even if they boasted a more literal interpretation of Bible doctrine than their Catholic predecessors. If the Catholic Church was wary of giving credence to such superstitious hokum as the malign influence of Satan, the evangelical churches revelled in it. And the influence of evangelism is especially strong in these mountain villages: appalling, ear-rendingly amplified evangelical 'rock' is played from dawn to dusk in Todos Santos and the surrounding area, and each week more villagers are welcomed into the fold. The influence of the churches was strengthened in the wake of General Rios Montt's military coup in 1982 – the general, as well as presiding over the genocide of rural Mayans, is a fervent evangelist.

If Christian organisations had a hand in fomenting the distrust of foreigners which led to the Todos Santos lynching, it would not be for the first time. In the mid-nineteenth century, when the failed Republic of Central America was in the throes of civil war, priests in Guatemala took advantage of a cholera epidemic to persuade the indigenous people that foreigners had poisoned the waters; the clergy, angered by encroachments on its property and power by the ruling Liberal Party, hoped to swing the balance of power back in their favour by encouraging popular hatred of foreigners. A bloodbath ensued.

In that particular case the rationale for encouraging distrust is easy to work out; it is more difficult to explain why evangelical organisations should today wish to provoke hatred against foreigners. Indeed, many of the foreigners working in the region *are* evangelists: glassy-eyed American preachers and Bible translators, spreading the good word with aggressive bonhomie. If evangelical churches were the source of the rumour, perhaps it stemmed simply from a realisation that unity is far stronger against a common enemy: if people were not part of the evangelical movement, they were part of the problem.

Ritos satanicos – satanic rites – appear again and again in Guatemalan newspapers. A year before the Todos Santos lynching a schoolgirl in the town of Huehuetenango was brutally raped and murdered, in what was considered to be part of a Satanic ritual. Newspapers published during the fortnight after the Todos Santos incident show a number of cases involving Satanism, usually concerning groups of criminally minded young men.

This may be the result of pure pop Satanism: the influence of heavy metal culture worldwide is huge, and any Satanic iconography found during police raids might simply have been taken from the covers of Black Sabbath and Slayer records. It is also conceivable that once people have heard about the power of the He-goat, they will expect a better return on their spiritual investment by joining his monstrous cabal than by siding with the Nazarene.

A local cultural feature is also worth bearing in mind. The Japanese tourists, in their monochrome bus and wearing principally black clothes, may have seemed harbingers of death in a community in which the importance of colour can be difficult for an outsider to understand. Red, the principal colour on villagers' clothes, symbolises the life blood of the people and the warmth of the sun. Black is its symbolic opposite, linked to death and the withering cold of the mountain night.

Fear of Satanists has led to attacks on tourists elsewhere as well. In a similar, but less serious, recent case, an Austrian visitor to Edremit in Turkey was stoned by locals convinced he was a devil-worshipper. 28-year-old Sascha Michael Mariacher had dyed his hair red, was dressed in black and had facial piercings, all of which led villagers to suspect his religious persuasion; police took him into custody for his own protection. He was not seriously hurt in the attack.

CHILD-SNATCHER

The root of the child-snatching rumour is harder to pin down. Stories that foreign missionaries were kidnapping Mayan babies to make soap were circulating as early as 1907, and the contemporary belief that Mayan children are routinely stolen for the sale of their vital organs recalls organ theft rumours throughout the developing world, as we'll see later.

A notice in four languages in the most popular tourist hang-out in Todos Santos explained that a number of incidents had occurred shortly before the lynching to equate Westerners with child-snatchers in local minds. In Peten department, in the far north of the country, the remains of nine children were found near the house of Billy Bruce, a US citizen; his son was at the time of writing awaiting trial for kidnapping two children. The notice further stated that before the lynching another rumour had circulated, involving a local child who was kidnapped and killed by a local man.

This writer heard another story about an American citizen being arrested early in 2000 in Coban, in the central Alta Verapaz department, for trafficking in children; the story may stem from the Bruce incidents. While it was never explained in these stories precisely what was to be done with these children, another story, also told in an attempt to explain local distrust of foreigners, was more specific.

In this story a US citizen is crossing a border in Central America, say Guatemala to Mexico. He is carrying a child, which is heavily wrapped up, and explains to border officials that the baby is very ill. When officials ask to inspect the child the American refuses, for the sake of the child's health, or so he claims. Officials persist in their request and finally remove the child forcibly. Unusually, it doesn't scream or cry out. It is dead: the brain and innards have been removed, the body stuffed full of drugs and the incisions sewn up.

The tale has all the characteristics of an urban myth – a grisly punchline and a viral urge to be retold – but may have some basis in fact: smugglers have been known to carry surgically implanted drug packages themselves, after all. What is unlikely is that a baby would be kidnapped and killed specifically for this purpose – especially a baby whose racial type did not match that of the ostensible parent.

While there is little hard evidence of foreign tourists stealing Mayan children, there is a thriving trade in adoptions, many of which are arranged by Western evangelical organisations for substantial profit. For Mayan people, long accustomed to extremely close relationships with their children, the coercive techniques used by some adoption agencies to acquire children can breed considerable resentment. (Traditionally high infant mortality rates have led mothers to take great care of babies; there are no daycare centres here, and children spend their first years strapped to their mother's front or back.)

In 1994 an Alaskan woman was beaten into a coma after Mayan villagers mistakenly believed that she had stolen a child. The belief is still current – this writer was threatened with a stoning by women who accused him of being a *ladron de ninos*, a child snatcher, while walking in a village north of Todos Santos – and it is possible that such concerns are encouraged by conservative politicians, keen to have as few foreigners as possible witness the unravelling of the Guatemalan peace process.

Another explanation offered for the protectiveness of the Cuchumatanes people towards their children is that this is the legacy of a bloody civil war in which hundreds of thousands of villagers were 'disappeared' by the military, and their children widely dispersed. Several hundred inhabitants of Todos Santos were slaughtered on one day in 1982 by soldiers, after the military saw that rebels had raised a flag bearing the image of Che Guevara in the town. The killings not only brutalised the community but also taught it that violence was an effective means of dealing with undesirables.

These mountains saw some of the fiercest fighting of the war, and a distrust of North Americans – to most rural Guatemalans any Westerner will automatically be assumed to come from *El Norte* – makes sense insofar as the US was heavily involved in both initiating and subsidising the war. But the soldiers who fought in the conflict were Guatemalans; and the distrust of foreigners is so strong among these mountain people that it is difficult to attribute it solely to the factors considered so far.

Perhaps it has a deeper root, one considered in other societies to be the essential cause of racism and xenophobia – a desire to protect their culture. The Cuchumatanes people have had their lives and culture severely threatened over the ages – by warring tribes, by the Spanish, by soldiers during the civil war – and perhaps now they face the most insidious threat of all: tourism. The distrust of foreigners – notwithstanding the friendliness exhibited by many locals on an individual level – may be an instinctive attempt to stem the tide of assimilation into a foreign culture that invariably accompanies tourist development.

It is not only tourism but Western influence in general that is distrusted here. The growing crime rate in these traditional villages has been blamed on materialistic Western influences, brought back by those who have travelled to the US or the larger Guatemalan cities looking for work, and spread by imported programming on radio and TV. At a town meeting in the late 1990s the mayor blamed a spate of robberies on a group of long-haired young heavy metal fans, the sons of the local elite, in a bid to undermine local confidence in their fathers as potential candidates for the mayoralty. He encouraged people to take matters into their own hands and, when one young man came to challenge the mayor for evidence to support his claims, that is exactly what they did, beating him and holding him down while one man went to find some petrol. Eventually the youth broke free and managed to escape. His crime? Having been influenced by Western culture. It would have been the first lynching in Todos Santos.

ORGAN THEFT

Baby snatching. The removal of body parts. The stories are common among poor people in shanty towns from Africa to

South America. In Brazil the ghoulish rumours centre around large blue and yellow vans driven by American or Japanese agents, which scour poor neighbourhoods in search of stray children. When children are found they are captured and put into the back of the van. Their eviscerated bodies are found later, dumped by the roadside, missing eyes, heart, lungs and kidneys.

In East Africa some talk of brothels in which men are drugged while sitting on chairs above trapdoors; as soon as they are unconscious they drop to a basement in which they are operated on, their skin and organs removed and their blood drained. Other African rumours feature vans abducting people for the removal of their organs, to be used in *muti* (magic) rituals, or for their blood.

The blood rumour has been especially strong in Malawi recently, where stories of vampires have led to numerous lynchings of strangers acting suspiciously. The unpopular government of President Bakili Muluzi, so the rumour goes, employs the creatures to extract blood which can be exchanged for food with international aid agencies. Muluzi's protest that 'No government can suck the blood of its people' has only added fuel to the fire. Similarly in South America, where government officials have made radio statements protesting that tales of forced organ removal are false, the denials exacerbate the situation. Children are locked away at home; strangers and foreigners are shunned.

The easiest way to explain the popularity of such rumours is that they are true as metaphors. The developed world *does* suck the blood of the developing world; the bodies of the poor *are* used by the rich, from Free Trade Zone sweatshops to sex tourism brothels. But they are also true in a more literal sense: illegal organ harvesting of the bodies of the poor is common in the developing world, and has even occurred in the UK, and the shady practices of some adoption agencies in Brazil and Guatemala might legitimately be described as baby snatching. It's unsurprising that in the minds of many the thriving trade in adoption is confused with the trade in organs; perhaps these babies are worth more dead than alive.

It's also true that a global black market for body parts from living donors exists. In the early 1980s, 131 patients from three renal units in the United Arab Emirates travelled to Bombay where they bought kidneys, through brokers, from living donors; and in 2002 a British GP told undercover journalists that he could arrange for a dying man to travel to India and purchase a kidney from a living donor for £3,000. It is not difficult to extrapolate from these known facts to beliefs that the rich will have potential donors killed for their organs.

The stories have now spread to the developed world. One rumour which has circulated in both the worlds of tourism and business travel involves a Western man being drugged and having organs stolen, usually both kidneys. A typical telling of the tale, which in common with urban myths the world over has never happened to the teller, is the following, told to anthropologist Nancy Scheper-Hughes during her research for a paper entitled *Theft of Life*:

> [T]his Mexican lady who works in the kitchen of 'Noah's Bagels' told me about a friend of hers who had gotten drugged and abducted from Spengler's [a seafood restaurant]. The guy was just sitting at the bar and minding his own business when a businessman, dressed up to kill in a Giorgio Armani suit, sat down next to him and bought him a few drinks. Well, the guy finally passed out cold and the next day the police discovered him still unconscious in a dumpster. He was OK but he had a very fine little incision on his stomach, like it was done by professionals, you know.

The story is probably untrue; many tests for compatibility have to be carried out before successful organ transference, and the American National Kidney Foundation, alarmed by the damaging effect of the rumour on voluntary organ donation, asked in a press release dated 4 April 1997 for 'any individual who claims to have had his or her kidneys illegally removed to step forward and contact the foundation'. So far nobody has taken them up on the offer.

What is interesting here is the spread of these stories from the impoverished to the privileged, from developing to developed world. The popularity of the rumour in the West may stem from a guilty fear: a recognition that poor people often do not have control over their bodies, and that the inequalities which lead to this situation are fostered by the developed world; with this recognition may come a fear of a socio-economic backsliding, of becoming like these poor people. Perhaps the retelling of the story has its roots in a talismanic urge, a conviction that through repetition and representation lies protection.

Perhaps, finally, the guilt behind the story is altogether simpler, especially in respect of the variants which involve a male victim being approached by a woman in a bar. The theme of punishment for sex, or even for desire, is long established; this telling of the organ theft story may be little more than a peculiarly modern addition.

5. STAYING ON

THE TOURISTS THAT NEVER MAKE IT BACK

'I went a little farther,' he said, 'then still a little farther – till I had gone so far that I don't know how I'll ever get back. Never mind. Plenty time . . .'
Joseph Conrad, *Heart of Darkness*

John is 53. Originally from Belfast, he settled in Australia during the 1970s, one of a wave of emigrants drawn by the lure of free flights, cheap living and perpetual sun. He got married and had children, but his two sons have now grown up and left home, his wife has left him and he can find no solace in his work. There is nothing for John in Australia any more, and he wants to vanish. He wants to start a new life in Thailand, where the food, beer and rent are cheap and where the girls can make him feel young again.

John's case is not unusual. Former generations had the French Foreign Legion as an escape route; in an age of cheap travel and easily forged papers, we have the developing world. And not only the developing world – a similar phenomenon occurs within Western countries themselves, with people running away from debts and bad marriages to start a new life elsewhere in the same country. And as anyone who has been the victim of bank fraud is aware, it's not difficult to construct new identities or to hijack existing ones anywhere in the world.

Every year thousands of tourists fail to make it home. Some, like John, want to vanish. Forged documents are readily available in the developing world and, if you have money, nobody will ask too many questions, as has long been known by expatriates fleeing domestic problems with the authorities, whether they are Nazi war criminals hiding in Paraguay or bail-skipping North Americans drinking themselves to death in the gringo haunts of Latin America.

In a sense this voluntary resettlement is the logical extension of other factors key to modern tourism. The ability to toy with one's own personality, to construct new personae while travelling (see 'The Hippie Hippie Shakedown'), is a dry run for setting up a permanent fake identity abroad. The identities don't even need to be new. Some tourists, recognising the high market value of, for instance, a British passport, will sell theirs and apply for a replacement at the nearest consulate. For around a thousand dollars they have to endure nothing worse than a pointed interview with a bristling consular official. Others are relieved of their passports unwittingly; and what is sold or stolen here is, in a sense, nothing less than an identity, a second-hand role the new holder is obliged to play.

However, many of those who get away and resettle in their newfound paradise find that escape is not the answer. Some simply disintegrate when removed from the societal control of their homelands, sinking into a cycle of alcoholism and depression – whatever their problems were, they tend to accelerate in a climate of cheap alcohol, *laissez faire* attitudes and an absence of family and friends – that often ends with a shot to the head.

Some embark on crime sprees that end in disaster. When 23-year-old German tourist Joseph Schwab arrived in Brisbane, Australia, in June 1987 he hit the ground running, defrauding the ANZ bank by falsely claiming that his traveller's cheques had been stolen; after collecting the replacement money he promptly cashed the cheques at another bank. After buying a shotgun, three rifles and a large amount of ammunition, he drove in a hired vehicle to the Northern Territory, where he robbed and killed five Australian campers in two separate incidents. Police were able to link the murders because in each case the victims had been shot in the back, their bodies stripped naked and their vehicles set on fire.

A massive manhunt ensued, and on 19 June, four days after the last murder, a helicopter pilot spotted Schwab's vehicle, which was heavily camouflaged in the bush. Armed police duly surrounded the vehicle and demanded that the gunman give himself up; when a volley of bullets answered their request, police opened fire. They fired teargas grenades at the vehicle in an effort to drive the gunman out, and accidentally started a small bush fire; when the smoke cleared Schwab was found dead outside the vehicle, having been killed by a single shot to the heart.

Police at this stage had no idea of the gunman's identity and issued a statement to the press that the gunman had been found in possession of a vehicle rented by Schwab; they feared that the tourist might have been another of the gunman's victims. It wasn't until the following day that Schwab was identified as having been the killer himself.

But such an incandescent end is rare. Most perpetual tourists survive, although many are unprepared for the financial obligations of their new lives. Work abroad can be hard to find, especially outside the specialised areas of language teaching and bartending, and some, as their savings rapidly dwindle, find themselves faced with a choice between an ignominious return to their home country, tail between their legs, and crime. Many choose crime. And not just any crime either, but one they have a good chance of getting away with – hustling tourists.

DRY HUSTLE

Anyone frequenting the more popular byways of the international tourist trail has met the harried traveller claiming to have lost his wallet the day before he flies home. He just needs $100 to pay for one more night at his hotel, a taxi to the airport and his departure tax; he swears he will pay you back, and wants to give you his address as proof of his sincerity. Occasionally, of course, this is a valid request for help, and this writer has met people who have lent strangers money and duly had it returned. These are, however, exceptions, and in most instances this is a popular scam often perpetrated by tourists on other tourists.

Other scams and hustles include drug sale rip-offs, often from tourists who have severe drug problems themselves, whether the acid-burned freaks of Goa and Kathmandu or the crack addicts of Central and South America; hotel scams, in which tourists overwhelmed by Bangkok or Delhi trust blindly in a self-professed tour guide from their own country who meets them at the airport or train station and persuades them to pay in advance for non-existent hotel rooms; and timeshare or 'holiday club' scams.

The latter are extremely common in Spain and the Canary Islands, where they are thought to be fronts for organised criminal activities such as money laundering and drug trafficking. Here's how it works: you're out walking along the beach, perhaps with your boyfriend or girlfriend, and are approached by a friendly, chatty young person, usually from your own country. You are handed a scratch card, and told that you have won something – a free holiday, a bottle of champagne or a sum of money. Your bubbly new friend is terribly excited and tells you that to collect your prize you need a credit card, just to prove your identity, and must attend a presentation, often some distance from where you are now. There you are plied with alcohol and forced to endure a long sales pitch that aims to convince you that cut-price luxury holidays can be yours. You are told there is a get-out clause, and that there is no way you can lose your money.

Leaving the presentation can be difficult, and the sales-people may refuse to give you your prize or gift unless you sign a contract. Elderly couples are particularly targeted and have been subjected to presentations lasting up to nine hours, after which their resistance has been broken down and they have signed a contract. Once an elderly lady with a stomach bug was followed into the toilet to stop her using her mobile phone to call for help, and others have been effectively imprisoned in strange buildings far from their hotel rooms – until they signed on the dotted line.

Once a member of a 'holiday club' you are given a telephone number to book your holidays. The most common result is that no holidays are available for the requested period, or that the phone remains unanswered; if holidays are provided they are normally in substandard accommodation which would have been far cheaper to rent through a high-street travel agent.

The basis of the 'holiday club' agreement is similar to timeshares, but they are proving a more popular scam now that timeshares are covered by the EU Timeshare Directive. 'Holiday clubs' are usually drawn up for just one month short of three years – thereby putting them outside the remit of the directive – to avoid legal interference.

Timeshare presentations are very similar, although rather than discounted holidays, you pay a one-off price plus an annual maintenance fee to occupy a holiday home for a set period (usually a week) each year. What you won't be told is that the maintenance fee will usually rise steeply year after year, and you may also be forced to pay 'special assessment fees' of up to £800.

The key to the success of these scams is that tourists trust their fellow countrymen; there is a common language, a national bond. Perhaps the tourist and the hustler will discuss sport, or news from home, with a familiarity lacking in relationships with locals against whom a tourist is often more vigilant. The locals, to many minds, not only look different and speak an incomprehensible language but are also not to be trusted under any circumstances.

But tourists – or those masquerading as tourist-friendly expatriates – pose, in many parts of the world, the most serious threat to other tourists, whether in low-level crimes such as robbery or high-level crimes such as rape or murder. It is said that in Sydney, Australia, Britons have most to fear from other Britons, many of whom have gone there looking for work only to end up running out of money and hustling tourists. And the success of Charles Sobhraj as a criminal stemmed principally from his ability to pass as a Frenchman and guide his supposed countrymen through the pitfalls of the East.

On the beaches of Goa and Ko Phan Gan and the cafés of Bangkok's Khao San Road, emaciated travellers move in ever decreasing circles, unwilling to stay, unable to return home, human rubble disguised as career tourists, looking disdain-fully on the gap-year holidaymakers who are ripe fodder for their light fingers and long cons.

The following account of one such character is given by a traveller who searched Thailand for the missing son of a friend and posted her findings online (www.netlistings.com/outofcountry.htm):

. . . a tall ghost of a man – who knows how old (maybe 50, maybe 60), made his way down the hallway towards us and captured my attention. He actually looked like he was a hundred years old. He had bad hair, bad teeth, bad skin and was just a sack of anemic bones. He was wearing only a short tie-dye sarong wrapped around his bony hips. His large callused feet loosely sported floppy worn-out rubber thongs. I could have counted his ribs. He walked casually, like he was out for a morning stroll. He carried a tattered tea-bag and balanced a cup of weak tea with his scrawny long fingers that were oddly graced by long fingernails. He sat down next to us.

He was not Thai. He was not friendly. He was not unfriendly. He was just there. I said hello and he replied with a lazy hello in an accent I did not recognize. I asked him where he was from.

'Holland,' he replied as he dipped his tea bag slowly in and out of his hot brew. I asked him how long he had been in Thailand. Oops. He paused, looked at Gary. Of course I gathered he was no backpacker nor was he just on holidays. Bad question, I guess. I got no reply.

'Do you also work in biology like Gary?' I asked. No reply. OK, I thought, he is not being rude, just hesitant, so I will push a little. I asked him, 'What do you do?'

'I rob people,' he replied as he cautiously sipped his hot tea.

'Rob people?' I repeated.

'Yes, when I need money I just rob some damn backpacker. They can afford it.'

'Do you hurt them as well?'

'Not always.'

One doesn't have to travel long before encountering such characters. Events such as the following are commonplace: in a dormitory room shared by ten tourists in Quito, Ecuador, one tourist comes up with an idea for breaking the ice. Why doesn't everyone show each other their passports? They can have a laugh over the inappropriate photographs, or admire each other's visa stamps. The other tourists readily agree, and reach into their money belts, unwittingly revealing where they keep their valuables. The next morning the tourist who'd suggested the cut-rate entertainment has gone, along with all of their money and passports.

'Drug and rob' schemes are also not uncommon among Westerners. Witness the following account, which is similar to those given by the surviving victims of Charles Sobhraj, and is taken from a website run by a Western expatriate in Thailand (www.philipwilliams.freeservers.com):

I had a great friend in England called Jim. All his life it had been Jim's dream to come to Bangkok and find himself a nice Thai wife, and now at the age of 61, he had saved enough money to live comfortably for the rest of his days, but wanted someone to share the twilight of his life with him.

Jim booked a flight-only deal from the UK, and I arranged his hotel in Bangkok. Unfortunately, on the day he arrived, I was not able to meet up with him, so as you do, Jim, being full of excitement at being in wonderful exotic Bangkok, dumped his suitcase in his hotel, and took a mid-day stroll along the Sukhumwit where he decided to have a beer in a pretty innocent-looking bar. After a short while, he was approached by an Englishman who struck up a friendly conversation. Although the stranger was a good bit younger than Jim, they got on well and the beer flowed. After about 2 hours, the man suggested that Jim accompany him to one of his favourite bars a short taxi ride away, and Jim agreed. He was only too happy to have such a friendly guide on his first day in Bangkok.

When they got to the second bar, Jim noticed that it was nothing special, rather dingy and run-down in fact, and what few customers there were seemed to be drunken Thais who looked like they had no fixed abode. The two new customers ordered a drink at the bar, and proceeded to chat and sip their ice-cold beers. After a while, something very strange happened. The stranger got up and left Jim sitting at the table. Not a word was spoken. The stranger eventually returned some 15 minutes later holding two hamburgers, and offered one to Jim. 'I bet you must be as hungry as I am.'

Jim hadn't eaten since on the aircraft that morning and he did feel a little peckish. He gratefully accepted the burger and proceeded to devour it hungrily. That was the last thing that Jim remembered.

He awoke from a deep sleep to find himself lying on the floor of a dirty shack in the middle of a slum area, miles from anywhere. As he stumbled out into the daylight, he realised that his money and passport were gone from his money belt. Also his watch had been removed. Fortunately, he had had the foresight to slip a hotel card into his pocket when he first arrived, and luckily, a taxi driver understood his situation and delivered him safely to the hotel, where the police and I were waiting. Jim had been missing for three days. At a hospital later that day, the doctor told him that he had been given a dose of a drug that would have killed a less healthy man. Sadly Jim could remember nothing about the bar he went to, or indeed very little about the smooth-talking stranger, but the police told us that he was in fact Australian, not English, and the Thai police had been after him for a long time. That was in 1990, and . . . I always remember [Jim's] words: 'You never prepare yourself for a situation like that. Because he was my fellow countryman, my guard was down.' Welcome to Bangkok.

The long arm of the law finally caught up with the Australian in 1996 when, acting from a tip-off, the police raided his apartment to find among other things, a stash of false passports and at least two handguns. He was jailed for fifteen years.

'Jim' was at least luckier than the tourist visitors to Bangkok who got a ride in Egyptian Ghanam Elsayed Mohammed's illegal taxi. Mohammed is alleged to have killed at least six foreign tourist passengers – two Frenchmen, a German, an Arab, an Iranian and an Austrian – who were stabbed in frenzied attacks, their belongings stolen and their mutilated bodies dumped around Bangkok. Mohammed's unique taxi service was finally brought to an end when the Thai fiancée of one of the French victims called police after waiting at the airport for six hours, sparking off a wide-ranging enquiry. As one policeman explained after Mohammed's arrest:

> . . . some wide-eyed arrivals fall for conmen who claim they'll help steer them clear of the bad guys. This may explain why quite a few of the criminals who prey on tourists turn out to be foreigners: they can plausibly claim to be 'on their side' against the Thais.

The stories above are only a small selection of the many scams perpetrated on tourists by their countrymen and other expatriates; there are many more. But not all tourists who stay on hustle other tourists. For some their protracted stay is less voluntary, as we'll see in the rest of this chapter. Some end up chewing clay in a bid for enlightenment in an Indian ashram; some end up chewing cockroaches in a hellhole jail; and some simply vanish.

GETTING WITH THE PROGRAMME

> It's very easy to get into a movement, and it's very difficult to get out.
>
> Wolfgang Dobrowolny, producer of Ashram

Holy Smoke, directed by Jane Campion (The Piano) and released in 1999, tells the story of a tourist – played by Kate Winslet – whose embrace of an Indian guru's teachings in an ashram and subsequent refusal to return home so alarm her parents that they employ a crack 'de-programmer' – played by Harvey Keitel– to rescue her.

The tale is not as improbable as it might sound. Since the first wave of hippie travellers to the Far East in the 1960s, ashrams, ostensibly Hindu retreats in which the faithful can pursue an ascetic life away from the trappings of modernity, have attracted millions of Western tourists on a spiritual quest. For many in the West, God may be dead but spiritual needs remain, and they are unlikely to be satisfied by consumer capitalism; Eastern religions, with their typically anti-consumerist bent and the allure of ancient, exotic wisdom, offer an attractive alternative.

The flirtation of beat writers such as Jack Kerouac and Allen Ginsberg with Zen and Eastern philosophy opened the gates, and the chronic LSD use of the late 1960s held them open; the popularity of the novels of Herman Hesse and mass-market paperback editions of *The Tibetan Book of the Dead* further strengthened the appeal of this inner quest through the 1970s, and laid the groundwork for the contemporary New Age industry. Today, budget travellers are particularly likely to experiment with such belief systems as they often travel at formative times in their lives: they are open to new ideas, ready to flirt with radicalism in one guise or another, and are often willing to shed the baggage of their lives at home.

The character played by Kate Winslet in *Holy Smoke* is typical of this group, and Harvey Keitel's 'de-programmer' is typical of another. De-programmers – who seek to reverse the malign 'brainwashing' effect of a cult with their own fiery brand of indoctrination – have often been employed by well-to-do parents alarmed by their child's shaven head, novel sartorial choices and anti-materialist babble. Some critics argue that the techniques employed by de-programmers are often more damaging than the activities of cults themselves; and many of those who recruit de-programmers are relatively conservative Christians whose principal motivation is resentment towards their children's rejection of their faith. Given that the principal difference between a cult and a religion is size (and its attendant respectability), the motives of those who employ de-programmers can often be regarded as suspect.

But this doesn't mean that ashram gurus and their 'cults' are always beyond reproach themselves. Ashrams are today one of the main attractions for the Indian tourist industry, a fact that has dismayed many Hindu traditionalists who resent the presence of 'sightseers', many of whom use narcotics, and the consequent overcrowding of many ashrams.

Critics of ashram gurus claim that their objectives are anything but spiritual: that the money given by acolytes to their gurus is used solely to enrich the latters' personal fortunes; that the cleansing and purification rituals practised in many ashrams are not only functionally useless but actively dangerous; and that the amoral 'free love' that has been practised in some ashrams is crassly exploitative and has occasionally led to the abuse of minors. The harshest critics are those who are ex-believers themselves, such as Andrew Harvey, a former disciple of Mother Meera, who wrote in an exposé of the 'cheap Hollywood version of the Indian trip' that ashrams are 'lunatic asylums, filled with jealous and needy people'.

The activities of some of the more notorious gurus appear to bear out at least some of these criticisms, with Indian Bhagwan Shree Rajneesh providing an illuminating example of what happens when a guru goes wrong. Bhagwan's concept of tantra – the idea, basically expressed, that the road of excess leads to the palace of wisdom – proved so attractive to Westerners in the 1970s that the population of his ashram in Poona was around 10,000, at least 6,000 of whom were Westerners.

His popularity was helped by the fact that his female disciples, many of whom were extremely attractive, wore loose-fitting robes with no underwear; and by his message that people should not confuse sex and love, or love and possessiveness – that they should not deny sexual desire but rather indulge it with full awareness. Sexual experiments were advised for anyone who had phobias: women were routinely told to practise oral sex if they feared rats or spiders. 'Shoes and minds' were to be left at the gate, and total surrender to Bhagwan encouraged.

But not everyone subscribed to Bhagwan's ethos of indiscriminate sex. Rape was common at the ashram, with group leaders justifying such activity as necessary for the victim; in one instance a Canadian woman, mourning the death of her parents, was forced to have sex against her will in front of a group. Children were considered as unwanted baggage, and disciples – known as sannyasis in the Poona ashram – were encouraged to undergo sterilisation. But in India in the 1970s this was a dangerous operation, and after two women nearly died following the operation during one week in 1979 the ashram turned to vasectomies as a safer and cheaper option.

Many Indians were offended by Bhagwan's teachings, which were not only critical of Hinduism but also disrespectful of traditional Indian ideas about sex. A number of attempts were made on the guru's life, and Western members of the ashram were routinely attacked, with several women being raped on the street and one shot in the thigh with an air rifle.

Violence was also common among members of the ashram community itself. One of the more popular activities at Poona was the encounter group, a gathering in which the sannyasis would be encouraged to relax, to open up and express their emotions, whether they be positive or negative. Many of the sessions ended in broken bones, the predictable result of endemic malnutrition coupling with the sexual hostility and jealousy that accompanied Bhagwan's 'free love' policy. However, Bhagwan's sometime bodyguard Hugh Milne maintained in *Bhagwan: the God that Failed,* an exposé of the ashram published in 1987, that 'It seemed that there was some kind of release and relaxation when a bone was broken, triggering the letting go of deep-seated tensions.'

One sannyasi murdered another about a mile from the ashram, and another was found under a nearby bridge, killed by multiple stab wounds. A third suffocated himself with a plastic bag, inspired by a passage written by Bhagwan which argued that holding the breath with enough determination would lead to immediate enlightenment.

Disease was rife at Poona but generally considered a sign of 'negativity' rather than the result of a reluctance to observe basic hygiene rules or to eat properly. Some sannyasis developed hepatitis, which often led to permanent organ damage and, occasionally, death, and tuberculosis and pneumonia were far from rare. Sexually transmitted diseases (STDs) began to run like wildfire through the ashram during the mid-1970s, leading first to an edict that gloves and condoms should be used during intercourse, then to an eventual ban on the practice of free love that had attracted so many disciples.

Bhagwan had no truck with anti-materialism, the Poona ashram taking between $5 and $7 million in its final year, mostly through merchandising of his books and videos. The owner of 93 Rolls-Royces and two aeroplanes, Bhagwan believed that 'spirituality is the luxury and privilege of the rich'. Enlightenment was available – but only at a price – and after a while even the rooms at the ashram were charged at an exorbitant rate. Many of the female sannyasis turned to prostitution to support themselves, taking a train to Bombay and making themselves available in the lobbies of luxury hotels. The preferred clients were moneyed Arabs, but soon the problems with STDs at the ashram spread to the hotels, and sannyasin women were routinely barred from entry to the hotels.

For those unable or unwilling to take to prostitution, drug running was another option. The runs were occasionally officially sanctioned, if very discreetly – runners would even ask Bhagwan for oblique advice on the best day to go. Three English girls were caught and arrested in 1979, and their story did much to popularise the notion of Bhagwan in England as an 'evil cult' leader who 'brainwashed' his charges. A psychologist who worked on the case told the court that 'those who left the sect were found to have regressed to the mental age of twelve'.

When the Poona ashram finally closed in July 1981, Bhagwan taking a select group of sannyasis to the USA, many were unable to cope with life apart from their guru. Unaware that Bhagwan had planned to move elsewhere, they found the break too severe, the betrayal of trust too great. Many suicides were reported, and the local psychiatric hospital began to overflow with damaged sannyasis; other acolytes turned their attention to other gurus, their egos now so weakened by surrender to Bhagwan that they were unable to function without someone else making decisions for them.

Bhagwan purchased a farm in Oregon where sannyasis were used as slave labour to build Rajneeshpuram, 'America's first enlightened city'. His empire finally collapsed in 1985, amid a welter of recriminations and criminal charges. Bhagwan was deported from the USA and fined, after authorities heard evidence that the Rajneeshees had poisoned US citizens with salmonella and shipped in homeless people to make up the numbers at a local election; the homeless had been drugged to keep them docile, a process which left at least one dead.

While the case of Bhagwan Shree Rajneesh is especially notorious, the exploitative practices of many of those associated with ashram culture and the intersection of Eastern religion and tourism continues. From sleazy yoga instructors who offer special massages to favoured students to pickpocketing sadhus rifling through clothes left at meditation centres, many see tourists who embrace Eastern religious practices as easy prey. In some cases they have a point. Rich, naive and gullible, those tourists who claim to espouse asceticism while paying huge sums for exclusive retreats, who nod sagely at poor beggars while eating vegan slurry, clad in a pashmina shawl, provide a ready and willing supply of victims – for those cynical or opportunist enough to take advantage – that shows no signs of drying up.

But exploitation, whether sexual or financial, is one thing; murder is another. 32-year-old Italian Alessandra Verdi's parents didn't even know where she was until an Indian sadhu wrote to them in July 2001 explaining that she had vanished while owing him money. It turned out that she had lived in Manali, in the northern province of Himal Pradesh in India, for six years, smoking chillums with the sadhu, Baba Mast Ram, who came from nearby Vashisht. After receiving the sadhu's letter Verdi's parents contacted the Italian embassy in India, which in turn contacted local police. The police searched the house she'd rented, and found bloodstains on the sheets, along with photographs of Verdi with the sadhu.

Her parents flew over to look through the local file on unidentified bodies, a grisly collage of body parts in various states of decomposition. They were eventually able to identify their daughter's body, which had been found on the banks of a river in August, its legs snapped off below the knee by the force of the river's flow. The sadhu was tracked down and arrested.

Verdi isn't the only tourist to have been murdered by a self-professed holy man. Joanne Masheder's adventurous backpacking holiday through rural Thailand during the mid-1990s ended brutally when she was raped and killed in a cave by an amphetamine-addicted Buddhist monk. Initially the Thai authorities regarded her simply as one of the hundreds of Western tourists who go missing annually; it took a determined investigation by her father to track down her body and discover what had happened to her. The case drew attention not only to the vulnerability of lone female travellers around the world but also to Thailand's growing problem with rogue monks. Worried that the fraternity of Buddhist monks was attracting an undesirable criminal element, often on the run for crimes committed as civilians, the Thai authorities pledged in the wake of Masheder's death to regulate entry into the system more strictly.

BANGED UP

It's not difficult to picture the scene. You're on Hat Rin beach in Ko Pha Ngan, Thailand; it's the monthly full-moon party, and around 10,000 people are dancing around you. You can get anything here – pills, speed, acid, mushrooms – and most people have taken advantage, if their dilated pupils are anything to go by. You've joined in; you're on holiday, and it's the kind of thing you do at home anyway. Everyone else is doing it, so the authorities must turn a blind eye; they're probably just happy to have the tourist trade.

By the morning you're tranced out and start to walk back to your beach hut. You're stopped on the beach by two Thai men who demand to see your papers. You don't have them with you – they're in the hut. They tell you they are plain-clothes policemen and search you. You're still buzzing, and not too worried – you've taken all the hard stuff and just have a bit of hash left. Surely they won't be interested in that. But they are. And they also want you to accompany them to the station for a urine test.

In Thailand possession of less than twenty grams of any illegal drug leads to a jail sentence of at least one year; taking drugs, as proven by a urine test, can lead to a sentence of anything between six months and ten years. The Thai authorities have come down hard on recreational drug use recently, with a Ministry of Justice spokesman warning that:

> We would like to be tough on drugs and we arrest everybody who involve [sic] in drugs and send them to jail. If they do not realise this and come to Thailand and take drugs, because in some countries in Europe they are more lenient, they will be treated as the Thai who takes drugs and that will make their lives miserable.

Miserable indeed. Many Westerners do not survive their stay in Thailand's prisons, probably the most notorious of which is Bangkok's Bang Kwang, otherwise known as 'Big Tiger', to which prisoners serving sentences of thirty years or over – or awaiting execution – are sent. Conditions are said to be so appalling at Bang Kwang that most foreigners become heroin addicts, using homemade syringes fashioned from biros and dispensary needles, in order to cope with the degradation. Cells are chronically overcrowded, with no furniture and prisoners lying on the floor head to toe with each other. Many longer-term Western prisoners tell of having seen ghosts in the cells, the existence of which are taken for granted by the Thais.

The average life expectancy for new prisoners is said to be as low as two weeks, as bottled water is not supplied and dysentery and other water-borne diseases are rife. The food given to prisoners is so minimal and unhealthy that unless visitors bring extra food or enough money can be earned from prison work to buy extra rations, survival is difficult without eating rats. Some rodents are farmed by prisoners and particular cuts especially favoured, although eating sewer rats is frowned upon. In the darkrooms – punishment cells crammed full of prisoners who are allowed light for only five minutes every day – cockroaches are caught and fattened up on prison food then mashed into a pulp with salt and pepper added to taste. Westerners who refuse to eat this, their only available source of protein, normally do not survive the minimum one-month darkroom sentences.

Torture is common and inventive, following the Thai philosophy that sinners are worthless, and that those who destroy them are backed by divine justice. One at Bang Kwang involves a blindfolded prisoner standing in the yard, circled by guards wielding canes. The guards strike the prisoner at random intervals, so that he never knows where the cane will land next. Some are caned to death, and Westerners are not exempt from such treatment, or from milder punishments such as having to stand for hours on end up to their necks in raw sewage.

In another Thai prison, Maha Chai, a game was sometimes played that became legendary in prisoner circles. A prisoner would be placed inside a small ball made of thatched bamboo, which would often have nails driven into it. Guards would push the ball around before leading an elephant into the yard. The animal would be shown how to tap the ball, and would roll it around the yard until tiring of the game and stamping on it, crushing the unfortunate inhabitant.

One saving grace about Thai prisons is that homosexuality is frowned upon, except as practised consensually with *katoeys* – ladyboys, who dress in frilly underwear to ply their trade – and other prisoners seeking to augment their meagre food ration; rape is uncommon. According to Warren Fellows, an Australian who spent twelve years at Bang Kwang for smuggling heroin, most sex at the prison takes place between prisoners and pigs. For the Thai prisoners, at least, there is no reason to stray from heterosexuality just because of a new species: male pigs can be had for only two packets of cigarettes while female pigs cost five packets.

* * *

The British Foreign Office estimates that more than 3,200 British citizens are currently residing in foreign prisons; of these around half have been charged with drug offences. The statistics are similar for some other European countries, Australia and America, with around 2,500 US citizens arrested annually abroad. Jail sentences in Southeast Asia are routinely as long as forty or fifty years, while many popular holiday destinations in and near Europe have surprisingly harsh drug laws. In Spain, for instance, sentences of twelve years are common for possession; Cyprus's zero tolerance policy means that possession can lead to life imprisonment, as in Greece; and in Turkey some death sentences are given for drug offences, although for Westerners these are normally commuted to life. And the authorities of many of these countries are not shy of handing out maximum sentences: the exportation of British drug culture to islands such as the Balearics and Cyprus's Ayia Napa has led to severe clampdowns on tourist drug use recently.

Tales of local drug dealers colluding with police to have foreign tourists arrested are legion, everywhere from Turkey to Colombia, although most policemen have little interest in actual arrests, earning far more from the bribes paid by panicked tourists to avoid incarceration. In some instances tourists have been arrested by people simply masquerading as policemen, although it can be difficult to judge authenticity in an alien environment; as a rule of thumb, if they're armed it's probably a good idea to pay them.

Smuggling has long been an attractive option to tourists seeking to prolong their holiday. During the early to mid-1980s many did the 'milk run' from Hong Kong to Korea or Japan to sell cameras, calculators and watches at vastly inflated profits. But nothing gives a higher profit than drugs, where crossing one border alone can increase the value of your consignment by ten times. The methods for smuggling narcotics are legion – bags with false bottoms, hardback books, cans of food, 'balloons' swallowed or packed up the backside – and the rewards legendary. Until you get caught.

Drug smugglers receive the worst treatment of all in foreign prisons, being routinely given life imprisonment. Thailand's

Article 27, a military law providing for immediate execution without trial, is often used to dispatch drug traffickers, although the Prime Minister has to be petitioned first and the law is only rarely used against Westerners. There is a political edge to the heaviness with which the governments of many developing countries come down on drug smugglers: in order to receive aid or other support from the USA they must show that they are playing a key role in the 'war on drugs'.

When Briton Robert Davies was convicted of smuggling hash in China in the early 1990s he found another political twist; not only had clampdowns occurred to divert funds from heavily Islamic hash-producing areas, but he also found the prosecutor recalling the Opium Wars, accusing him of exploiting the hard-working Chinese much as had British sea captains during the 1850s.

Most smugglers are unlikely to be as fortunate as Billy Hayes, whose successful bid for freedom from a Turkish jail was immortalised in the book and film *Midnight Express*, a modern Orientalist horror story whose tone says a lot about Westerners' presumptuous disrespect for local law and custom. The film is even stronger than the book, with its overblown depictions of Turkish sadism meted out by filthy homosexual guards – Hayes, by contrast, remains resolutely heterosexual (one of many changes from the book), clean-shaven and freshly laundered, even as he shrieks to his captors, 'I hate you! I hate your nation! I hate your people! I fuck your sons and daughters!'

Hayes's story is, however, typical in one respect, featuring as it does the financially and emotionally devastating effect that incarceration abroad has on the prisoner's family. Some families move abroad to be closer to their imprisoned loved one and to help ensure their continued health, and many families are ruined by unscrupulous or simply unsuccessful lawyers.

While escape is rare, it is not unusual for Western prisoners in Thailand to skip bail if it is given to them; anything to avoid the Piranesian labyrinth of the Thai prison system. In February 2000 a British couple, 25-year-old James Gilligan and 21-year-old Judith Payne, were jailed in Bangkok after being charged with possession of half a kilo of cannabis and six grammes of heroin. Gilligan admitted that the drugs belonged to him and that Payne had nothing to do with them, but under Thai law she was held responsible as the drugs were found in her room. After their families posted £5,000 bail for each of them they fled the country, crossing the border into north-east Malaysia on foot. Although their passports had been seized, they were returned by the British Embassy in Bangkok, enabling them eventually to fly back to the UK. Neither could face returning to the Thai prison, where Payne reported she'd been in a room with eighty other women.

Thai police have often been accused of planting large quantities of drugs on people and charging them with drug trafficking, as Thai law allows the country's poorly paid policemen to collect a percentage of the street value of any drugs seized. Visa infractions have also been exploited by unscrupulous police and prison officials, as shown in the following tale told online (www.netlistings.com/outof-country.htm) by a visitor to a Thai prison:

> There was a very emotional English girl sitting nearby. Her English boyfriend had overstayed his visa by only a few days. The hotel owner turned him in to the police (probably for a fee), and the police in turn took him to prison. The fine for overstay was supposed to be 200 bhat per day, payable at any port or immigration office. The police had taken 1400 bhat and had extorted more and more money every day, thousands of bhat. The authorities knew the couple had credit cards and had forced them to max them out. Now the girl had no idea what to do because the prison officials continued demanding money; they'd suggested they wire home for more money. Her story was not unique.

Probably the worst example of known police corruption in Thailand occurred during 1994, when a gang of rogue policemen killed an average of two tourists a month for their valuables over seven months of slaughter; the victims were mostly Chinese, which may explain in part why the case was virtually ignored by the Western media.

Many prisoners will claim to have been framed by the police, although it is virtually impossible to verify such claims. Some smugglers also claim to have been unwitting drug mules, and have been known to have their sentences commuted if their stories are believed. Birmingham teenagers Karen Smith and Patricia Cahill travelled to Thailand in 1990 on a holiday paid for by a British man they hardly knew, and were arrested before flying back to the UK with 66 kilos of heroin in their luggage, the largest haul ever recorded in Thailand. They were finally released after three years in jail, as a result of heavy petitioning from the founder of the British organisation Fair Trials Abroad, solicitor Stephen Jakobi, and requests by the British Government for clemency. Still unanswered are some key questions: why would a drug trafficker trust two teenage girls with such a large amount of heroin? And could the girls really have been naive enough to think that an acquaintance would pay for their holiday expecting nothing in return?

In a more recent case 22-year-old Briton Daisy Angus was arrested in November 2002 when customs officials in Bombay discovered 10 kilos of hashish in her suitcase. She claimed at first that she had been set up by an Israeli friend, 37-year-old Yoran Kadesh, but later confessed to her mother that Kadesh had offered her $10,000 to carry the suitcase. Her only hope of a swift release is on health grounds, as she contracted malaria in jail and her health has since declined rapidly.

In some other cases the innocence of the prisoner charged with smuggling seems almost assured. Take for example the recently released Briton Ian Stillman, a deaf, diabetic amputee aid worker who had for 30 years worked with India's deaf and underprivileged before being arrested in August 2000 for smuggling 20 kilos of cannabis in the Kullu valley. It happened when Stillman, in his early fifties, was investigating facilities for the deaf in the valley, and was taking a public taxi back to his hotel late at night. When the taxi was stopped at a police roadblock, 20 kilos of cannabis were allegedly found in the back of the car, and Stillman was arrested, alone out of the group of young backpackers also in the taxi. The Indian authorities suggested that his artificial NHS leg was hollowed out for the purposes of drug smuggling, and that he was not deaf but merely slightly hard of hearing. His trial was carried out without an interpreter, and he was given documents in Hindi to sign; he says that on at least one occasion his signature was forged. The courts sentenced him to ten years in jail, a sentence later upheld by a Delhi Supreme Court judge.

Pressure from his family led to British MPs' awareness of the case and a cross-party petition was sent to the Indian government urging a judicial review of the case, described during a debate in the House of Commons as 'the worst case of injustice of a Briton abroad'. Stillman was finally released in December 2002 after the British Foreign Secretary, Jack Straw, intervened on his behalf because jail conditions were adversely affecting his health. He has not, however, been acquitted of the charges, and vows to clear his name when his health has recovered.

A backpacker from the British Midlands was accused of smuggling heroin from Afghanistan to Pakistan in March 2002 and jailed in the notorious Peshawar Central jail. Roger Jowett, 31 at the time of the arrest, was caught attempting to cross the border without a visa – to buy a new motherboard for a computer he'd broken, according to him – and accused first of being an Al-Qaeda spy, then, when known Al-Qaeda prisoners failed to identify him, a drug smuggler. The Pakistani authorities had recently arrested two Britons allegedly carrying three suitcases of heroin, and assumed that Jowett was working with them, although both he and they claimed not to have met each other before.

A British reporter who interviewed Jowett in prison stated that he seemed delirious, and that he asked at one point for a razor or some rope, to kill himself. Jowett also begged the reporter to ask his parents not to come, as he didn't want them to see him in this state.

Guilt by association also led to the arrest of 24-year-old Rachel McGee, who accepted the offer of a cheap holiday in Cuba from Karite Clacher, a friend of her boyfriend. Acting on a tip from drug smugglers who had been caught arriving from Jamaica with 15 kilos of cocaine, police raided Clacher's room at the hotel and arrested him and two acquaintances. McGee had been leaving the hotel in a taxi when she heard the commotion and returned, only to be arrested as well, although no drugs were found on her. The trial was conducted in Spanish and her name was never mentioned, until she received a fifteen-year sentence in jail.

Offers of cheap or free holidays – as with timeshare and 'holiday club' scams – are rarely what they seem, and are best avoided. As for deliberate drug smuggling, the final word should come from a Western inmate of Bang Kwang, writing for www.farangonline.com:

> There's a message in here somewhere, and it's not just targeted at you hell-man adventure cowboys and you ennui-plagued, insouciant heiresses-in-waiting who are out to shock the world – maybe your parents – by taking the fateful walk from the conventional wild side into something you feel exudes a truly radical allure – like an impulsive jaunt into narco-trafficking, for instance.
>
> There's no glamour here, no promise of success, no proverbial pot of gold to pick up on the other side; just a sweaty, inanimate existence riddled with the futile dreams of what could've been, mingled with aching regret of having let so many good people down – especially yourself.

In the wake of films and TV movies such as *Brokedown Palace* (1999) and *Bangkok Hilton* (1989), prison visits are all the rage among backpackers in countries such as Thailand. Many hostels and cafés post notices with prisoners' names and building numbers, and both the Lonely Planet guidebook and the Khao San Road website (www.khaosanroad.com) give details of how to find Bang Kwang and what to take for prisoners.

Most prisoners are grateful for visits, although visitors are warned not to make promises – to write letters or send emails on behalf of the prisoner – they do not intend to keep. But some prisoners are suspicious of the visitors' motives, alarmed at being yet another attraction on the beaten track. According to Susan Aldous, who runs a non-governmental organisation working with prisoners in Thailand, 'There are a few who won't come out. They don't want to be a monkey in a zoo.' Those visitors who do see someone often find that they have got more than they bargained for, dealing with prisoners who have either been reduced to squawking insanity or who regard them as a last hope in their bid for freedom.

MISSING IN ACTION

The Kullu valley in Himachal Pradesh, northern India, has been called the end of the habitable world. Kipling wrote of it that 'Surely the gods live here; this is no place for men', a view shared by those who dubbed Kullu the valley of the gods. Pine forests flank the mist-wreathed mountains, and ancient Buddhist temples dot the hillsides; its beauty is undeniable. But the hikers and mountain climbers are now starting to stay away, put off by the lawlessness of this land of *charas* hashish cultivation and the propensity for its visitors to go missing.

The fate of some is clear. In July 2000 two German trekkers were attacked as they slept in their tent. One, 28-year-old Adrian Mayer-Tasch, escaped with four shotgun wounds to the leg; his companion, 26-year-old Jorg Meihrauch, was not so lucky. His killer was never found.

A month later 32-year-old British civil engineer Martin Young, his 34-year-old Spanish girlfriend Maria Girones and her 14-year-old son, Cristobal, were also attacked in their tent. Young was the only one to survive, and later described how the attackers had thrown the boy off a cliff. Again, nobody came forward with information about the attack, although Young's passport and some valuables were handed in anonymously to a police station once word got around that he had survived.

In December 2001 the corpse of an Israeli military pilot, Nadav Mintzer, was found near the village of Malana. His body, which had lain undiscovered for over a year, had been ravaged by wolves. Before he was found, his passport was offered for sale in the markets of Manali, a tourist boom town at the foot of the valley which now hosts a thriving trance party scene.

Exactly what has happened to other tourists is less clear. Still unaccounted for are Briton Ian Mogford, 21 at the time of his 1996 disappearance, and a student at Bristol university; Canadian Ardavan Taherzadeh, missing since May 1997; Maarten de Bruijn, a young Dutchman missing since May 1999; and Russian economist Alexei Ivanov, who vanished in April 2000. These are only the recent names: the Kullu valley police department has several files full of accounts of tourists who visited the valley and never returned.

Many of the missing tourists' families, disheartened by the police's ineffectiveness in tracing their loved ones, conduct their own investigations, and some have teamed together to form an amateur investigative network, trading emails and leads. But local apathy and an unwillingness on the part of Kullu natives and expatriates to discuss the disappearances mean that their questions go largely unanswered, and their 'missing' posters are ignored. Ivanov's mother, a colonel in the Russian army, even employed a private security firm to scour the mountains around the spot where he had last been seen, but the only trace they could find of him was a Russian-made oxygen bottle discarded on a hillside.

The British Group 4-Securitas company has now joined forces with several foreign embassies in New Delhi to conduct a private investigation, and has unearthed a number of pieces of evidence missed by the police. The company warns prospective visitors not to trek alone past Manikaran, a village in the upper reaches of the Parvati valley that features in the cases of many of the missing tourists.

Local police have a number of theories concerning the disappearances, although the official line is expressed simply in a photocopied warning handed to those who request information: 'Due to some unfortunate incidents in the last few years, we do not recommend that you go trekking alone.' Privately, some officials blame the influx of Nepali immigrants, who are reputed to work harder than locals for less money, thus driving the now unemployed locals to crime; some point to the easy access to guns in the valley, licensed weapons ostensibly issued for the protection of crops from wild animals; some maintain that the missing tourists have simply fallen off mountain trails; and others point to *charas*.

Ask any hash smoker what his favourite kind of hash is and the answer will almost invariably be *charas*. The substance, a kind of hash cream, has long been associated with the Kullu and Parvati valleys due to the history of its production locally and the favourable climatic conditions.

But where *charas* used to be used as a religious sacrament it is now big business, routinely commanding the highest prices in Amsterdam's coffee shops and exported in massive quantities from the valley. It is so popular among tourists that a new prison has been opened at Kanda, near Shimla, to deal with the massive numbers of tourist arrests on drug charges in Himachal Pradesh.

The trade has also had a powerful effect on the local community. What used to be closed, insular communities given over to subsistence farming have become in the past few years grossly materialistic. Fruit and vegetables have to be imported from neighbouring regions as all available land is given over to marijuana cultivation. *Charas* can make a cultivator more money from one crop than they could hope to earn otherwise in a decade, and its value has risen sharply in the last few years. Not everyone can make money out of its cultivation, however, and some prefer to take a short cut to the wealth displayed by their neighbours – by robbing, and often stabbing or shooting, a tourist.

It is not only the locals who grow and sell *charas*. A confidential Indian police circular estimated in 2002 that between seven and nine thousand foreigners live clandestinely in the hills around the Kullu and Parvati valleys, all dependent on the 10,000 kilo-a-year *charas* trade. Many of those who

fill the police files of missing tourists have vanished voluntarily, retreating further into the hills to protect their lifestyles
as mainstream tourism encroaches on their Shangri-La. Some
become mystics, as described by Kullu Superintendent of
Police Anurag Garg:

> They want to lose themselves here. Khirganga village is full of
> foreigner sadhus. We have come across people who have
> written letters to their families that say, 'I no longer
> remember you. I am very happy here and I want to stay here
> and forget everything else.' One so-called missing foreigner
> was traced after eight years in a village where he had been
> living. Many of them marry locals.

Some have been missing for so many years that their
embassies have forgotten about them. In 1998 an unkempt
woman in her fifties requested a passport at the British
embassy; she explained that she'd been a British Airways
stewardess and had arrived fifteen years before, but now
wanted to go home. Some of the foreigners living in the hills
deny their nationalities when approached by the authorities,
and it is possible that a few, their minds numbed by a heavy
diet of *charas* chillums, have forgotten where they are from.

But many have chosen this life, fleeing bad debts and
boredom at home for a life without constraints in the
wilderness of northern India. They are not interested in
helping families locate their loved ones – 'the missing don't
go looking for the missing', as one Kullu expatriate put it.
They live there illegally and cannot go to the police; and in
any case, like the locals, they have too much to lose from
police interference with the *charas* economy to welcome
investigations. This might help to explain the police apathy as
well: official police pay is eclipsed here by *charas*-funded
corruption, and most police have too much to lose from a
concerted investigation.

Himachal Pradesh is not alone in having more than its fair
share of tourist disappearances. The same nexus of cheap

drugs, voluntary disappearances and police apathy applies in Thailand. Many, like John from Belfast at the beginning of this chapter, are seduced by the Thai culture: one in which people keep to themselves, mind their own business and avoid confrontation; one in which people can do whatever they want, if they have the money. These features, so appealing to some, also make it virtually impossible to trace a missing person in Thailand; an added appeal to those who, for whatever reason, do not want to be found.

Many parents have gone out to the land of smiles to search for their missing sons and daughters, only to be appalled by the lack of police interest in the cases – they are routinely simply shown a book of photographs of corpses washed up on beaches or found in fields – and the apathy of other backpackers, who don't want their holiday spoiled by anything as heavy as the possible death of an acquaintance. Even when parents make a concerted effort to spread information about their child's disappearance, such as putting up posters and notices in guesthouses, these are normally removed as soon as they have left. The tourist trade is crucial to the Thai economy, and nobody wants to see it hurt by horror stories of tourist disappearances.

Some backpackers, wanting to make the most of the cheap and readily available narcotics, overdo it and lose their sanity. *Ya-baa* (literally 'bad shit') is the local name for methamphetamine, popular among Thai prostitutes and, increasingly, tourists, but seriously detrimental to the user's mental health. The drug, manufactured principally by the Burmese United Wa army, had been largely ignored by the Thai government until the first few months of 2003, during which a crackdown led to 600 deaths in twenty days and a 300 per cent increase in the drug's price. Three million people, out of the Thai population of 62 million, are estimated to be addicted to the pills.

While some parents fear that their children have been driven mad by drugs used to spike their drink before they are robbed, the drugs used in such robberies tend to be sedatives and unlikely to cause mental damage. The condition of characters such as the following, again from www.netlistings.com/outofcountry.htm, is far more likely to be self-inflicted:

> *A poor sap came up to me on the street. He was barefooted, wearing shorts and a tank top. He had long, stringy, matted blond hair and was completely skin and bone. His body was a mass of infected, bloody open wounds and bites. If he had been an animal someone would have put him out of his misery. 'Uh, can you give me some money?' he said in a strong English accent.*
>
> *'My God,' I said, 'you look awful. Where are you staying?'*
>
> *'Uh, I dunno. I slept on the corner,' he replied. He seemed so dazed.*
>
> *'Well, where are your things?'*
>
> *'I dunno.'*
>
> *'Do you have your passport?'*
>
> *'Na, dunno, don't have nothin',' he replied with great difficulty.*
>
> *He was disoriented. I asked him about his sores. He told me he thought they were from rats.*

Rumours still circulate about an enclave of backpackers living in isolated paradise somewhere in Thailand, a traveller myth given form and focus by Alex Garland's 1996 novel *The Beach*. Ironically enough the novel has helped to strengthen the rumour even while presenting it as fictional, and some backpackers travel the length of the country hoping for a chance encounter with a hand-drawn map.

A community such as that described in the Kullu valley above is in a sense similar to the one Garland describes in his novel. But both the Kullu valley and *The Beach* have their sordid overtones of death and corruption, and the same would seem to apply to any attempt to establish such a paradise community. As in the novel, travellers talk, and 'unspoilt paradises' are soon overrun by backpackers and people looking to make a fast buck. The 'paradise' may last for a while, but it is never sustainable, and by the time it collapses the local inhabitants have seen their culture irreversibly damaged and their environment horribly degraded. Many countries in the developing world are now clamping down on illegal expatriates: even the Kullu valley, long considered beyond the reach of authority and the modern world, is now witnessing a crackdown on expatriates who overstay their visas.

The trajectory of tourism on the island of Koh Samui in Thailand is sadly all too characteristic of what happens when an 'unspoilt paradise' is 'discovered'. Hippie travellers built small huts on the beach and exported Goan full moon party culture to the island during the late 1980s, dissatisfied with the growing commercialisation of the Goa scene; the parties eventually became so popular that around 10,000 people would attend once a month, and organised criminals moved in during the mid-1990s. The island is now run by the Russian mafia, with budget establishments steadily pushed out so that luxury hotels, nightclubs and restaurants can take their place. Every so often decapitated bodies are washed up on the increasingly soiled beach, victims of a trademark Russian mafia killing.

It is not only backpackers who vanish, and it is not only the developing world in which tourists go missing. In March 2001 David Eason, a 46-year-old British advertising executive, flew to Melbourne, where he visited friends before travelling to Sydney. There he joined a group heading out on a fourteen-day trip up the east coast, stopping at the Great Barrier Reef and Cairns.

On the morning of 28 March Eason visited Fraser Island, a world heritage site famous for its dingoes and for being the largest sand island in the world, in a tour group travelling in a four-wheel drive minibus. The group spent the morning wandering around the island, and at lunchtime they were dropped off at the One Tree Rocks surfing beach where they had the option of staying on the bus or walking the well-marked path to nearby Lake Wabby. Eason and four others opted for the walk, agreeing to meet back at the car park at 3 p.m.

As a smoker on a non-smoking bus, Eason welcomed the chance to have a cigarette, and also perhaps some privacy, a rare treat on an organised tour; so he sat on the beach, telling his fellow walkers that he'd catch them up. He hasn't been seen since.

Various searches have been carried out, the first on foot that evening and later ones involving helicopters with heat-seeking equipment. It is unlikely that Eason would have gone swimming: the sea was rough that day, and sharks and undertows are very real dangers on Fraser Island. Eason is reported to have been a good sailor with a respect for the sea and a great fear of sharks. In any case, police are convinced that if he had gone in to the sea there would be some trace of him by now; it is also unlikely that he would have taken his backpack and clothes, which are also missing, with him.

Eason's family, who have criticised local police for not doing enough to find him, are convinced that he has not chosen to go 'walkabout'. He left his passport and tickets in his hotel, and could easily have opted for independent travel rather than an escorted tour if the former had appealed to him. They believe that something more sinister has happened: that Eason may have been the victim of an aggravated robbery, and been buried in the sand; or that he may lie in a sandy grave after having been hit by one of the four-wheel drives that are allowed to roar along the beach.

Shortly after Eason's disappearance a nine-year-old boy was killed in a dingo attack on Fraser Island, but police didn't think that dingoes were involved in Eason's case. They believe at the time of writing that Eason is still on the island, but that if he is alive he does not want to be found. If Eason's disappearance was a faked or even a real suicide, however, there is a strong likelihood that he would have left behind some sign of his intention.

STOP PRESS: As this book was going to press, David Eason's skull was found by a British tourist on the perimeter of Lake Wabby. The police are currently treating the death as 'non-suspicious'; Eason's family released a press statement stating that they are pressing for an inquiry into the practices of the Queensland police, in the hope of preventing 'such a travesty from ever happening again'.

6. THE HIPPIE HIPPIE SHAKEDOWN
THE LIFE AND CRIMES OF CHARLES SOBHRAJ

I never killed good people.

Charles Sobhraj

Who are you? The clichéd image of the traveller journeying the world to 'find' him or herself has, as do all clichés, some truth to it. For many people a long period of independent travel – three months' backpacking around Asia during a year off, say – is their first experience of a life that is not shored up by the familiar. Our environment to a large degree constructs our identity, and family, friends and institutions – whether educational or job-related – help to define it still further. Behaving 'out of character' is usually frowned upon, as though our characters were something static with an obligation to consistency, and we internalise this curtailing of our range of potential identities early on; whether we are aware of it or not we often behave according to how we imagine others see us.

Here lies part of the attraction of a large city for those from the provinces: the freedom of anonymity, the chance to explore identities with no fear of repercussion. And here too lies one of the benefits of independent travel – nobody knows who you are. If you are shy you can pretend to be outgoing; if you detest your job you can pretend to be involved in something more interesting. It's often tempting to play with your identity even if you *are* happy with what you do – endlessly reiterating your background and occupation to strangers tends to pall fairly quickly, and having to keep a story straight adds an extra frisson of excitement to an otherwise ordinary encounter. Once you've started signing false names into hotel registers it can be hard to stop.

Most people don't take it this far, of course, and prefer to retain their name but enjoy the lack of pressure to conform to expectation; the fact remains that it is easy, and often tempting, to toy with different identities while travelling. That this has long been one of the chief attractions of solo, independent travel is pointed to in the following quotation from William Hazlitt's *Tabletalk*, first published in 1821:

Oh! It is great to shake off the trammels of the world and of public opinion – to lose our importunate, tormenting, ever lasting personal identity in the elements of nature, and become the creature of the moment, clear of all ties – to hold to the universe only by a dish of sweet-breads, and to owe nothing but the score of the evening – and no longer seeking for applause and meeting with contempt, to be known by no other title than 'the gentleman in the park!' . . . We baffle prejudice and disappoint conjecture; and from being so to others, begin to be objects of curiosity and wonder even to ourselves.

Some might argue that the adoption of different identities is a mark of insecurity; that, like Britain's notorious 'King Con' Paul Bint, who has masqueraded as a doctor, a lawyer and an aristocrat, people who play with identity do so because they cannot bear to be themselves – in Bint's case a failed trainee hairdresser. And yet there is something of the essential spirit of play in this, the urge that informs games of 'dressing up' or 'let's pretend' in our youth and only survives into adulthood through the realms of acting or sexual role-play – or the con.

It's easy to have a grudging respect for con artists. The most professional, of course, never get caught; but some spectacular stories have filtered down from others. Take for example Frank Abagnale, who masqueraded as an airline pilot: he flew a Boeing 737 untrained, travelled for a year with a team of trainee air stewardesses who never guessed that he was not what he claimed to be, and eventually had a film of his life, *Catch Me if You Can*, made by Steven Spielberg.

For a culture that sets such store by self-confidence, by image, the con artist is the unsung hero. But while it's not difficult to admire con artists who are content simply to take money from their professional endeavours, and who never harm others, sometimes their abuse of trust shades over into something much darker – murder.

A SPOONFUL OF SUGAR
The students considered themselves lucky to have met the man who called himself Daniel Chaumet. For this tour group of 60 French engineering students from Tarbes, sightseeing in Delhi for a few days before flying to Bangkok, it was a rare treat to meet someone who spoke French rather than the barbaric English endemic to the region; and rarer still to meet someone who knew so much about the area, was happy to share his knowledge and seemed to expect nothing in return. He'd come up to them at the Taj Mahal and they'd been charmed straight away. He seemed to know a lot about gems and helped some of the students who, he insisted, had been ripped off, to secure refunds; he was also accompanied by some spectacularly beautiful girls. The combination – the raffish charmer with his stunning girlfriends and exhaustive knowlege of precious stones – proved glamorous in a way few could resist.

He also knew a lot about the intestinal problems common to the region; most visitors to India contracted dysentery at some point, he maintained, and some of the students concurred, having already suffered from severe bouts of the illness. Chaumet poured scorn on Indian doctors – their remedies were worse than useless – and distributed tablets of his own, telling the students that these would help protect them against stomach upsets. What they didn't know was that most of the pills were placebos, with a few among them designed to give the takers diarrhoea: those students who'd taken the placebos would now have a greater trust in his medical abilities, as they watched their fellows writhe in gut-cramped agony. Building up trust was very important in his line of work.

Chaumet had arranged to meet the students at the restaurant of the Vikram Hotel on their final evening in Delhi. It didn't look like they planned to have a quiet night: bottles of vodka had already been opened, and they clearly wanted to make it a night to remember. Chaumet had other plans for them, however, and distributed more pills around the room, again telling the students they were protection against intestinal problems. About half of the students took them, delighted to receive free, reliable medical advice. Chaumet knew they'd start passing out soon, and tried to hurry them to bed. But the students were in a festive mood, passing the vodka around and becoming increasingly boisterous; they were touched by their new friend's concern, but felt he was being over-cautious. They felt fine and there was no way they were going to bed early on their last night in India. Then one of the women collapsed.

Some turned to Chaumet – what had happened? The self-professed medical expert asked if they'd been taking anti-malarial tablets. On hearing that they had, he told them that the quinine in their tablets had probably reacted badly with the vodka. This seemed to reassure the students, until a few more fell unconscious. One or two began to vomit, and Chaumet looked distinctly nervous. The leader of the tour group called for the manager: surely they had food poisoning? Faced with a room full of angry and bilious Frenchmen the manager found it difficult to calm them down: the food was fine, he insisted, and he told them that he would call for an ambulance. One of the stricken women crawled across the floor towards him, and the manager bent down, keen to soothe the troubled guest. Her response was to bite his leg.

Before the scene descended into anarchic farce, one of the students who hadn't taken Chaumet's medication realised that all of the members of the party who were suffering had. He pointed this out to a friend, and the two of them rounded on the possible culprit. Chaumet, after realising that his placatory hand gestures wouldn't work here, bolted for the door, but now the wrath of the remaining fit members of the tour group was fixed on him, and he was held. He attempted to keep them off using karate – the students were surprised by how strong and nimble he was – but the sheer number of them, some of whom were rugby forwards, kept him there until the police arrived.

Little did the students know that the raging man they had cornered, smooth tour guide and unreliable apothecary, was Charles Sobhraj, a master of disguise wanted in three continents and suspected of having killed over fifteen tourists. The bikini killer's reign of terror was finally about to end.

STUCK IN THE MIDDLE

Vietnam, 1940. The wetlands had little to offer fourteen-year-old Song. She was beautiful and ambitious, but could see only a lifetime of farming and tending water buffalo ahead if she stayed with her family in the countryside. Saigon, with its promise of opportunity and a taste of the high life, beckoned. Her family were appalled: as far as they were concerned, girls who left the countryside for the city usually ended up working the streets.

But Song went anyway, and her looks soon helped her find work as a waitress in a café, where she was flattered by the attention paid her by the establishment's regulars. The owner himself not only appreciated that she brought in more customers but also hoped that she might one day share more than a working day with him.

Of all the men courting her, one in particular held her attention. Hotchand Bhawnani Sobhraj was an Indian tailor from a town near Bombay; he was in his early forties and had settled in Saigon. While he lived and worked in just one room, he had grand plans for expansion, and Song was impressed by his quiet determination. She moved in with him.

When Song fell pregnant, Sobhraj was appalled. He maintained that the child was not his: she flirted with all the customers of the café, and who knew what else she got up to with them? It could belong to any one of them. The café owner was similarly unimpressed, and sacked her, angry that she'd elected to enjoy the favours of another man over his. With all the trouble the child had already brought her, Song regretted not having had an abortion, but the child, a boy, was born on 6 April 1944. The tailor didn't visit her in hospital and agreed to let them stay in his shop only on condition that they understood that he wasn't about to admit paternity of the boy or take responsibility for his upbringing. The boy was called Gurmukh, but had no official identity other than a hospital record, soon lost in the tumult of war.

In August 1945 Saigon was ravaged by violence as the Ho Chi Minh, less than fourteen days after the Japanese surrender to the French, seized power in Hanoi and claimed that the Viet Minh would soon unite the country. Kidnappings became commonplace, especially of foreign nationals; Indians were especially targeted, as many had grown wealthy from lending money to the Vietnamese to feed the national obsession with gambling. One day, when Song had taken Gurmukh out for a walk, they were both kidnapped by Viet Minh partisans, who duly demanded a ransom of $10,000.

Sobhraj didn't have that kind of money, and even if he did, he was unlikely to spend it freeing a child he didn't believe to be his and a woman he believed to have cheated him, but he told a valued customer, a British army officer, what had happened. The officer gathered a small group of soldiers together, found out where the mother and child had been taken and raided the house, retrieving them both unharmed. Sobhraj made each soldier a new suit as a token of his gratitude. But he blamed Song for the abduction; if she hadn't dressed like a rich man's girlfriend then none of this would have happened.

The relationship deteriorated further. Song discovered a letter from the tailor's wife in India, and was deaf to his protestations that it had been an arranged marriage which did not concern her; he in turn accused her of infidelity again, this time with French soldiers. She left him, and she and Gurmukh moved into another flat. She was young, not yet 20 years old, and good looking; she wanted to have a good time now that she was free of the staid tailor. But it wasn't easy to find a job, and her situation worsened dramatically when she found that she was pregnant again; by her calculations the child's father was again Sobhraj.

A friend advised her to find another man quickly – a young lover could forgive her pregnancy, and even learn to love the child as his own, but most would be put off by a new-born child. Song started to go out every night, partly in search of a man but also to enjoy Saigon's nightlife in a way she had been forbidden when living with the tailor. But every time her son saw her dressing up to go out he would scream and wrap his arms around her legs; once he even cut up her best dress with a pair of scissors.

Just the fact that she already had a child put off many suitors, and Song didn't want just to have casual sex or, worse, to prostitute herself, but eventually she met Alfonse Darreau, a French officer. When she told him she was pregnant he didn't mind, and after a brief period of courtship they married on 15 September 1948. Darreau accepted legal paternity of Song's daughter Anne-Marie, but not of Gurmukh. The boy was the only stain on the couple's new picture of domestic harmony: he hated his stepfather, once tearing the brass buttons from his uniform, and idolised his real father, boasting of how Sobhraj would soon rescue him, although in truth the tailor had by now lost all interest in the boy.

Gurmukh's behaviour became so antisocial that he had to be locked in his room when Darreau's officer friends came round for dinner. He wet his bed until well into his teens. Song took him to see a doctor, who told her that the problem was psychological and stemmed from his unstable upbringing. Upset that he had been prescribed no physical cure, Song resorted to one of her own, tying a piece of string around the base of his penis at night.

The boy spent more and more time on the streets, and Song didn't press him too closely about his whereabouts; the less he was around the house the better, as far as she was concerned. One day he was brought home by the police on suspicion of having stolen a bicycle, and Song locked him in his room. Gurmukh climbed out of the window and escaped, leaving his mother to enjoy a few days' peace until a phone call from the tailor revealed that he'd found the boy hiding in his shop. Deaf to the boy's protestations that he wanted to stay, Sobhraj returned him to his mother, who tied him to his bed as punishment: he wouldn't be embarrassing her so easily again.

Darreau was transferred back to France in 1949. Song was delighted – at last she would experience the civilisation of Europe, a far cry from the rice paddies of her childhood – but her son was horrified at the thought of being uprooted again and taken so far from his father. But as the boy lacked legal documentation proving his identity, it was unlikely that he'd be able to travel to France in any case; the only option appeared to be to persuade the tailor to take him back. Song and Gurmukh visited him to ask if the boy could stay for a while while Darreau arranged legal guardianship. The tailor, whose plans for expansion were by now being realised, was reluctant until the boy put his arms around his father's legs and begged. Sobhraj finally agreed – the boy should learn a trade.

Three years later, in the wake of renewed aggression from the Ho Chi Minh, Darreau was posted back to Saigon. Song had never kept her promise to send for the boy, and now she had three more children to look after, but she was still looking forward to seeing Gurmukh again. On visiting the tailor she found that he had taken a new Vietnamese lover, Sao; the couple already had three children. Sao hated Gurmukh, a living reminder of the tailor's involvement with Song, and treated him badly; the boy responded by running away and making a living on the street, leader of a group of urchins who hustled tourists and soldiers and stole food to survive. Song and Darreau searched the streets for the boy until they found him holding court over his gang, ragged children carrying knives and living in the remains of a bombed-out house.

On seeing his condition, Darreau decided to take care of the boy, telling Song that his behaviour probably derived from the fact that he had no official identity and no stable family unit. Legal custody was given to the officer, although Darreau refused to give the boy his name; after consultations with the tailor, the boy was finally officially named Hotchand Bhawnani Gurmukh Sobhraj.

As the combat worsened Darreau, who normally worked at a desk job, volunteered for front-line duty. He soon returned with severe shell-shock, unable to abide the slightest noise and unfit for work of any kind. He was told to return to France to recuperate, and would this time be allowed to take Hotchand with him. Despite the boy's protestations that he wanted to stay close to his father the family moved to France and then, following a new posting, to Dakar in French West Africa, where Darreau was given a large mansion and another administrative post.

Song now had seven children, and Darreau's extreme sensitivity to noise meant that most of them spent their days away from the house. Hotchand, as the oldest and wiliest, became their leader, and was especially adored by his half-brother André, who was eight years younger and awed by the older boy's confidence and control. Hotchand led them in games of make-believe and dressing up; an accomplished mimic, he took the nickname of 'Charlot' after impersonating Charlie Chaplin. The nickname stuck, and when the boy was formally baptised in 1959 his name was given as Charles Gurmukh Sobhraj.

'THERE ARE ALWAYS FOOLS'

The change of environment hadn't changed his behaviour, however, and he was poorly behaved at school, although clearly one of the most intelligent students, as well as being well known to Dakar police as a practised thief. He befriended the son of a local Wolof tribesman, and both went thieving together; the local boy would also run errands for Charles, who told his mother that 'There are always fools who will do what I tell them to.'

As France's colonial empire dissolved the family moved to a small house in Marseilles. Charles was by now sixteen, still a bed-wetter and a chronic liar, and his relationship with his mother oscillated between extremes of love and hate. When police brought him home with the news that he'd been threatening people with a knife outside a department store, Song and Darreau agreed to send him to a boarding school known for its strict discipline – perhaps this would teach the intractable boy to behave. After being told of the decision,

Charles tried to board a freighter headed for the East, desperate to be reunited with his father, but was caught.

He escaped from the boarding school in a similar manner, and proved so difficult a pupil that Song had to beg the institution to keep him, allowing them free rein over the means of punishment for the teenager. But Charles hated the school, subjected as he was to racist abuse – France was at the time at war in Vietnam – and ran away again. This time Song told them that she washed her hands of him; let him run back to his father, she had six other children to look after.

Charles made it as far as Djibouti before being caught. He told the captain that his father would pay for his passage, but there was no reply to the cable duly sent; when he was threatened with a stint in an African jail he contacted Song, who picked him up when the freighter returned to Europe – she wouldn't be able to break contact with him so easily.

Song arranged for him to work in a friend's kitchen in a Paris restaurant, but Charles was a less than model employee, unable to last long in any job until he began to work as a busboy at La Coupole – being close to the capital's rich and famous appealed to Charles, and his behaviour began to improve.

One day the tailor, now wealthy enough to travel to Europe casually, visited him at the restaurant. He was touched by Charles's story of lack of opportunity and dead-end education, and impressed enough by the young man's bearing as a busboy to take him back to Saigon and teach him the tailor trade. Charles was delighted – his father wanted him – and once the legal niceties had been taken care of through a contract of employment that allowed Charles to leave France, the two set off for Saigon.

But the situation there was far from how Charles had imagined it; his father was too busy with work to spend much time with him, and Sao's attitude had not softened with the years. The work was harder than any he'd done before, too, and he soon took to slipping away early then not turning up at all. When he was jailed on suspicion of car theft his father, convinced that his behavioural problems stemmed from his lack of legal citizenship of any country, tried to arrange Indian citizenship for him.

For this Charles would have to spend a year in India and learn one of the subcontinent's languages. When the tailor told Charles that he wanted the young man to stay with his cousins near Bombay, Charles was distraught; he felt like he was being abandoned again, but the tailor explained that it was his last chance to gain citizenship of a country.

Far from being in Bombay itself, Charles found his cousins living in the countryside some way outside the city, speaking only Urdu and most living in one room. He hated it and ran away twice: the first time he was thrown off a boat while boarding it, and the second time he made it as far as Saigon and was caught only because he rushed on to the deck to see the city. The police contacted the tailor, who told Charles that he had to return to India. He had stolen from his cousins and had to work for them to pay them back; this was his last opportunity. If Charles failed then the tailor didn't want to see him again.

But Charles was not even to have the opportunity to make good his debt: when the boat returned to India he was not allowed to disembark as he lacked the requisite funds. He was jailed, awaiting a response from his father, which, when it arrived, curtly expressed the wish that he should be sent to his mother in Marseilles. Song wasn't too pleased to hear from her son in this way again, but couldn't bear the thought of him trapped as a pauper in an Indian jail, and paid for him to enter France – a loan, which he was expected to pay back. The French authorities gave him a three-month non-renewable visa, with which he was not allowed to work, and Song told him that the loan was all she'd do to help him – he couldn't stay with her.

Charles was now in a difficult position. He needed to make money but could not work legally, and he was too proud to join the thousands of other illegal migrant workers in unskilled labour. There seemed only one avenue open to him. After his visa expired Charles was caught speeding in a stolen car, out on a joyride with a young woman. He was jailed for six months, then on his release told that he would be deported in thirty days. He made contacts easily in the Parisian underworld with other Vietnamese criminals, one of whom, Romain, taught him karate.

Romain could see potential in the young man, who was bold and intelligent, and wanted them to work together on large-scale robberies, but first Charles would have to secure a passport or *carte d'identité*. Romain knew where he could buy one, but he'd have to get hold of the money first, so Charles embarked on a string of petty robberies. Shortly before he'd earned enough, however, he was again caught speeding in a stolen car with a young woman, without any papers. The judge presiding over his case decided to make an example of him, as a warning to other immigrant criminals he warned were flooding into the country from France's former colonies – Charles Sobhraj was sentenced to three years in Poissy prison.

THE VISITOR

Before Félix d'Escogne met Charles Sobhraj, he was told two things: the prison priest, who first approached him about the case, told him that Charles would try to take over his life, and a prison social worker warned him that he would have to be consistent in his visits – Charles needed stability in his life.

D'Escogne, a man of independent means in his late thirties, had been a prison visitor for some years; like others from a similar background, it mollified his social conscience. The job normally involved little more than writing letters for inmates and providing someone to talk to – many of the visitors otherwise had nobody on the outside to help them – but his relationship with Charles soon developed into something far more involved.

The young prisoner was an interesting case; he had been asking the priest for books on Nietzsche, Jung and character-ology, a French system for classifying people and predicting their behaviour, and now turned his requests to Félix. His ability to read and retain was extraordinary, matched only by his effusiveness as a correspondent – he wrote to Félix constantly, often sharing his interpretations of his readings, particularly Nietzsche, in passages such as the following: 'It really is true that nature divides the strong and the weak. There are people who are weak from the moment they leave their mother's breast. They are condemned. I believe I am in the category of the strong.' The visitor responded by agreeing to help Charles to attain citizenship.

Félix conducted his own enquiries into Charles's family: the tailor told him that if and when his son was truly rehabilitated he would be welcome in Saigon, but not before then; when he went to visit Song he found her accompanied by a Marseilles detective masquerading as Darreau, as she'd feared her son had sent someone to rob her. Félix also saw something of Charles's attitude to his father in a letter the young prisoner had written:

> You bore a son, but you ignore him. You abandon him worse than a dog, worse than for the lowest beast!!! From you I will carry only the name you gave me. The faithful love I had for you, I have still, unfortunately. But I will fight it. You are no more my father. I disown you . . . I will consume you. I will make you suffer. I will make you regret that you have missed your father's duty. The fortune, I will get without you. And I will use it to crush you.

Félix soon found a legal loophole which should provide Charles with French identity, a rarely used clause involving citizens of French Indochina who had been obliged to flee after France's withdrawal. They were entitled to full French citizenship if they resided permanently in France; the only conditions for Charles's entitlement were that he should be available for military service and that he would not be allowed to live in Paris for a set period after his release due to the nature of his crimes.

On Charles's release Félix offered to look after him for a while, to smooth his re-entry into society. He let the ex-con stay at his flat, invited him to parties and lent him money to buy clothes, but from the outset Charles abused his minder's generosity, failing to repay loans and treating his belongings with scant respect. At one party Charles met a young woman, Hélène, a twenty-year-old from a bourgeois family who was instantly charmed by Charles's ripe talk of love and poetry. Félix was less impressed by Charles's demands that he take the two of them out to smart restaurants, where Charles would hold court while eating, food falling from his mouth.

'ETERNAL WOMAN, LITTLE GIRL, YOU ARE MINE'
Finally Félix had had enough of his young charge's mannerless behaviour and kicked him out; but Charles continued to appear at odd intervals, always able to make his way into Félix's flat, even when the locks were changed. Things came to a head when Charles tried to borrow 1000 francs on top of what he already owed. Félix refused, telling Charles that he needed to stop being so reliant on his former visitor; Charles agreed, telling Félix that prison had ruined him, thereby established a pattern whereby blame for his actions would always fall on somebody else. He also told Félix that he had got rid of his emotions; his feeling of vengefulness towards his father had deformed him, and he now aimed to be pure intellect.

Charles took Félix's advice and found work as a fire-extinguisher salesman. He was too lazy to work well, however, and spent most of his time flirting with the secretaries, many of whom were happy to lend him money, and some of whom complained when he was finally sacked.

Perhaps understanding that the job market could not offer him the easy money and glamour for which he yearned, he contacted some of his former jail cronies. One, a giant Spaniard known as Porto, disfigured since a prostitute had thrown boiling olive oil in his face, asked him if he'd like to join a small gang committing local robberies. Charles's counterproposal was to draw up detailed plans of rich people's flats and houses to be robbed – through Félix he had been invited to a substantial number of these and remembered their layouts well. He would take 50 per cent of the proceeds for this alone, with an upfront payment of 5,000 francs, repayable if the robbery was to fail. Police later discovered that he planned to secure the blueprints for houses of officials whose lives had shaped his – judges, attorneys and prison officers – to take a private revenge.

Hélène knew little of his past, but was charmed by his air of worldliness, his exotic tales of different cultures, and his unashamedly romantic letters to her, of which the following extract is typical: 'Eternal woman, little girl, you are mine. I simply cannot bear the hours we are not together. I toss in my bed unable to sleep, summoning portraits of you that fill the walls of my room. There *is* a god, *chérie*, and he sent me to you.' But her parents were less impressed by her boyfriend – he didn't seem quite respectable – and when he proposed to her they were adamant in their refusal; she asked him for more time.

But patience didn't come naturally to Sobhraj, whether for women or money. He had begun to gamble, and one evening took Hélène to the Deauville casino, where he lost heavily. Speeding back in the car, he was upset by his poor luck and demanded a demonstration of commitment from his girlfriend. For the last time, would she marry him? She finally relented – it seemed better than putting up with his incessant wheedling – only for him to lose control of the car, spinning out and crashing it into the roadside.

It could have been worse – Porto was later said to have been waiting at Charles's flat, ready to kill him and take back his 5,000 francs and any other floorplans or blueprints he had – but it was bad enough. The car was stolen, as was his driving licence. Charles was sentenced to eight months in Rouen prison. It would have been longer, had it not been for Hélène's statement that she planned to marry him, and Félix's – supported by a psychiatrist – that he could still be rehabilitated.

While in prison Charles wrote to Félix, long letters explaining how he was a victim of circumstance. Disgusted by the self-pitying tone, Félix wrote Charles a critical character appraisal, stronger than anything he'd told his charge before. On reading it Charles became hysterically angry, breaking up his prison furniture then eating the letter before the guards could take it away from him. He wrote back to Félix, a cold letter lacking his characteristic effusiveness, asking the visitor to stay out of his life.

Sobhraj busied himself with studying French law during this stint in prison, and continued to send perfumed missives to Hélène, who had decided to side with him over her increasingly alarmed parents. He also received visits from two Asian men who brought him jugs of stew; when he returned the jugs he would hide blueprints of potential burglary sites inside, and in this way earned 15,000 francs while imprisoned.

After his release he married Hélène. He apologised to Félix, who was his best man at the civil ceremony, and even her parents seemed impressed by his efforts to better himself – he began to do odd jobs in restaurants and seemed to have put his criminal leanings behind him. Hélène was soon pregnant. Charles was called up for military service but given a medical discharge after a few weeks, apparently having been able to raise his temperature at will – tricking doctors was to become something of a speciality in his criminal career.

If Sobhraj appeared to have changed, it was in appearance alone. He stole 6,000 francs from his sister, who pressed charges and had him arrested; only Félix was able to persuade her to retract the charges, promising her that the money would be repaid in full. Shortly afterwards the tailor came to visit his son. Charles, keen to make a good impression, put on a lavish reception for him, buying him gifts and driving him to Geneva. He had bankrupted himself preparing for the visit, and passed bad cheques during his father's stay. When they were alone together Hélène told the tailor that Charles had money problems – she didn't know how he could afford to be so generous. The tailor advised her to leave him. But she loved Charles; he was the father of her child. How could she leave him?

AROUND THE WORLD

Charles 'borrowed' a car from Félix, planning to drive to Asia to join his father in Saigon. He hadn't paid his sister back, and his bad cheques had been traced back to him – he was duly sentenced to one year's imprisonment *in absentia*, and permanent expulsion from France. He wrote to Félix, apologising for his abrupt departure and the impromptu loan of the car; the visitor also heard from the tailor, who wanted him to pass on a message. Charles was not welcome in Saigon.

It was 1970, and Charles Sobhraj's career as an international criminal had just begun. In Rhodes he stole a hire car, left his hotel without paying and left a bad cheque at the casino after losing heavily at baccarat. The casino was also the setting for his first known 'drug and rob' crime. An Englishman called Converse had won at roulette and, on hearing at the bar of Charles's losses, boasted of his winnings. After drinking a nightcap with Charles he woke up in his hotel room the next day, robbed of several thousand drachmas, his passport, £200 in traveller's cheques, an airline ticket to London and some English money. In Sobhraj's hotel room police found several chair legs, the ends carved with imprints of Greek entry and exit stamps.

It was not known whether the woman accompanying him had been a party to his crimes, and he was sentenced *in absentia* to one year's imprisonment on charges of fraud and theft. Using other people's passports did not present a problem to Sobhraj. A criminal friend had taught him the art of disguise, and his features, while unusually strong, lent themselves well to it – he could pass as Indian, Japanese, Vietnamese, southern European, Malaysian or Indonesian with ease.

The couple drove towards India, selling the car at the Pakistan border and taking a train to Delhi. On 15 November 1970 Hélène gave birth to a baby girl, Shubra, in a Bombay hospital. The family soon made their mark in Bombay society: they seemed chic and sophisticated, falling in with both the French expatriate community and the Europhile upper-class Indians. It didn't take long for Charles to hit upon an ingenious way of making money, using contacts he picked up at parties.

Demand in India for European or American cars was huge, but the red tape surrounding their importation made buying one legally an interminably slow and expensive process. Charles could get cars delivered much more cheaply. He took orders for individual models with a deposit of around $2,000 in a stable currency, such as Swiss francs. He would fly to Teheran and pick up a stolen car of the desired model that had been driven from Europe, and have new ownership papers made up assigning the car to him. He would then drive into India, bribing the border officials to turn a blind eye, and arrive in Bombay, where the car would be stripped of almost everything. Now barely driveable, the car would be taken to a forest near Bombay and crashed into a tree, taking care not to damage the bodywork too much. Charles would report the car stolen; the police would find it and contact him, and he would tell them to auction it off as junk. He would then find out where and when it was to be auctioned, buy it in the name of the customer, repair it and sell it for around $20,000.

Charles made good money from the scam, but Hélène felt neglected. She was often consigned to the house while her husband travelled on 'business', and when on one occasion he did take her with him, to Hong Kong, he wouldn't have sex with her. They moved to Macao, partly to be closer to a large casino where Charles could satisfy his gambling urges. He sometimes won, but more often lost, and any gifts he'd given to his wife were soon sold to cover his losses. Hélène wanted to go home – she didn't like the way he'd often leave her in strange hotels with no money and nobody to speak to – but she wondered how guilty she was of sharing his crimes. She knew that at the very least they often left hotels without paying; who knew what else he was up to?

LOBO

After losing $40,000 in a Macao casino, Charles was approached by an Englishman named Maurice, who'd known Porto and who offered to loan Charles money to pay the casino back if he took part in a jewel raid. The plan was to persuade an American dancer, La Passionata, that he was the director of a casino interested in hiring her as a dancer and thereby gaining entry into her hotel room, which was above leading Delhi jeweller the Rajasthan Emporium. Charles agreed and began to prepare his identity as J. Lobo, casino director, having a number of business cards printed.

He introduced himself to the dancer at one of her shows, and she was flattered enough by his attentions to invite him to her room; but instead of offering her a job he tied the artiste to a chair and, with the help of an accomplice, attempted to drill through the floor. After a couple of hours they gave up – there appeared to be a thick sheet of solid steel above the ceiling of the jeweller's. Sobhraj hit on the plan of asking La Passionata to call the jeweller and ask him to bring a selection of the shop's most extravagant pieces of jewellery to the room. She did so, and Sobhraj tied up the jeweller, stole the keys to the shop and robbed it of as much as he could carry.

He was to leave from Delhi airport, and took the bag of jewels as hand luggage with him. Just as he was about to board the plane he was called back; there was some irregularity in the currency he'd used to pay for his ticket. When he'd dealt with the problem, he found to his alarm that customs officials were searching every bag before letting people on to the plane, and he could see from the other direction the jeweller, accompanied by several policemen, walking towards him. He climbed out of a window in the nearest gents toilets, leaving the bag behind and walking out of the airport. Ironically customs hadn't even found the jewels in his bag; it had been marked 'OK' and passed.

Sobhraj explained to Maurice what had happened. The Englishman had already read about it in the papers; it wasn't Charles's fault, but he still owed Maurice money, and would have to do another job for him in a few days. It never happened. Sobhraj was stopped on the street and arrested for car theft; one of his old customers had given his name and description as an excuse for their papers not being in order. Sobhraj protested that they'd stopped the wrong man and pulled out some fake ID, unfortunately including one of his 'J. Lobo' cards. The name had been all over the newspapers, and the arresting policeman couldn't believe his luck.

While in jail awaiting trial Sobhraj tried to be moved to the hospital, which would provide a far easier means of escape than the prison itself, but took his act too far and ended up having his appendix removed. Hélène came to visit him in hospital and they chatted until the guard finally fell asleep; she took his keys and released Charles, then climbed into bed in his place. But Sobhraj didn't get far; his operation had left him weak from loss of blood and lacking in his characteristic ingenuity when it came to disguise. This time he was caught masquerading as an Untouchable – a *Harijan*, a member of India's underclass – trying to board a train.

Hélène was jailed but then released on bail posted by a friend, and tried to raise money for the trip back to France, but when she heard that Charles was dying she couldn't resist seeing him again. He had sent his Indian lawyer, Rupinder Singh, on a round trip to Saigon to ask the tailor for bail money. Incredibly the tailor agreed – he was near death in any case – and gave Singh a 40,000 rupee loan. Hélène agreed to wait for Charles and, after sending Shubra back to France, survived on money smuggled out of prison by her husband on visiting days. When Singh posted bail the couple left the country immediately, buying forged passports from one of Sobhraj's contacts and stopping off in Kabul for him to conduct more 'business'.

It would be the pattern of Sobhraj's criminal career that while he aimed high, attempting to defraud the rich and naive in the lobbies of smart hotels, he often had to settle for far lower targets – hash-soaked young men with little worth robbing save a passport and $100 in traveller's cheques. Kabul was full of hippies like this. Charles despised them as weak, decadent drug addicts; they deserved to be robbed.

But they were valuable to him in other ways as well: from them he would learn about the different kinds of tranquilliser, freely available in Asian chemists, and their effects; among them he would find the women he could manipulate into helping him rob richer tourists. Having rejected the morality of their parents' generation, they were easily convinced of the revolutionary potential of Charles's crimes, whether these involved defrauding consulates or robbing rich tourists.

When they were about to leave Kabul in July 1972 and continue their journey west, they were arrested for non-payment of a hotel bill, stealing a rental car and attempting to cross a border illegally. Sobhraj was sent to Damazan, a prison in which no food was served at all, and at which if a prisoner had no means of raising funds he would die. Sobhraj planned to escape at the earliest possible opportunity, and began to dig a tunnel outside with a Frenchman; the dirt from the tunnel was packed into the floor of the cell, and others played bongos to disguise the sound. When the tunnel was finally ready Sobhraj crawled out, only to be seen on the outside by an off-duty prison guard. The Western prisoners were now all moved to maximum security, but Sobhraj was able to escape even from here, feigning a haemorrhage and chloroforming hospital guards.

In September Sobhraj planned to free his wife from jail, and hired a Chevrolet as a getaway car. By Afghan law all hire cars came with a driver, an inconvenience that didn't bother Sobhraj too much. He drugged the driver with Largactyl and put him in the boot of the car, hoping to dump him near a village, only to find when he opened the boot that the man had died.

Sobhraj was accompanied by a Dutch girl who he'd paid to come with him, planning to use her as a decoy to free his wife; he persuaded her to help him dispose of the body in a river. Later she would make a report to Interpol in Teheran about the death of the Chevrolet driver, discovered to be Mohammad Habib, 35 years old, the father of three children. His body was never found.

A murder charge was brought against 'Damon Seamen', who'd hired the car; Charles was using a bewildering array of names at the time, including Dr Jalian Clair, Charles Sounder, Adolph Nomer, Dr Marshall Golian and Salim Harady among others. He succeeded in freeing his wife from jail, but was shortly afterwards arrested in Teheran, this time for smuggling passports.

This was a serious crime in Iran, as passports were extremely useful to the anti-Shah terrorist underground, who were indeed Sobhraj's clients. To avoid torture and probable death, he told SAVAK, the Shah's secret police, the names of two Iranians active in the anti-Shah network, and was released on bail near the Turkish border.

This time Hélène left him for good and travelled back to France after telling Charles that she would file for divorce and change her name in the hope that he wouldn't be able to track her down.

KEEPING IT IN THE FAMILY

André couldn't believe how much his brother had changed. He'd received a call to join Charles in Istanbul, and had leaped at the chance. He'd always known his brother would be a success, and now look at him – a multilingual charmer who seemed to know everybody and everything. But it took some time for Charles to reveal the true nature of his business. First he told his brother that he was now known as 'Alain Gauthier', and showed him around Istanbul while explaining the way he dealt with people: 'Psychology is very important to me . . . it is the principal weapon in my business. I use psychology like stupid people use guns.'

He went on to expound his personal philosophy: life, for him, was a series of tests or crises, that could either strengthen or destroy a man depending on his nature. The world was divided into inferior and superior beings, and André should never let himself become a follower. Charles had in the past blamed his upbringing for his shortcomings; now he felt that it had strengthened him.

His room was littered with books: non-fiction dealing with gemology, global economics and languages – Charles could speak French, English, German, Spanish, Italian and Vietnamese, as well as some Greek and Hindi; and a selection of novels, cheap espionage paperbacks mixed in with the works of Somerset Maugham, Greene and Conrad. When André asked his brother what purpose the novels served, Charles replied that the authors had covered the territory before him.

It is tempting to imagine how Sobhraj conceived himself in relation to his taste for gin-soaked tales of Europeans in the tropics: as a huckster Kurtz, ruling over his minions through terror and an inhuman bravado; or as a secret agent in the Greene mould, a spy in so deep he had become his own cover story.

When Charles finally explained that he was a thief, André was ready to join him – he idolised his brother more than ever before. He was trained by Charles to be his accomplice, learning what kinds of clothes to wear, how to converse fluently on current affairs and business matters, and what kind of prospective victim to approach. The French were Charles's preferred nationality, as they were typically over-joyed to find someone who spoke their language and regarded other nationalities as grossly inferior.

Once a casual meeting had been arranged, André was to probe for weaknesses. Everyone had one, whether it was drugs, jewels, girls – even boys – and André was to admit that he could procure the goods at a cut-rate price. But it was crucial to establish confidence first; it didn't do to appear a crass hustler, and so the offer of gems or girls was to be made almost as an aside, an afterthought. When the victim had agreed, they would be taken to their hotel room, drugged – normally using Valium or Mogadon – and robbed.

There was one key rule: use nothing that could be used as evidence, whether weapons or narcotics. It was good to keep a clear mind in any case; Charles despised those who used drugs. He trained his brother in karate, and showed him the way he recruited beautiful women, usually from the USA or Europe, to help him in his crimes; he would sometimes even steal them from their boyfriends, and André would later describe Charles's appeal to women: 'He represented mystery, intrigue, romance. He was a woman's fantasy of one moment of adventure – and danger.' The female accomplices were also well rewarded for their pains, often leaving with several thousand dollars in cash as well as expensive gifts.

The victims chosen would usually be in Istanbul for only a couple of days, so that there was little chance of their identifying Sobhraj or his brother after being robbed; as extra insurance the brothers stayed in small hotels on the outskirts of the city for a few days after committing each robbery. They were usually successful, but the overheads of their set-ups were so large that their profits were never enough; Charles always wanted more.

One particularly elaborate con involving a Turkish couple, Anton and Krista Kecvic, earned them enough money to leave Istanbul. The equipment required included pillowcase hoods, drugs, syringes, toy pistols, new calling cards and a book on Eastern mercantile commerce. Charles sat near the Kecvics' hotel restaurant table for a few days, picking up background information: Anton was a gambler, interested in exporting clothes to Japan.

Charles engineered a chance meeting in the hotel casino, and told Anton that he was a French-speaking Japanese businessman in the textiles industry. On Anton's explaining his export plans, Charles told the Turk that he knew exactly the Japanese businessman to speak to – Mr Saito – and asked him to come to meet Mr Saito in his hotel room the next day.

Anton was keen to follow up the lead, but when he paid a visit the next day he was disappointed to find that Mr Saito had not yet arrived. Charles sought to placate him, offering him coffee – drugged, of course – and asking him to wait just a little longer. Anton drank the coffee, but it didn't seem to have the desired effect, and when Charles could stall no longer André, following a pre-arranged signal, leaped out of the bathroom and tied the Turk up. Charles then tranquillised him intravenously, only to find when searching his pockets that he had almost nothing of value with him.

He called the Kecvics' room to speak to Krista, telling her that her husband wanted her to come to the room to celebrate the closing of a deal. On her arrival he knocked her out with an injection and took her room key, then stole all their valuables. The Kecvics were found two days later by a cleaning lady, barely alive.

That night the brothers left Istanbul. Charles told André of his plans for a business in which all of the family could take part – then they would surely love him. They travelled to Athens, Charles using Anton Kecvic's passport. The robberies continued: of a Japanese professor there to see the ruins, Charles posing as an academic; and of an Egyptian called Khymal, for whom Charles recruited a buxom ex-hippie as a honeytrap.

It didn't do to stay too long in one place – hotel police would become suspicious after two or three similar robberies locally – and the brothers soon set off for Beirut. While they were on a shuttle bus at the airport André played with a laughing doll he hadn't been able to resist taking from Khymal's luggage; it was unfortunate for them that the Egyptian was on the same bus.

The brothers were arrested and their luggage searched; it was full of incriminating evidence, including the Kecvics' passports. The Turkish authorities requested that the criminals be extradited, to deal with 'these depraved bandits who violate the peace of Turkey by assaulting our tourist guests', to use the words of a high-ranking Turkish policeman; but first the Greeks wanted to dispense justice themselves.

The brothers were taken to Korydallos, a fairly lenient prison, to await trial. Charles hit on a ruse to ensure their early releases: if the brothers swapped identities, then 'André' would be released soon, as this was his first offence in Greece; once Charles was safely out he could then contact the authorities to tell them they'd released the wrong man, obliging them to release the real André in turn. André trusted his brother's scheme, but its first flaw soon became apparent: the Greeks were in no hurry to release 'André' anyway.

Charles duly planned to escape. He acquired a set of the prison plans, and enlisted the help of two Americans in a nearby cell, in which a tunnel would be dug. The Americans were opposed to the Vietnam War, and it didn't take long for Charles to convince them that he'd been driven to crime by US aggression in his own country, or that their own sentences (for hash possession) would see them in Korydallos until they were old men.

Charles and André dug most of the tunnel, but their plans were foiled when they struck a water main, which caused the water to back up in the toilets in other cells. While the tunnel itself wasn't found, guards were now posted outside all the cells, making it impossible to continue. The Americans were soon released in any case, their families paying a lawyer to buy them out, and Charles – hoping for preferential treatment – revealed that they had built a tunnel and planned to escape. He received, for his pains, double milk rations, and when the prison governor heard of his own involvement in the escape plan, which didn't take long, the brothers were sent to Aegina, a reportedly escape-proof island prison.

Charles knew that he had to be sent to the mainland hospital to have the remotest chance of escaping, and after a year he bruised his ribcage and complained of a stomach complaint, hoping the prison doctor would suspect a haemorrhage. It worked – he was sent to the hospital – but the doctor there sent him back to the island.

In the two minutes he was left alone he managed to steal a bottle of perfume, and in the prison van on the way back to the dock, Charles asked for a light for his cigarette. He then doused the inside of the van with perfume and set it on fire. The drivers stopped the van and opened the rear doors, Charles taking advantage of the smoke and confusion to walk away. He'd done it again.

SMALL-TOWN GIRL

On 4 May 1975 a Boeing 747 on its way to India stopped for refuelling in Teheran. Among its passengers were French airline reservations clerk Jeanne Paumier and her friend, reservations agent Christian Rucher. They were approached by a scruffy, long-haired yet chic man who told them he was a photographer employed by *Paris Match* to take photographs of India; he gave his name as Alain. When he heard they were going to Kashmir he told them he was too; he knew the country well and could help to show them around and ensure they weren't ripped off on renting a houseboat.

When they arrived in Srinagar they met another couple with whom they arranged to share a houseboat; the prices, even taking into account Alain's bargaining prowess, were exorbitant, so it made sense to share. Marie-Andrée Leclerc was 29 and had barely left Canada before, let alone travelled to Asia. Her partner, Bernard, an older Canadian, hadn't swept her off her feet – he was convenient, a safe option, for whom she'd settled because she felt she was plain. Marie-Andrée didn't love Bernard, but she fell for Alain instantly. He was charming, dominant, worldly and a little dangerous, everything Bernard was not.

But he didn't respond to her obvious interest; not, at least, at first. He was more interested in Jeanne, although the Frenchwoman found his constant preening and posing more than a little off-putting. The atmosphere in the houseboat became slightly awkward, with Alain chasing Jeanne, and Marie-Andrée chasing Alain – and what of Bernard? But Alain ensured there was enough to occupy the group, taking them on trips to spectacular waterfalls and helping them bargain for rugs and antiquities; and he remained aloof, occasionally talking to hippy girls from the other houseboats and never remaining in the frame if one of the holidaymakers was taking a photograph. All they had of him, they realised afterwards, were a couple of blurred images, as though his character were too ill-defined to be pinned down.

When they returned to Delhi, Alain made Jeanne a business proposal: would she smuggle gems for him? She refused, surprised that he'd wanted her to know he was a crook, and he turned his attentions more fully to the Canadians once the French couple had flown home. He took over their holiday, arranging flights to Nepal and to Thailand, where Bernard fell ill. Fortunately for them Alain knew a great deal about local illnesses and gave Bernard some pills that sent him to sleep; he was unconscious long enough for Alain finally to seduce the shy if willing Marie-Andrée at the end of her holiday.

She hoped it wasn't just a holiday romance; she'd never met anyone like Alain before. And he appeared to see her the same way: from the moment she returned home he bombarded her with love letters, begging her to return to him; he wanted her to have his child, to be with him forever. Marie-Andrée was not given to making rash decisions; her innate conservatism had ensured that she'd barely ever left the town she grew up in. But her trip to the East had given her a taste for something more exciting, and so she ignored the advice of her family, who wondered what a playboy such as Alain saw in plain, unadventurous Marie-Andrée.

What indeed? Marie-Andrée was everything Charles Sobhraj was not: small-town, respectable, staid, representative of permanence, homeliness, the embodiment of the qualities Sobhraj had never had. She would also be easy to manipulate and would make the perfect smuggler – nobody would ever suspect her – and the perfect accomplice: who would imagine that a man with a partner so bland would be intent on drugging and robbing them?

She accepted Alain's offer of a round-trip ticket to Bangkok, withdrew $2,000 in safety money and flew out to meet him in early August 1975. Her dream lover shattered her expectations from the moment she arrived. He met her at the airport accompanied by May, a pretty Thai girl who he introduced as his 'girlfriend'; Marie-Andrée was described to May, by contrast, as his 'secretary'. As soon as they were alone together she rounded on him: this wasn't the true love he'd been writing of. But he calmed her by explaining that the girl was an expert gemologist and a crucial contact for his work – he was only pretending to seduce her. Marie-Andrée wanted to believe him, although she wasn't convinced; but she couldn't return to Canada so soon, couldn't bear the snide remarks and nosy gossips, so she vowed to stay. If he was seeing May, then she would try to win him back.

Sobhraj had told May a similar story – he was only pretending to seduce Marie-Andrée for his work. He soon exhausted his 'secretary''s safety fund in loans, which she realised he would never pay back, and when her tourist visa expired he claimed he'd have it renewed but never did. Bureaucracy didn't seem to bother him very much. Marie-Andrée was appalled: it all seemed so far from what she'd expected. Her belief in his promises of international travel, of a pure, strong love, made Marie-Andrée feel naive. 'Alain' had an altogether different kind of travel – a different kind of excitement – in mind for them.

KANIT HOUSE

September 1975. Australian PhD candidate Russell Lapthorne and his Indonesian wife Vera were on holiday in Pattaya, Thailand, on their way to the less commercialised beach of Hua Hin. When they heard that Parisians Jean and Monique Belmont were also travelling to Hua Hin, they decided to go together, and on arrival took adjoining hotel rooms. Monique took them a couple of chocolate milkshakes as a neighbourly treat, but soon afterwards the Lapthornes both fell ill with diarrhoea; maybe they'd eaten some bad seafood. They soldiered on, ill but lying in the sun the next day, while Jean asked them how much money they each earned, and how much they'd brought with them in traveller's cheques.

The following morning they felt a little better, and gladly accepted more chocolate milkshakes from Monique; this time the drinks left them unconscious. When the cleaning lady found them she alerted the hotel owner, who rushed them to hospital to have their stomachs pumped; they might not otherwise have survived.

The Belmonts had gone, and had taken with them almost everything the Lapthornes possessed. The couple tried to explain to the Thai police what had happened, but found the language barrier insurmountable; six months later Interpol would take a stronger interest in their story, showing them photos of Charles Sobhraj and Marie-Andrée Leclerc, who the Lapthornes would identify as the Belmonts. Marie-Andrée had joined in with Sobhraj's drug robberies just one month after her return to Thailand.

Sobhraj and Leclerc now rented a flat in Kanit House in Bangkok, where Marie-Andrée tried to ignore her partner's continuing affair with May and threw her energies into decoration and domestication. It wasn't long before they began to entertain guests.

Dominique Veylau, a 24-year-old French tourist, was about to return home when he met Alain and Monique Gauthier in Chiang Mai; they took him out for a meal, after which he fell ill. Alain told him that he had dysentery, and offered to take Dominique back to his hotel room. He accepted the offer gratefully, and was only a little surprised to find the couple in his room when he woke up. He wouldn't be fully well again for some time, Alain told him; why not stay at their apartment in Bangkok and convalesce?

Dominique couldn't believe his luck – the couple would attend to his needs, regularly bringing him medicine and even offering to look after his passport and traveller's cheques. The only thing that puzzled him was that his illness seemed to be getting worse, not better. He asked Alain if he shouldn't see a doctor, but his host insisted that Thai doctors would not be able to help. He was in the best possible hands exactly where he was.

In October a new couple moved into the block. They were French – Remy Gires had taken a job as a sous chef at a leading Bangkok restaurant – and quickly got to know the other French couple, Alain and Monique. Remy's wife Nadine and Monique took to spending their days together, while both of their husbands were at work. Nadine thought that some things about their set-up didn't quite make sense – what exactly did Alain do? And why was the Frenchman in their flat not getting better? But Remy told her not to ask too many questions. He'd rather she didn't spend too much time with them in any case. Her suspicions were raised to a higher pitch when she saw handcuffs in Alain's apartment, as well as an open safe full of passports. When she asked Monique about these she was told they were essential for Alain's work; a candid enough answer.

Unable to find the victims he wanted in the upmarket hotels, Alain took to frequenting budget hotels, and at the Malaysia he met two French ex-policemen, Yannick and Jacques. When he found that they wanted to stay longer in Thailand, Alain explained that he could help them find work in Pattaya, and a few days later he took them there, along with Marie-Andrée and Dominique, who was now well enough to travel. They rented a bungalow and went out for a meal on the first night. Alain excused himself during the meal to make a long phone call, and when the group returned to the bungalow they discovered that Yannick and Jacques's possessions had been stolen.

The Frenchmen were distraught, until Alain generously offered to let them stay at Kanit House until they'd arranged new passports; of course they'd have to pay their way by running errands. Dominique, similarly, owed him now, and would have to work for him as soon as he was well; but Dominique never seemed to get well, although the ex-policemen were soon doing favours for Alain all over Bangkok.

The flat was already crowded when Alain invited another acquaintance to join them: Ajay Chowdury, an Indian from New Delhi whose father imported foreign cars. Chowdury's various business ventures had failed, but he proved an ideal accomplice for Alain, smooth, well spoken, smartly dressed – and willing to kill on demand.

THE BIKINI KILLING

Born in southern California in 1955, Teresa Knowlton was a child of her times. Her parents split up while she was still in her teens, and Teresa moved in with her grandparents; she soon began to experiment with drugs, sex and esoteric belief systems, and was eventually thrown out of the house. Her downward spiral appeared to stop when she began living in an informal Seattle foster home with other drop-outs, and at eighteen she started to go out with Christopher Ghant, a boyfriend who dabbled in yoga and white magic.

They travelled together through Europe, following the overland route that was already becoming *de rigueur* among their peers, working in Greece for a while to earn enough to continue east. While in Goa Christopher heard about the Kopan monastery in Kathmandu, a Buddhist retreat that would test his mettle as a practitioner of the middle way; Teresa reluctantly agreed to accompany him. In the event it was she who took to the monastery life, perhaps not having had such a fixed idea of what to expect as Christopher. The ascetic pursuits brought her a peace she hadn't known before, and she felt that this was what she'd been seeking through her teen experimentation.

But her world collapsed when Christopher broke off their affair. Back in Seattle she tried to throw herself into work, going to college to study biology and holistic medicine with a view to caring for the elderly. But when she saw Christopher with his new girlfriend Francine, she finally realised that the relationship really was over and fled the city to a meditation retreat in southern California. There she decided to return to Kopan to become a Buddhist nun.

She arranged her flights – Seattle to Hong Kong and Bangkok to Kathmandu – and set off. On the day before she was due to fly to Kathmandu to surrender all her earthly desires, she met Charles and Ajay. Was she tempted to have one last fling? To enjoy being the life and soul of the party as she had throughout her teens? We will never know; but she arrived at the Kanit House flat on 15 October 1975 and was an instant hit with the other guests, dancing and enjoying everyone's attention. Not one to be upstaged, Charles demonstrated his karate skills, asking to be punched in the stomach by each of the guests.

Charles and Ajay took Teresa to Patpong, Bangkok's notorious sex district, where they were seen in a strip club. It is not known whether they drugged her or whether she went willingly. In the morning she was found dead, half-naked and face down in the water on Pattaya beach.

The local police didn't want to involve the bureaucracy of Bangkok, preferring to deal with inconvenient events such as tourist deaths themselves. They made a cursory check of the major Pattaya hotels to see if any Western guests were missing, then, unable to identify the corpse, hurriedly proclaimed 'death by accidental drowning' and sealed the remains in a plastic bag before burying them in a paupers' cemetery. Later, when the investigation into the 'bikini killings', as they came to be known, was under way, the body was exhumed for an autopsy; but nobody could be quite sure exactly where it was, and several groups of remains were removed before the corpse of Teresa Knowlton was found.

Alain and Monique were just the kind of couple Roger and Giselle Klebar enjoyed meeting. The Canadian dentist and his teacher wife were seasoned travellers, and happy to tell

Monique all the news from her home country, well aware of how homesick long stays away from home had made them in the past. The couples met in Pattaya and went out for a meal together, after which they went dancing.

Later that night both Roger and Giselle fell ill. Alain and Monique offered to let them stay at their Bangkok flat while they recovered, and even gave them medicine, Monique insisting that she'd worked as a nurse in Canada (in fact she'd been a medical secretary). The couple slept for hours, and agreed when Alain suggested that he take their passports and traveller's cheques for safekeeping.

The success of Sobhraj's ploys can seem difficult to believe, especially in today's climate of crime-conscious tourism. In the 1970s cities like Bangkok or Kathmandu would have seemed far more alien and threatening to a Westerner than they do now: the level of tourism – and attendant Westernisation – was far smaller. Most tourists, bewildered by their strange and alienating surroundings, would be grateful for any help they received. Charles's gem expertise is important too in this respect, as though the degree of authenticity of the tourists' gems he inspected conferred a sense of authenticity, or trustworthiness, on him. Most tourists are prepared to be ripped off; few expect to be drugged and robbed with a smile.

Roger soon realised that he always felt worse after taking Monique's medicine, and decided to stop. But he wouldn't tell her, as she always seemed so insistent if he questioned her medical skill; he didn't suspect that anything was amiss, beyond the fact that she was probably giving them the wrong kind of medicine unwittingly. He told his wife to stop too, and soon both were strong enough to leave. But when they asked Monique for the return of their passports and traveller's cheques, she told them to wait for Alain, who hardly ever seemed to be there. And the flat was filling up with guests again.

THE BANGKOK RUN

Vitali Hakim was born into a Sephardic Jewish family in Istanbul. His parents' hard work ethic rubbed off on their first son Israel, but Vitali had his own ideas about how to live life, and at twelve decided to leave school and work for his brother; three years later he travelled to Israel alone. Unwilling to tie himself to the mundane world of career and family, he left Istanbul for good at seventeen, travelling to Paris, London and New York, and working as a cabaret performer, magician, poet and tour guide. Twelve years after leaving Turkey he was arrested for possession of cocaine in Spain.

Stephanie Parry had been invited to Ibiza in the early 1970s by a distant cousin, Zazi, about whom dark rumours of narcotics and loose living had spread through the extended family. To Stephanie she may have represented an exotic opportunity for adventure, and a rebellion against her bourgeois upbringing; but by 1975 it was apparent that the dressmaking business Stephanie had tried to set up had failed, and she told her cousin that she was broke and ready to return to Paris. Zazi introduced her to Vitali.

Stephanie had never met anyone like the Turk before. He was larger than life, a joyfully intense bear of a man; she was smitten, and soon moved in with him. Her love life and her business were both looking up, until her work materials were stolen. Vitali told her not to worry; he proposed that they move to Bangkok and get married. He would fly out now, and she could follow shortly afterwards. He had a business deal lined up there, so they'd have money. All she would have to do was take some gems back to Europe from Thailand for him.

Stephanie wasn't so naive as not to realise that she would be smuggling, and initially refused, but Vitali's persistent good humour won her over in the end. What she didn't realise was that she wouldn't be smuggling gems at all. Vitali's plan – the seed money for which had been put up by Zazi – was to use Stephanie as a drug mule, carrying the morphine he was to buy from a Burmese connection in Bangkok to Europe.

When Hakim arrived in Bangkok in November 1975 he found that the contact address he'd been given by Zazi didn't exist. At a loss for what to do, he was delighted to meet Alain and

Ajay in the lobby of his hotel; they told him they could provide him with cut-price jewels direct from the Chantaburi mines, which would ensure that his trip had not been in vain. He could also stay with them, and he left a note at the hotel telling Stephanie where he would be.

With the arrival of the Turk the flat was too busy. Both he and the Canadian couple made demands of Alain: Hakim wanted to make a major gem purchase while the Canadians wanted their passports back before they visited Chiang Mai. When the Turk fell ill his demands for a quick buy vanished; all he wanted to do now was rest.

Alain offered to drive the Canadians to Chiang Mai, and gave them some medicine for the trip. A few hours into the trip he seemed annoyed that the Canadians were still awake – they'd thrown the medicine away, while telling him that they'd taken it – and drove back to Bangkok at 3 a.m., irritably telling them that he'd taken a wrong turning. Their persistence in staying awake probably saved their lives.

The next day Alain and Ajay drove to Chantaburi with Hakim. They left after 10 p.m. and returned before dawn. When they came back Hakim was not with them. Roger knew that Chantaburi was a six-hour trip each way; they couldn't have made it that far. He asked after the Turk and was told that he'd met friends in Pattaya and decided to stay with them. Roger thought it strange, then, that he'd left his luggage in the flat, but Alain and Ajay looked tired, dishevelled and irritable, in no mood for further questions.

This time when the couple pressed Alain for the return of their documents Monique joined in, and their passports and traveller's cheques were finally given back to them. Pages had been torn out of their passports, and others inserted, and about half of their traveller's cheques were gone, but they were happy just to get away. Something was very wrong in Kanit House.

On 29 November 1975 labourers a few miles from Pattaya found Vitali Hakim's body, although the correct identity would not be established for many months. He had been clubbed about the head, doused with gasoline and set alight while still alive. The pathologist who conducted the autopsy commented that at least two people had been involved in the killing.

BURNED ALIVE

Life in Bangkok was beginning to feel a little too frantic even for Charles. While he and May were no longer lovers but still met for business reasons, Charles had met a twenty-year-old Thai girl, Suzy, who was said to closely resemble his mother. He appeared besotted with his new love, showering her with gifts and proposing to her. Marie-Andrée was furious – how could he treat her this way after all they'd been through?

Charles was also having money trouble. He had made several contacts with whom he planned to start a legitimate jewellery business, but was having problems raising the $25,000 he needed as a start-up fund: the proceeds from his various scams were high, but so were his running costs. He decided to go to the Macao casino, where he had done well before, to improve his finances, and flew alone to Hong Kong. On arrival at the casino he ran into an old acquaintance, who warned him that the security had tightened up and that they would be on the look-out for undesirables such as Sobhraj, who had passed bad cheques there before.

His stalwart earner seemed less of a gamble, and he met a Dutch couple, 29-year-old Henricus 'Henk' Bintanja and 25-year-old Cornelia 'Cocky' Hemker, in the lobby of the Holiday Inn. He had previously warned his brother not to bother dealing with the Dutch – they were suspicious and parsimonious – but other opportunities were thin on the ground.

Bintanja had recently finished an MsC in chemistry but was struggling to find work commensurate with his abilities, so he and his girlfriend, a nurse, had decided to see some of the world before settling down. Alain Gauthier must have seemed the embodiment of the exotic potential of travel to them, and they were soon hooked by his charm and helpfulness. Cornelia wanted to buy a sapphire ring but was disappointed by the high prices in Hong Kong; after leading her around some local jewellers Charles sold her a ring from his own collection for $1,600. She was delighted by the bargain, and they eagerly accepted his invitation to stay with him in Bangkok.

When Stephanie Parry arrived in Thailand she found Hakim's note telling her that he was staying at Kanit House. She visited the address and was told that her friend was travelling and would be back in a few days; she waited, along with the Dutch couple, who seemed to be very ill. Nadine had seen the Dutch couple too, during a visit one day when Alain, Monique and their young French charges were out; it had scared her, to see the two of them sitting in the darkness. They looked close to death.

Stephanie didn't stay at Kanit House long. Her body was found on the morning of 15 December on a beach near Pattaya, naked and with her neck snapped. She had been strangled, but at the time the murder was assumed to be just another unidentified tourist drowning, and after the cursory check of local hotels the body was buried; it would not be exhumed and identified until much later.

The next day the Dutch couple also left the flat. Charles and Ajay dragged them down the stairs and bundled them into a car, driving away after midnight. Charles and Ajay returned just before dawn, their trousers muddy and stinking of petrol.

The *Bangkok Post* ran a feature when the bodies were discovered, 60 kilometres south of Bangkok. Both had been strangled, and the woman had been hit on the skull with a heavy object. They had then been doused in petrol and set alight, but were still alive when they began to burn. The bodies had only been partially charred, however; some of their clothes remained unharmed, and the fact that one garment had been made in Australia led the authorities to assert that the victims were Australian.

Remy and Nadine went on a short holiday and returned on 22 December. When they dropped in on Alain and Monique they found that the couple were in Kathmandu, but Yannick, Jacques and Dominique were still there. They looked very worried and didn't need much prompting to tell Nadine why: they thought Alain was a thief and a murderer. It was the only way to make sense of the facts.

They showed Remy and Nadine the passports in the safe – many belonging to people they had all seen staying at the flat, as well as their own. Pages had been torn out of almost all of them, and some carried visa stamps for countries they'd never visited. They then told the Gires about the abrupt departure of the Dutch couple and the recent discovery of the charred corpses. They were adamant that Monique knew exactly what was going on.

Nadine wanted to go to the police. Remy was less keen; he'd heard stories about what happened to foreign nationals who created problems a long way from home, and didn't want to get involved in any legal hassle. They decided to give the Frenchmen money to get home, and arranged for them to contact the police there: Yannick and Jacques were ex-policemen, after all, and had contacts at Interpol. But Remy and Nadine heard nothing further from them after their holiday, and began to worry about how to explain their absence to Alain and Monique.

Meanwhile, Charles and Marie-Andrée had checked into the Hotel Soaltee-Oberoi, Kathmandu's most luxurious hotel, as Henricus Bintanja and Cornelia Hemker on 18 December: it was typical of their travels that they used the passports of their most recent victims. Charles lost heavily at the hotel casino and failed to make a connection with any of the other guests, so turned his attention again to smaller fry: the backpacking denizens of the notorious hippy mecca Freak Street.

DEAD MAN ON THE RUN

Like Teresa Knowlton, Connie Jo Bronzich was from California, although she came from a substantially richer background. Born in 1946, she was a bright only child, whose formative early travelling experience involved being sent to

Italy to see her maternal grandfather when she was ten; although he died while she was there she loved Europe, and never felt at home in the US again. After leaving high school she spent two years working around Europe and the Middle East, and on her return met and married an old schoolfriend, John.

The marriage soon turned sour – John drank heavily and used hard drugs, and was reputedly jealous of Connie's relationship with a major Santa Cruz drug dealer. She moved out of their house, and a few days after an argument with John, in which he begged her to come back to him, he overdosed on heroin and died.

Connie became severely depressed, blaming herself for the death. Therapy didn't help, and she finally decided to go abroad. She'd revisit Europe, revitalising herself so she had the energy to start all over again; and she'd work in a hospital in India, penance through selflessness.

But nothing ever stays the same. Europe seemed different this time, harsher and colder, and she rushed through the Continent on her way to Bombay, keen to start working. However, the state of the first Indian hospital she visited convinced her that this was no place to seek solace. She met another American in Delhi who seduced her then vanished; he'd given her a false name and lied about where he was staying. This was not what she'd come out for.

She decided to head back to the US, but wanted to buy some gems and stop off in Kathmandu first. On the bus from Delhi she met a 23-year-old Canadian, Laurent Carrière, who was obsessed with Everest. His youthful enthusiasm boosted Connie's flagging self-confidence and they decided to stick together for a while; some accounts state that they were both now heroin addicts, which may have provided an added incentive to team up.

Carrière was no stranger to adventure, coming from a family of seven children descended from French-Canadian pioneers and growing up on a 200-acre farm accessible only by dirt road. A foreign exchange programme during high school had sent him to France and he'd been bitten by the travel bug; so much so that he hadn't yet completed college.

He'd promised his parents he would, but wanted to go on one last tour of the world before settling down to work; he earned the money for his trip during three gruelling months on a fishing boat in the Arctic. His brother accompanied him when he set off for Europe, but they separated in the Middle East, vowing to meet in Bangkok or New Zealand in 1976. But Carrière's journey ended when he met Charles Sobhraj.

Laurent and Connie spent ten days together in Kathmandu, growing ever closer as the days passed. The Canadian was disappointed to have missed an organised trip to Everest base camp, which meant that he'd have to wait two weeks for the next one; going alone seemed unwise as the decapitated body of a young American had been found in fields near Kathmandu a few weeks before.

The couple met Charles and Ajay on 19 December and were treated to what was now for Sobhraj a standard preamble to robbery. They were taken out for luxury meals and the gems they'd bought were inspected, Charles telling them that they'd been ripped off and that he'd help them get a refund in Delhi later.

On 22 December the burning body of a Western man was found in a terraced field a few miles from Kathmandu; his throat had been cut so deeply that he had almost been decapitated. Another corpse was found a few days later; this was of a Western woman who had been stabbed four times below her left breast then drenched in petrol and set on fire.

The Kathmandu police worked harder than their counterparts in Thailand; they soon found that Carrière and Bronzich were missing from their hotel room, and arranged for a group of Australian tourists who'd met the couple to identify the bodies. Connie Jo Bronzich was easily identified from a ring and the remains of her clothing, but they couldn't be sure the man's body belonged to Carrière.

The police assumed that it was probably his until they found a Nepalese exit card apparently filled in by Carrière on 23 December, the day Bronzich's body had been found, stating that he was heading for Bangkok. Interpol were notified: Carrière was suspected of the murder of his girlfriend and an unidentified Western man. When the Canadian's parents made enquiries, worried by their son's continued silence, they were shocked to hear that he was wanted for double murder.

'EVERY EXIT IS AN ENTRANCE'

Sobhraj, after fleeing Nepal on Carrière's passport, only spent one night in Bangkok before returning to Kathmandu as Bintanja; police later theorised that he left to throw suspicion on Carrière and to sell the couple's jewels, then returned to Kathmandu promptly to throw anyone who might suspect the truth off his scent. He had also left Marie-Andrée waiting for him in Kathmandu. When he went to Kanit House, however, he was horrified to find that his entourage had vanished. He visited Nadine's flat, distraught, and she told him they'd returned to France. His reply is revealing: 'But they needed me! They loved me! They were my family!'

Back in Kathmandu, the car seen at a number of the dump sites (where victims' bodies had been found) was traced to Henricus Bintanja at the Oberoi Hotel. Police questioned Sobhraj, who posed as a professor of social sciences under the Dutchman's name. When Marie-Andrée was taken into another room to be questioned separately he protested that they were Christians – could they not celebrate Christmas in peace? The police relented but kept the couple under surveillance, noting that despite his protests Sobhraj spent Christmas Day gambling in the hotel casino.

One detective, Preman Bizra, was particularly puzzled by items found in the boot of the car, which included a pair of jeans suitable for a tall man, six foot or more; 'Bintanja' was short. Sobhraj was called in again and was, as before, full of blustery annoyance – he'd never seen the trousers before – while Marie-Andrée was let off questioning for 'feminine problems'. Bizra was convinced that something was wrong – Sobhraj was too glib, not nervous enough – and checked on him again the next day.

But the couple had fled during the night, leaving their hotel bills unpaid. The airports and Kathmandu road exits were alerted but Charles, Marie-Andrée and Ajay were already well on their way to the border in a taxi, and were soon in Calcutta, having travelled non-stop by car, horse, ferry and aeroplane.

In early January 1976 Sobhraj met an Israeli student, Avoni Jacob, who was researching comparative religion. When he discovered that Jacob was travelling to Varanasi 'Alain Ponant', as Sobhraj styled himself for this encounter, decided to accompany him. The setting was appropriate: Varanasi's principal industry is death, and Sobhraj and the student cruised down the Ganges to look at bodies burning on the ghats.

On 6 January a cleaning woman found Jacob's naked body in his hotel room; he had been drugged and strangled, his belongings stolen. They didn't amount to much, only a few hundred dollars, and the killer had used Jacob's passport to cash some of the student's traveller's cheques at a nearby hotel. Most of the pages in his diary had gone too, but the final entry remained: 'I would like to stay in Varanasi until I understand more. Every exit is an entrance. If one believes strongly enough, life can be lived without fear of death.'

THE ACTION COMMITTEE

When Nadine heard nothing from the Frenchmen who'd left Kanit House she decided to do some snooping of her own. She persuaded the housekeeper to lend her the key to Alain's flat, and found what she was sure were possessions belonging to the recent murder victims inside. Now convinced of Alain Gauthier's guilt, she contacted a British diplomat who, though sceptical, sent a report to the Thai police. When Nadine still heard nothing she contacted the French Embassy, where she was told not to get involved.

Charles, Ajay and Marie-Andrée were still in India, and arrived in Panaji, Goa, on 7 January 1976. That evening they met three Frenchmen, who narrowly escaped with their lives after having been given whisky laced with valium then injected with a tranquilliser and robbed. Their unconscious bodies were put in their van which was started, a rock placed on the accelerator, and steered towards a cliff; fortunately the van hit a tree instead, and the three woke later in an Indian hospital.

The Dutch Embassy in Thailand had been contacted by the parents of Henricus Bintanja and Cornelia Hemker, and Herman Knippenberg, the embassy's second secretary, was put on the case. Abrasive and doggedly undiplomatic, Knippenberg was destined not to go far in the service, but those same qualities stood him in good stead in attempting to unravel the mystery of the Dutch couple's murders.

He investigated the case of the 'Australian' corpses found near Bangkok and soon found that this presumption of nationality was solely due to the presence of an item of clothing made in Australia; correct identification followed receipt of the couple's dental records from Holland. This was the extent of Knippenberg's diplomatic duties, but he didn't trust the Thai police to solve this double murder without international pressure. He began to do some detective work himself, hoping to prepare a dossier that would convince the Thai authorities to take the crimes seriously.

Knippenberg was given a letter from Hemker describing a French gem dealer, 'Alain Dupuis', but was unable to track down anyone of that name in hotel registers. In the course of his investigation into another French gem dealer, Artur Gabreaux, he heard stories about 'Alain Gauthier', who was darkly rumoured to kill tourists. He also heard a story from the Australian Embassy of a tourist couple who'd survived a drug and rob attack – Vera and Russell Lapthorne, whose description of Jean and Monique Belmont closely matched the information Knippenberg had unearthed on Alain Gauthier.

News spread quickly in diplomatic circles of Knippenberg's investigation – indeed it embarrassed the Dutch Embassy so much that he was later forced to take a brief leave of absence – and he discovered that the British Embassy had Bintanja's diary. They wouldn't initially admit to its possession, but Knippenberg persisted; when they gave it to him, they also showed him a report they'd made, an *Aide Memoire* compiled from information given by the French policeman, Yannick, and the Gires. Knippenberg was incensed that the document had not been shared with the Dutch Embassy. Not only did it name Gauthier and give his address, but it also explicitly mentioned evidence crucial to the case of the murdered Dutch couple, as well as others:

> YANNICK, after . . . relating his suspicions that GAUTHIER had been responsible for not only these murders [of the Dutch couple] but for others including the two European girls found in Pattaya recently, a Turkish murder and possibly the two murders of young Europeans in Nepal, left with his girlfriend suddenly for Europe. Since then the GIRES claim to have sighted in the GAUTHIER flat clothes belonging to the Dutch couple, their diary in Dutch . . . their tape recorder and their passports together with clothes and passports belonging to others, up to 10 in number, kept in GAUTHIER's safe.

Knippenberg and a number of other young diplomats formed an 'Action Committee' determined to have Gauthier arrested. He visited Nadine and Remy and debriefed them over the course of a few days; Nadine agreed to spy for them, keeping a record of who came and went, drawing a plan of the apartment and taking photographs. Gauthier always eluded the lens, however – strange in a man so self-obsessed if not uncommon in career criminals; she could only ever get blurry images of him.

Sobhraj had a new business partner, Jean Dhuisme, a Frenchman evidently lured by Charles's promise of a fast buck. Nadine overheard them discussing leaving Bangkok, and told Knippenberg. The diplomat took all the evidence amassed so far to the Thai police and suggested a raid.

THE EVIDENCE MOUNTS

At 4 p.m. on 11 March Thai police raided 504 Kanit House. They had promised to call Knippenberg just before the raid began, so that he could be on hand to view the evidence; in the event he wasn't called until 10 that evening, when the suspects and the safe were at police headquarters. The Thai police told the diplomat there'd been a mix-up: there was no Alain Gauthier at that address, only an angry American citizen, Robert Grainer, whose passport showed that he'd been in Sri Lanka at the time of the Dutch murders. Knippenberg was unable to convince the police to keep 'Grainer' and his wife in custody overnight, but their passports were confiscated for scrutiny by a US Embassy official in the morning.

When Charles and Marie-Andrée returned in the morning, the safe was opened – it was empty. A US DEA agent, Sam Anson, grilled Charles over the contents of Grainer's passport, and all his answers except one were word perfect; but to Anson this mistake was highly suspect, and he told the Thai police to keep the couple in custody until the passport had been checked out. Charles and Marie-Andrée were told to wait on a bench in a corridor; by the time Anson returned they were nowhere to be seen.

Nadine, who had been suffering from sleepless nights ever since Knippenberg's investigation got under way, received a call from Charles in Malaysia. He claimed to have bribed a police official with around $15,000 to turn a blind eye to his departure, although Bangkok police later denounced the suggestion.

Knippenberg persuaded the Thai police to let him study Gauthier's apartment. The police had missed plenty of evidence in their initial raid, including:

- Fifteen kilos of pills and medicine, mostly sedatives and including a botttle marked 'Kaopectate', which is a medicine to aid recovery from diaorrhea, but actually containing a drug designed to increase its severity.
- A well-used pair of handcuffs.
- A handkerchief smelling of petrol.
- Letters apparently written by Hemker, along with her leather shoulder bag.
- A plastic make-up bag given to Teresa Knowlton by her friends as a leaving present, and a book marked on the flyleaf with her name.

- Used hypodermic needles, with a document featuring instructions as to their use, believed to have been written by Marie-Andrée.
- Records of gem sales, hotel bills, drivers' licences, etc. many from different people – these included car insurance papers and bank statements belonging to Vitali Hakim.

Police would later wonder why, if Sobhraj was guilty, he had kept so much incriminating evidence. The question also applies to another serial killer who preyed on tourists – Australian Ivan Milat, who kept camping equipment and other objects easily identifiable as belonging to his victims. The answer is the same: an arrogant belief that they would never get caught, as well as the urge to keep souvenirs, trophies of their skill and power.

Nadine received a postcard from Charles in Switzerland and told Knippenberg, who was convinced that they were heading for France, where both Sobhraj and Dhuisme had connections. They made a report to the French authorities, who were unperturbed by news of such distant crimes.

Knippenberg's hunch was right: Sobhraj, Leclerc and Dhuisme had left Thailand in a rental car, walked across the border to Malaysia and holed up in a cheap hotel in Pinang, where Ajay had met them with a batch of gems which Charles planned to sell in Europe. But Ajay didn't join them on the flight to Switzerland, and was never seen again. Charles and he had argued over money and gems, and Marie-Andrée would later assert that Charles had killed him.

In Paris Charles tracked down Félix, Hélène and Song in turn, and he and his entourage stayed with Song in Marseilles for three days before overstaying their welcome and being thrown out. Neither Charles's former guardian, his former wife nor his mother seemed pleased to see him. When Song later received a letter from a Marseilles lawyer stating that a Charles Sobhraj had swindled a woman in a jewellery deal, and that if he did not present himself grand theft charges would be filed, she wrote back saying that 'the name Charles Sobhraj is not known to me. He is not a member of my family.'

The trip to Europe had not been a success, and the trio left for the East again in Dhuisme's silver Citroën. In Karachi they picked up Mary Ellen Eather, a blonde Australian nurse Charles had befriended and promised work to on a previous visit. Marie-Andrée found an article about 'Alain Gauthier' in *Asia Week* and showed it to Charles; they were wanted by the Thai police on suspicion of murder. Charles was unperturbed, and decided that they should travel to India instead of back to Thailand.

This article, and a few in the *Bangkok Post*, finally spurred on a serious Thai investigation into the murders, which were being widely referred to in the press as the 'bikini murders' due to the fact that Teresa Knowlton's corpse had been found in a bikini. The tourist trade was threatened by such grisly details, and so the Thai police's 'immediate investigation' was at last under way.

Police Chief Lieutenant General Montchai announced that the case was 'the most shocking that has ever occurred in Thailand', and appointed Colonel Sompol Suthimai to lead the investigation. Suthimai was well known as an honest policeman in an endemically corrupt force, and was given an eight-man task force to help him solve the crimes, and an extensive debriefing from Knippenberg.

THE MAN WHOSE TEETH WERE MADE OF WOOD

In Delhi in mid-June, Mary Ellen was put to work, picking up three French tourists in the YMCA who were then drugged and robbed. As a contrast to Mary Ellen, Charles also recruited Barbara Smith, a dark-haired English girl, in Bombay; he met her through a Belgian acquaintance, Jean Huygens, for whom Charles also had plans. Smith had come from a broken home, and had been put into care when her father remarried, then ferried from one institution to the next until she saved enough money through part-time work to leave Europe. She had just been robbed of all her belongings in India when she met Huygens.

Huygens had worked in Brussels until the end of the 1960s as the foreman of a construction company. His stolid world crumbled with the divorce of his wife in 1967 and the death of his son a year later, and he fled Europe, drifting to India. He had married an Indian woman and now lived in a beach hut in Goa with his wife, two children and a crippling opium habit.

Sobhraj planned to make Huygens look like a diplomat in order to carry out a jewel scam. He invested heavily in the Belgian, buying him suits and a set of wooden dentures to cover his opium-ravaged teeth, and teaching him how to speak well. The girls were sent ahead to Delhi to scout out hotels and tourists ripe for Sobhraj's artistry, and reported back that the Imperial Hotel seemed ideal. The others joined them.

Huygens was nervous about his part in Sobhraj's plan – he felt sure nobody could mistake him for a diplomat – and his wife had threatened to leave him if he didn't return home soon. Instructed by Sobhraj to keep an eye on Marie-Andrée as she called her parents, Huygens stole her wallet and then took everything from the criminals' shared hotel room and returned to his wife.

Sobhraj was furious and travelled to Goa to look for him. Huygens and his wife had moved and were laying low, but the Belgian was worried that Sobhraj would eventually track him down and wrote to the Canadian Embassy – a curious choice, given the circumstances – about the proposed jewellery heist. The letter, a garbled mess of wheedling and imprecations, was duly forwarded to the Indian police.

The letter finally made its way to N. Tuli, the formidable head of the elite branch of Delhi's Crime Branch. Tuli was more successful than Sobhraj in tracking Huygens down, although the Belgian was at first reluctant to reveal his identity; eventually Huygens was persuaded to tell Tuli all he knew of Sobhraj, and he gave the policeman photos of Charles and Marie-Andrée, which were enlarged and sent to the major Delhi hotels.

Meanwhile the Thai investigation had resulted in arrest warrants for Alain and Monique Gauthier and Ajay Chowdury for conspiring to murder other persons by premeditation, forging and using forged documents, and receiving stolen goods. The non-renewable warrants were valid for twenty years and were issued at the end of May 1976, a fact that would not pass Sobhraj's attention. A report was also sent to Interpol, which scoured its files for an MO fitting what was known of Gauthier. In July 1976 Inspector Paul Delsart had a hunch that Gauthier was Charles Sobhraj.

BREAKING THE RING

Charles found out that a large French tour group was scheduled to arrive in Delhi soon; this was just the kind of opportunity he needed after the Huygens fiasco, but first he needed something smaller to pay for the preparations for a job of that size. The girls picked up a thin, bearded Frenchman in his mid-twenties, Jean-Luc Solomon, in the lobby of the Ranjit Hotel, and took him out for dinner with Charles. His food was drugged, and he was found two days later in his hotel room, barely alive. He died later that day in hospital.

Our account opened with the story of what happened to 'Daniel Chaumet' and the French tour group. Tuli was informed and he interrogated Chaumet, who was furious and extremely obstructive, insisting that he was an important businessman, and that unless he was released immediately he would sue. He claimed not to speak English, and to need an interpreter, but Tuli eventually persuaded him that this was unnecessary. The policeman sometimes feared the diplomatic nightmare that would ensue if he had the wrong man. Huygens's photo, as with almost all other photos of Sobhraj, was not quite clear enough for Tuli to be sure he had his man.

When Dhuisme, who had seen Charles being arrested at the hotel, returned to the girls and told them the story of the slapstick poisoning disaster they initially found it funny, but it wasn't long before it dawned on them that Charles might not get out of this one. They were penniless and began to panic, selling whatever they could and splitting up. The police caught up with them and arrested each in turn, interrogating them intensively in an attempt to find the weakest link.

Mary Ellen broke first, confessing to the Delhi YMCA robbery and the drugging of Solomon; she was being questioned with Barbara, who admitted her part in the crimes. Then Marie-Andrée confessed, signing a 32-page statement telling of her relationship with Sobhraj but not admitting to any complicity, insisting instead that she had been a prisoner all along. But Charles would still not confess, despite having Mary Ellen and Barbara paraded in front of him while their statements were read out.

Tuli remembered the notorious jewel heist, the Passionata case and the appendectomy Sobhraj had endured in his escape attempt. He called the doctor who'd performed the operation to inspect Sobhraj's appendectomy scar, but the doctor could not identify it conclusively as his work. Sobhraj's composure broke only after Tuli changed his tone; he began to compliment his prisoner, flattering him and his daughter and showing him photos of his own children. Sobhraj complimented Tuli in turn, telling him that he never thought he'd be caught in India. He confessed to drugging several victims, but claimed that if any had died it was at the hands of Ajay Chowdury.

India was at the time under the rule of Indira Gandhi, a rule which had led to considerable political unrest. She had recently invoked emergency rule, placing all prisoners – even non-political ones – under MISA (Maintenance of Internal Security Act), which meant that they could be held for up to two years without bail or a trial.

The five suspects were sent to the notorious Tihar prison in Delhi. Sobhraj's institution experience helped him quickly to secure a position of authority, running a network bringing in food and cigarettes and flouting prison rules by owning a small library of books, a radio and, later on, a television. He paid for his relative luxury with jewels he'd secreted in his mouth before being arrested, which he'd pass to visitors recruited to work for him on the outside.

The other prisoners were less fortunate. Barbara and Mary Ellen had turned state 'approvers', willing to testify against Charles and Marie-Andrée, so were Category B prisoners, with better conditions than Marie-Andrée, a Category C prisoner. The three soon fell out – unsurprisingly, considering the girls' readiness to testify against Marie-Andrée – and Marie-Andrée accused Mary Ellen of attacking her.

If the girls didn't believe in Marie-Andrée's innocence, the Canadian press did, with hand-wringing editorials in Quebec papers about this innocent lured to a terrible fate by a ruthless Oriental. Marie-Andrée later discovered that letters of support were being withheld from her, and went on a hunger strike both to improve her conditions and to receive her mail. Charles also maintained at first that she was innocent, telling the judge at an early court hearing that 'She is a victim of love ... she should not be accused of anything else'. However, when he later discovered her readiness to testify against him he claimed that she had been aware of his criminal activities and had been free to leave him at any time.

Marie-Andrée played her part with a mixture of shock and naivety, stating at a court hearing that she never wanted to speak to Charles again. But she was still in thrall to him, and continued to write letters, either accusatory or supplicating in tone.

One of Marie-Andrée's cellmates, an American woman known as 'Checkers', on her release discussed Sobhraj's 'family' with an American man who'd been a cellmate of Charles:

> They're all sick ... They've all got holes in their lives,
> unfulfilled aspirations, gaps, missing pieces of the puzzle, and
> Charles is smart enough to spot those weaknesses and use
> them. Any form of madness generates a higher energy level
> ... Charles makes the others feel that by clinging to him they
> can realize their fantasies. He is carrying the dream. He says
> that there is a pot of gold at the end of the rainbow, but he is
> the only one with a map.

A year passed before the trial, the heat of the Indian summer making the wait interminable. Tuli heard that Sobhraj had been putting pressure on the girls not to testify, threatening their lives; when he questioned them they denied it, although he was convinced it was true. They nearly saved Sobhraj the trouble, both attempting suicide by overdosing on barbiturates, but they were found in time and their stomachs were pumped. Sobhraj attempted to escape, but his plan, which involved a costume resembling an army uniform and an 8,000-rupee pay-off, was foiled after a tip-off.

IN THE DOCK

The trial finally began on 4 July 1977: Charles, Marie-Andrée and Dhuisme were to be tried for the murder of Jean-Luc Solomon. When India won independence, it abolished the jury trial due to its apparent potential for corruption, replacing it with a system whereby one evidently incorruptible judge decided the outcome. Indian justice also differs from Western systems in that all prosecution evidence is presented before the trial in the First Information Report (FIR); the job of the defence is to destroy the case as presented in the FIR.

The trial took place at the Tis Hazari Courts in Old Delhi, and was from the outset a ramshackle affair. The stenographer, instead of taking down what was said in court, took down what the judge instructed her to, an interpretation often some way from the actual substance. Judges were paid very little, even by Indian legal standards, and the trial judge here, Joginder Nath, was no legal genius. The showmanship was left to the lawyers.

Marie-Andrée was represented by S.N. Chowdhury and Frank Anthony, while Sobhraj employed Rupinder Singh, who was regularly fired and hired again when the killer tired of different attorneys; Singh was reluctant to leave for good because of the massive publicity given to the case. The Sobhraj story had glamour – a jet-setting playboy suspected of involvement in the deaths of bikini-clad beauties – and, crucially, was apolitical; the papers, banned from running any story on politics, had a field day with the case, and it was not only the Indian news media that were interested. Before the start of the trial Sobhraj had signed a contract with a Bangkok company to merchandise his life story in a book or film, and was being interviewed by British journalists Richard Neville and Julie Clarke, interviews which formed the basis for the book *Shadow of the Cobra*.

Public Prosecutor Daljit Singh started proceedings by questioning Barbara. Mary Ellen's resolve had already begun to weaken in custody, and she now maintained that her statement had been made under coercion. Barbara, by contrast, stuck to her story that Solomon had been poisoned, in the face of ridicule from Anthony: surely it was impossible to have spiked the Frenchman's food without him noticing? Anthony asked Smith questions which appeared arbitrary, such as the name of the examiner who had signed her O-level exam certificate; when she was unable to answer, Anthony triumphantly accused her of having an unreliable memory. He also asserted that she was a prostitute – 'I put it to you that you are a hot and sexy girl' – and as such inherently untrustworthy.

The defence maintained that Solomon was a drug addict, as track marks had been found on his arms. Another defence lawyer tried to make Smith admit that she'd attempted suicide because her conscience was troubling her over Solomon's murder – that she and Mary Ellen were prostitutes and drug addicts who were themselves responsible for Solomon's death, rather than the three defendants.

Mary Ellen was called and retracted her story on the stand, telling the court that 'nothing I know of' happened during the dinner; as far as she knew, Solomon was never given any drugs. Anthony read out her new statement that the police had fabricated her original statement, and that she had been coerced into signing the latter under the threat of being held in prison indefinitely without any legal recourse under MISA. Sobhraj later tried to have admitted at the trial a similar statement allegedly written by Barbara, recanting her confession and stating that it had been given under duress, but it was not witnessed or signed, and was refused.

Next called was K.S. Chaddha, a Sikh doctor who had viewed Solomon's body. It was he who had revealed that Solomon had fresh needle marks on his arms – possibly from a sedative injection administered by Sobhraj or Marie-Andrée – and he had been unable to ascertain the exact cause of death, which he had ascribed to 'unknown poisoning'. The defence suggested that Solomon was a drug addict who had died of an overdose, an allegation that Chaddha was unable to confirm or deny.

The trial dragged on for a year before the judge retired for his verdict. Sobhraj was found guilty, although not of murder; for the lesser crimes of culpable homicide, drugging for the purpose of robbery and voluntarily causing hurt to commit robbery he was sentenced to just seven years in jail. Marie-Andrée was found not guilty, but returned to Tihar to await trial on other crimes, including the YMCA case. Dhuisme was acquitted for Solomon's death but pleaded guilty in the YMCA case and was given three more months in Tihar. Barbara was pardoned and released, while Mary Ellen faced charges on the YMCA case and possible perjury.

TIHAR

Sobhraj paid a heavier penalty in a later trial for the murder of Avoni Jacob, being sentenced to life imprisonment. But the High Court overturned this conviction in 1983; even his conviction for the Solomon homicide was overturned in time, while he continued to plead guilty to various lesser crimes, clearly keen to minimise his time in Indian jails while avoiding extradition to Thailand, where the penalty for murder was death. There he faced charges relating to the poisoning of Russell and Vera Lapthorne, who had agreed to travel to Bangkok and testify in the event of a trial, and the murders of the Dutch couple, about which Knippenberg could supply a mountain of evidence.

Marie-Andrée Leclerc was diagnosed with ovarian cancer in jail and was allowed to return to Canada in 1983. She died there a year later. She maintained to the end that she had been a virtual prisoner with Sobhraj, staying with him only because she lacked the wherewithal to escape, although guards at Tihar later told journalists that she had continued to have sex with Sobhraj during her stay.

Sobhraj ensured that his stay at Tihar was as comfortable as possible. In 1979 he petitioned the High Court to have his leg shackles removed; this done, he strapped a tape recorder to his thigh and encouraged the unwitting guards to talk about their illegal activities – everything from extortion to dealing opium. He then took the cassette to the Superintendent, effectively blackmailing him into giving Sobhraj the run of the prison. As well as enjoying access to most modern conveniences, Sobhraj was also reputed to earn 40 per cent of the takings from all illegal moneymaking in the jail, and enjoyed 'conjugal visits' from the many women who wanted to marry him, excited by the accounts of this ruthless and dominant individual in the books about the case then circulating.

On 17 March 1986 two ex-cons arrived in a white Ambassador to help Charles celebrate his birthday, which was actually a few weeks off. Charles's position at Tihar, the prison's lacklustre security and a few well-placed bribes meant that this was not an unusual occurrence, and the guards were happy to join in the celebrations. They ate some cake that Charles's friends had brought, having first watched Charles eat some; but his piece must have been marked because, while he remained conscious, the guards promptly collapsed. The cake had been laced with powerful sedatives. The group took one unconscious warder with them, hanging his uniformed arm out of the car window to avert suspicion from the watchtower, and they drove through the main gate without being stopped once. Once again Sobhraj had pulled it off.

In one sense the escape was unusual: Sobhraj had successfully fought most of his convictions in the Indian courts and his jail time had by now almost elapsed. He later claimed that this escape was designed purely to ensure that he would never be extradited to Thailand; if he remained on the run he would enjoy the privileges of freedom, and if he was caught he would be jailed again for a period of ten years or so, after which the non-renewable warrant for his arrest in Thailand would be invalid.

It didn't take long for the Indian police to find him again, and he was arrested at a seafood restaurant in Goa following an Interpol wiretap. The sentence for his escape would have been ten years, but due to the congestion of the trial system he spent eleven years as an 'undertrial'. Changes at Tihar meant that he led a rather more restrained life at the jail now, but although by 1996 he had served more time than any Indian court could sentence him to and was able to leave at his leisure, he waited until the Thai arrest warrant had definitively expired before arranging his deportation to France.

CHARLES SOBHRAJ, SUPERSTAR

On 17 February 1997 Charles Sobhraj left Tihar and, after dealing with minor immigration charges, flew to France. There he was taken directly to a police station and questioned over charges relating to the attempted robbery and poisoning of the French tour group that had led to his downfall; but his lawyer successfully argued that he had already faced justice in India over the affair. Charles Sobhraj was a free man – and a celebrity.

Canny as ever, Sobhraj had charged so much for exclusive photography rights on his arrival in Paris that the photo-agency Sipa had to arrange for pool coverage with another photo-agency, Angeli. Four photographers followed him day and night and a number of interviews took place at pre-arranged times and undisclosed locations. Sobhraj claims that after three days he had earned half a million dollars.

His fees following this media blitzkrieg were $10,000 for an hour-long interview and $6,000 for half an hour; he has also been negotiating rights to his autobiography, ten chapters of which he wrote in Tihar. Crime, for Charles Sobhraj, has paid – handsomely. More recently he has been working with Indian movie idol Jackie Shroff on an Indian film of his life, entitled *Bottomline*, hoping to capitalise on his near-mythical status on the subcontinent.

'YOU HAVE THE RIGHT TO KILL'

Will Sobhraj kill again? It seems unlikely; he claims that his principal ambition in life has long been to write and he professes an enthusiasm for short stories. He clearly relishes his celebrity status, which is a boon for book and movie deals but something of a drawback for the indiscriminate slaughter of tourists.

Except that Sobhraj claimed that his murders were never indiscriminate – today, indeed, he claims that he killed nobody at all – and told journalists Richard Neville and Julie Clarke while jailed in Tihar that he had been employed to kill the tourists. His employers? A group of Chinese businessmen, based in Hong Kong, who were involved in heroin trafficking on a large scale. Amateur drug runners were often caught and caused problems for their larger operation; Charles's job was to kill such amateurs, often in such a grisly way that it would send a message to others.

He contended that all of his victims were involved in heroin trafficking, and that he had questioned each before killing them, in this way gathering the names of the next victims. For every successful hit a large fee would be paid into a bank account, and he was sent an assistant – Ajay – with whom to work.

Sobhraj even claimed responsibility for a murder with which he was never charged, telling Neville and Clarke that his first heroin-trafficking victim had been 56-year-old André Breugnot, who was found dead in a Chiang Mai hotel room on 21 September 1975. It was, for Charles, the perfect murder: he had drugged and drowned his victim, after extracting names of others in the trade, and the police suspected no foul play. Among the names given to Sobhraj were those of Vitali Hakim, who was said to be preparing to ship heroin from Bangkok to Europe via couriers, and Teresa Knowlton, who would be smuggling heroin herself from Bangkok to Kathmandu and thence to Europe and the USA, a route then in its infancy. Sobhraj went further in this unlikely confession, professing that the businessmen he worked for were under orders from the Chinese government, pushing heroin in the West as revenge for the Opium War.

Hakim was known to be involved in drug trafficking, and Bronzich had known associates involved with hard narcotics.

But for many of Sobhraj's other victims the idea seems ludicrous. The staid Dutch couple, for instance, seem an unlikely pair of international criminals, and Hemker's diary gives no indication of any involvement in the trade. The excuse of 'cleansing' smacks of a justification similar to that given by those serial killers who kill prostitutes.

But if Sobhraj's story is untrue, then what *was* his motivation? Was he amorally pragmatic in killing people, so that they could never identify him later? This seems unlikely given the kind of victim and the circumstances of his robberies. Or was he driven to kill, perhaps using the robberies as an excuse for doing so? His mother's explanation is a simple example of magical thinking – 'He gets his strength from the spirits of the people he killed' – but the truth may be more complex.

In a sense his murders can be seen as a form of revenge for what happened to him as a child: the lack of formally recognised identity, the disdain with which he was treated by his French stepfather (most of his victims were French), the constraints put upon his mobility. Assuming a bewildering array of identities at will, especially those of Frenchmen he'd robbed and sometimes killed, and flouting exactly the kind of laws that had so bedevilled him in his early years, those concerning identity, documentation and authenticity, must have exerted a powerful attraction. Indeed, his later life seems like a conscious attempt to emulate – but this time in control – the chaos of his early years. Sobhraj hinted at something of the sort when once asked why he'd committed his crimes: 'In some ways my life has been a protest against the French legal system which stole so many years of my youth ... All I wanted was to win them back.'

Sobhraj is similar in this to those serial killers who are violently abused as children, and who fantasise while enduring the abuse about becoming victimisers rather than victims. As adults they inflict on others what they were once forced to endure. Sobhraj's abuse consisted of being shuttled back and forth, an entity without legal identity – and as an adult he deprived others of their identity and their ability to travel.

Psychologist Erich Fromm, in *The Anatomy of Human Destructiveness*, has described the way that abuse – of any kind – at the hands of an adult can catalyse such an identification as a means of dealing with it, 'by doing actively what one was forced to endure passively: to rule when one had to obey, to beat when one was beaten, in short, to *do* what one was *forced* to *suffer . . .*'

Other factors from his youth are also important in understanding his adult behaviour. His unstable family background compelled him to surround himself with an entourage, a murderous Fagin lording it over his damaged charges; and the fact that he was a colonial child, part Vietnamese and exposed early on to the horrors of the French war, cannot be discounted. Nadine Gires once found in one of Charles's files a large glossy photo of a Vietnamese soldier holding in his hand a severed human head. Might his desire to kill – at the very least his callous disregard for life – not be in part a reaction to French military activity in Vietnam?

More pertinent, perhaps, is the fact that Sobhraj was a disadvantaged child, unwanted by either parent or country. The killer here fits anthropologist Elliott Leyton's theory, expounded in *Hunting Humans: the Rise of the Modern Multiple Murderer*, that serial killers are intensely class-conscious and obsessed with status. Most are adopted or illegitimate, and many are institutionalised in their youth, leading to a weak sense of identity which they seek to strengthen through international celebrity. Their victims tend to come from social classes above them, and the murders can be seen as a form of revenge on the established order, a blood-spattered protest against a perceived exclusion from society.

Tourists, being visible embodiments of the consumer society's ephemeralism, breed resentment among many of the world's poor with their flagrantly non-essential use of income; and the idea of privileged people feeling themselves entitled to travel for fun, when Sobhraj had been shunted around as a child by powers beyond his control, may have helped to confirm for him an idea of tourists as legitimate targets. The apparently arbitrary choice of murder victim may have its roots simply in a sense of power – he could choose who would live, and who would die.

Perhaps the final word on the matter should come from Sobhraj himself, who once asked journalists:

> Does a professional soldier feel remorse after having killed a hundred men with a machine gun? Did the US pilots feel remorse after dropping napalm on my homeland? No. Society condoned the soldiers, telling them: You have the right to kill; it is your duty to kill – the more you kill the bigger the promotion. Don't I have the same right? In the interest of my own minority?

7. ROAD KILL

THE AUSTRALIAN ROAD TO DRY AND DUSTY DEATH

*No parent saying goodbye to a son or daughter as they head
off to see the sights of Australia can feel secure in the
knowledge that they will return.*

Sydney *Sunday Telegraph*, 7/11/93

25 January 1990. Paul Onions was just about ready to give
up. People had told him that hitching was the best way to get
around Australia, to meet real Australians rather than the
Europhile townies he'd met so far, but he'd been waiting on
the Hume Highway for hours now and not one person had
stopped. When a 4WD pulled over, it looked like his luck
had finally changed.

The moustachioed driver offered Paul a lift to Canberra,
and he was delighted to accept. The driver, who called
himself Bill, had a moustache that reminded Paul of cricketer
Merv Hughes. He was friendly enough, if a bit nosy. Right off
the bat Bill asked him if anyone knew where he was, or where
he was going. Paul answered no to both questions, surprised
by the driver's solicitous tone, but then started to worry when
the questions got weirder. Did he have any Special Forces
training?

Like a lot of Australians Paul had met, Bill ribbed him
about being a bloody pom. But he was angrier about it than
the people Paul had met before, complaining bitterly about
the English occupation of Northern Ireland then going on to
rant about the 'gooks' in Australia. Then he just stopped
talking. Paul tried to lighten the tone with a few jokes, but
Bill didn't answer. Paul could feel the man's anger, and it
scared him.

The next time Bill spoke, it was to tell Paul that this far out
of Sydney the radio didn't work; he was going to pull over
and rummage around in the back for some tapes. The story

didn't add up – there were tapes between the front two seats – but Paul decided to play along. It wasn't like he could complain.

As Bill looked in the back of the car, Paul got out to stretch his legs, only to sit down again hurriedly as Bill shouted at him to get back in. When Bill returned to the front he felt under his seat and pulled out a gun, which he levelled at Paul. The young Englishman couldn't quite believe what was happening.

'This is a robbery,' Bill told him, and before Paul had had a chance to reply, Bill had pulled out a length of dirty rope. Now Paul was scared. As a hitch-hiker he was hardly likely to have any money, and his rucksack was barely worth stealing. What was Bill going to do to him?

Almost without realising what he was doing, he opened the door and stepped out. Then he was running, cars swerving to miss him as he sprinted down the highway. He heard shots from behind and turned, barely able to believe that Bill was shooting at him. Then the gunman was on him, and the two struggled. But even though Bill was far larger than him, Paul was terrified, and his fear gave him strength. He managed to get away again, running in front of a car which screeched to a halt. He could see that the driver, a woman, was scared; there was another woman in the passenger seat and four children in the back.

'You've got to let me in. There's a man trying to kill me,' Paul told the driver, barely coherent as he looked over his shoulder, wide-eyed with fear. The woman shook her head. 'You can't! I've got the kids with me. I can't help you!' But he'd got in by now, deaf to her protestations, and was trying to hide behind the front seats. His terror convinced the driver, who reversed for thirty metres then drove over the central reservation and sped off back the way she'd come. Paul hid until the car turned around, then looked up. He could see Bill standing by his car. He was sure the man who'd tried to kill him was watching him, and what stuck in Paul's mind most was the expression on Bill's face. He was grinning.

THE FOREST

On 19 September 1992 Keith Siely and Keith Caldwell were running in the Belanglo State Forest on an orienteering training exercise. It was the smell that made them stop – the sweet stench of death. They followed it to its source, sure they'd find the corpse of a kangaroo, or maybe a wallaby. But just beyond a makeshift fireplace they saw something far worse. Under a ledge in a sandstone outcrop was a human body, still clothed and covered in twigs and branches. But they could see enough to be sure of what it was. Horrified, they ran back to collect a mobile phone and call the police.

When investigators arrived they found that the body belonged to a woman. The T-shirt and bra had been pulled up over the breasts, but the shirt was still down at the back; the fly of the jeans was undone but the top button was still done up. A quick inspection of jewellery found on the body confirmed that it was Joanne Walters.

Walters, who was born in Maesteg, South Wales, in 1970, had been missing since April that year. She had been in Australia for a few months before then, working casually on yachts and picking fruits before landing a job as a nanny in Sydney. She'd met another British girl, Caroline Clarke, at a hostel in Sydney, and the two had rented a flat with a few other tourists while they worked.

Clarke, who'd grown up in the Surrey commuter belt in England, had decided to travel to gain experience before joining the police force. She'd been in Sydney since September 1991 and had worked in a factory. But nannying and factory work didn't allow them to spend much time outdoors, and on 18 April they'd set out to hitch to Melbourne, to look for fruit-picking work.

Their families hadn't heard from them since then. Joanne's father, alerted to the fact that something might be wrong when she didn't get in touch for Father's Day – she was normally so good at things like that – checked with her bank. She hadn't made a transaction since 16 April. The Walters contacted the police in Australia to register their daughter as missing, and managed to get in touch with the Clarkes from Joanne's effusive descriptions of her new friend.

Caroline's parents used their banking contacts to alert higher-ranking officers in the Australian police, and they started to take the disappearances seriously. The press picked up the story, and leads came in, but none proved helpful. Joanne's father travelled to Australia to keep press interest in the case alive, but there just wasn't any news – until now, when his worst fears were confirmed.

Police began to search the area in a spiral from where Walters's body had been found. They soon found another corpse, that of Caroline Clarke, covered just like the first with layers of twigs and branches; the head had been wrapped in red cloth which was riddled with bullet holes. Police searched the area around the bodies and found only cigarette ends and spent bullets – there was no trace of the girls' belongings.

The forensic pathologist assigned to the case found that Joanne Walters had been stabbed fourteen times, twice through the spinal cord at the base of the neck. Caroline Clarke had probably been killed by one of the ten bullets that had been fired into her head, although she too had been stabbed in the back. The shots to her head had been fired from various angles, indicating that it may have been used for target practice. There was no evidence of forced sex, although the bodies were so far decomposed that it was hard to tell; the fact that Joanne Walters's fly was undone indicated a sexual element to the attack. Vaginal swabs were taken in any case.

A ballistics expert was called in and charged with inspecting the bullets to determine what kind of gun had fired them, and whether or not they had any unique distinguishing features. He soon found that the bullets were highly likely to have been fired from a Ruger 10/22 made before 1982. He also found that the bullets had a distinctive marking on the head of the case, indicating a minor flaw in the firing mechanism. The sides of the cases were scratched, too, probably from a fault in a homemade silencer.

If they could find the gun, the mark was unique enough to identify it. Unfortunately the Ruger was one of the most popular .22s ever manufactured, and tens of thousands had been sold in Australia. Checking through all the registered owners alone would take years, and there was no legal obligation to keep a record if a gun owner sold a gun to somebody else.

Furthermore, the police weren't sure whether they were looking for one killer or two: the MO for each murder looked very different. Forensic psychiatrist Dr Rod Milton visited the scene of the crime, and favoured the two-killer theory: once people had started to kill they tended to follow a set routine. The differences between the frenzied knife attack on Walters and the controlled, leisurely shooting of Clarke – the cigarette ends near Caroline's body suggested that her killer had taken some time over the murder – were considerable. The first seemed a classic example of a disorganised and the second of an organised killing, key distinctions in serial-killer profiling.

One theory he kept coming back to was that the killers were brothers: one older and dominant, the other younger and rebellious but still submissive to his brother. Clarke would have been killed by the elder brother, Walters by the younger. The bodies showed no signs of having been restrained, which further supported the two-killer theory. Milton thought that the windcheater wrapped around Clarke's head was there to depersonalise her, so that her reality didn't ruin the fantasy being acted out; he also thought that the killers would live locally, with limited social lives. They clearly had a keen interest in guns.

The Walters made a tearful television appeal for information leading to the arrest of their daughter's killer. Calls flooded in and a task force was set up to sift through the information. Everything would have to be treated as potentially valuable, and the task force's computer system didn't help them to cross-reference material; it would take years just to check all the information called in. A reward of $100,000 was posted for information leading to the killer's arrest.

In October 1993 a local potter, Bruce Pryor, looked around the forest. Like everyone in their small community, he'd been horrified by the murders, and felt certain that the police had missed crucial clues in their search around the bodies of

Walters and Clarke. He had a permit for gathering firewood, and knew the forest well. Following a hunch about a track known as the Morrice Fire Trail, he found an old campfire, then a nearby bone, then a human skeleton. Appalled by his discovery, he contacted the police. When officers arrived they found yet another body; both had been covered with light brush.

One of the bodies belonged to Australian James Gibson. The nineteen-year-old had died from multiple stab wounds, including one through the spine. Once again his fly was undone, with the top button done up. The other body belonged to Deborah Everist, who had also died from stab wounds, although she had suffered from heavy blows to the head as well. Tights with knots tied in them were found near her body, indicating that she had been restrained.

Gibson, who was born in 1970, had been travelling to Confest, an alternative lifestyles festival on the New South Wales/Victoria border due to start in early 1990. Everist, who was also nineteen, had agreed to accompany him, although the free and easy hippie lifestyle wasn't really her thing. The last their parents had heard from them was a phone call from Deborah on 29 December 1989; she called her mother to reassure her that she was OK after an earthquake in Newcastle, 150 kilometres north of Sydney. Deborah promised to call her mother again on the 30th, and when she didn't call, Patricia Everist began to worry.

Patricia contacted Peggy Gibson, James's mother, and they reported the teenagers missing at Frankston police station. The police tried to reassure them, telling them that 86 per cent of people reported missing turned up again within a fortnight. Privately, they weren't too worried – two teenagers running off for the summer? Happened all the time.

But when James didn't contact his family for his sister's wedding on 21 January 1990, the Gibsons began to fear the worst. And when his empty backpack was found by the side of the Galston Gorge, 30 kilometres north-west of Sydney, it seemed to confirm their worst suspicions.

Pryor's discovery prompted a far wider search of the forest, and in early November 1993, days before the search was due to be called off, the body of German tourist Simone Schmidl was found in a shallow grave, again covered with twigs and sticks. Little more than the skeleton remained, but from that pathologists could see that there had been two stab wounds through the spine as well as six others which had marked bone. A length of wire tied into a loop was found nearby.

Schmidl was born in Bavaria in 1969, and in mid-1990 had decided to leave her job and visit Australian friends she'd met while travelling around Alaska. Her parents were not particularly worried by her decision – by all accounts Australia was a friendly and safe country. She bought new camping gear before going, writing her nickname, 'Simi', on some of it with a marker pen.

She planned to hitch to Melbourne on 20 January 1991 to meet her mother, who was coming out to see her – but she never met the plane. Her mother knew instantly that something was wrong – Simi hadn't arrived to meet her, and nor had she got in touch to say that she couldn't make it – and reported her missing to the police. Back home, Simone's father Herbert got in touch with the German cultural organisations in Australia, putting the word out about his daughter's disappearance. But they'd had no idea of what had happened to her – until now.

Three days later, two more bodies were found. A metre-high pile of logs, which it took three officers to move, covered one of the bodies, lending further support to the two-killer theory; the other body was covered by light brush fifty metres away. The first body was missing its skull and first three vertebrae; the second had six bullet holes in the head, as well as a broken hyoid bone in the neck, which suggested strangulation. Dental records confirmed that the second body belonged to Gabor Neugebauer, and there was a strong likelihood that the first was Anja Habschied, although in the absence of a head, skin tissue had to be DNA-tested for confirmation.

Neugebauer was born in 1970 in West Germany. He'd been travelling with a fellow German student, Habschied, who he'd met at a disco after finishing his military service. Unlike most of their peers neither of them smoked or drank, and they shared a love of travel; it wasn't long before they planned to take a long trip together. They decided to go to Indonesia in the autumn of 1991, but bad weather and volcanic activity prompted instead a trip to Australia.

On 26 December Gabor called his parents to tell them that he and Anja were heading for Darwin, where they had to catch a flight back to Indonesia. That was the last time their parents heard from them. They didn't return home on the flights they'd booked, or even make it to Indonesia, so the parents reported them missing and hired a private investigator to look into their disappearances. But the investigator was expensive, and didn't unearth any information, so the Neugebauers decided to go out to Australia themselves instead.

After appearing on television a number of times and attempting to retrace Gabor's steps, as a last resort they saw a Sydney fortune-teller, Margaret Dent. Dent told them that their trip had been in vain – the children were dead. She told them further that the girl had suffered very badly, although the boy had died quickly. Their bodies would, she said, be found within two to four years. The Neugebauers, devastated, returned to Germany.

Exactly how Habschied suffered will never be known. Her trials ended with her decapitation; the fourth vertebra was sliced in half, with a cut consistent with that coming from a sword, machete, heavy knife or sharp axe. The angle of the cut suggested that it had been an execution-style killing, with the victim leaning forwards on her knees. Police psychiatrists following the two-brother theory pointed to the decapitation as a show of strength by the older brother; a demonstration of dominance, an assertion that he was crazier than his companion.

Near the bodies police found a makeshift bondage device, a leash terminating in two wrist restraints, which was constructed from cable ties, sash cord, electrical tape and a brown leather strap.

The reward for information was increased to $500,000, and the Sydney *Sunday Telegraph* offered another $200,000, making the combined reward the largest in Australian history. Calls flooded in, with a number of people mentioning Ivan Milat as a gun fanatic who owned a 4WD – meaning that he could easily get around the rugged terrain of the Belanglo State Forest – and whose family had property near Belanglo.

Paul Onions, who was following the case back in England – the police at Bowral, where his rescuer had taken him, had done little more than warn him not to hitch again and loan him the money to get back to Sydney – called in his story a number of times, convinced that his experience with 'Bill' was important. But the investigation was swamped with information, and it took a long time before someone decided to follow up on the growing Milat file.

AT HOME WITH IVAN AND THE BOYS

Ivan Robert Marko Milat was born in 1944 to Stephen and Margaret Milat; Stephen had emigrated from Yugoslavia in 1926, while Margaret had arrived with her English father in 1912. The couple had thirteen other children – Olga, Alex, Boris, Mary, Shirley, Bill, Mick, Wally, George, Margaret, Richard, David and Paul – and lived in Moorebank, an industrial suburb of Sydney.

Stephen worked at a variety of jobs until settling as a market gardener, and encouraged his children to work hard by his side. They rarely worked hard enough for him though, and he would beat the children, often publicly, for the slightest infraction. Margaret would also beat the boys, once hitting Boris with a knife. There was violence between the parents too; Stephen began to drink heavily and would lash out at his wife at any provocation. The older children, Olga and Alex, left almost as soon as they were able to, marrying and moving away.

In 1956 the market garden was robbed and the entire crop of tomatoes stolen. Margaret insisted that Stephen get a 'proper' job, and he did, taking work on the wharves. Without him around to discipline the children and give them work to do, they ran riot around Moorebank, too much of a handful for Margaret to deal with on her own. They all had guns, and shot rabbits for the meat, which they could eat, and the skins, which they could sell. This was standard practice among their neighbours, but the Milat boys also shot birds, which was frowned upon locally, although their father did nothing to discourage them.

The boys quickly developed a tough reputation at school, but when the teachers met crime with punishment the Milats just stopped going. Truanting was far more fun: shooting out windows, shoplifting and indulging in boyish pranks. Margaret didn't dare tell Stephen about the truanting, or about the increasing number of times the boys were returned home by the police – he'd beat them savagely if he knew.

But she couldn't cope with all of the boys being around, and sent Ivan to a home for miscreant boys when he was thirteen. He was joined shortly afterwards by Bill. Ivan left after little over a year at the school, and never went back.

He began to work in a series of menial jobs, from the outset pilfering from shops he worked in and stealing from workmates. He was arrested for a string of petty robberies, and on his second conviction in 1962 was sent to Mount Penang Juvenile Institution for six months' hard labour.

Boris was the first of the boys to get a steady girlfriend, Marilyn Childs, and the couple had a child that same year. After Ivan's release, Boris became suspicious of his brother's friendliness with Marilyn and tried to punish her by refusing to sleep with her; but during this period she conceived. The child, Lynise, was Ivan's, as Boris would eventually discover; he came close to killing Ivan for his cuckolding on a number of occasions.

Ivan continued to commit robberies, often with his brothers, and never spent long out of prison: on parole he would almost invariably be sent straight back after being caught robbing a pub or stealing a car. He started to work out inside, a discipline he would maintain throughout his life, and in his brief periods of freedom he continued to see Marilyn behind Boris's back, as well as seeing Wally's on-off girlfriend, Maureen Parsons.

Both Marilyn and Maureen were drawn to Ivan because he seemed so much less violent than their boyfriends, as well as being less foulmouthed. He didn't drink much either, which was a boon. But he did scare them a little sometimes, when he talked of killing and dead bodies, although they treated it as just part of the survivalist banter most of the boys engaged in. When Maureen asked him once, half-jokingly, if he'd killed anyone, he replied that he'd killed a man and buried him in the bush. She also heard him talking at the Milat home about how to dispose of a body, saying that if you buried someone out in the bush and covered it with lime nobody would ever know.

Early in 1971 Ivan's sister Margaret was killed in a car crash in which Wally was also injured. Although Boris and Ivan had a truce for the day of Margaret's funeral, their relationship was worse than ever before, and by then they'd had a number of fistfights over Marilyn. Boris finally gave Marilyn an ultimatum – she could stay with her children or go with Ivan. When she chose the children, Boris married her, and the couple moved away. The marriage, coming on top of his sister's death, hit Ivan hard.

A few weeks after Marilyn's marriage Ivan picked up a couple of female hitch-hikers on their way from Sydney to Melbourne. He threatened the girls with a knife and told them that he was going to have sex with them or kill them; as he tied them up he told them that he'd done this before. One of the girls offered to have sex with him if he'd free them afterwards, and he agreed. But afterwards he refused to let them go, telling them that he'd look after them until the morning.

One of the girls insisted that she needed a drink, and Ivan stopped at a service station; the girl got out and told the cashier what had happened. Before Ivan could drive off the car was surrounded by the boss and two of his helpers, and both girls were able to get away.

They reported the rape to the police, and Milat's car was soon found. He denied the charges, although he later admitted that he'd had sex with one of the girls. Police doctors examined the girls but could find no evidence of brutality, although their wrists had raw marks consistent with having been tied up. Unsurprisingly, police found no evidence of knives or rope in Milat's car, but they still went ahead with the rape charges.

While out on bail Ivan joined his brother Mick's crew, holding up post offices and shops with shotguns. But one of the gang bragged to a girl he was trying – and failing – to impress, and was arrested after she told the police. It didn't take long for him to admit the identities of his accomplices, and Mick and Ivan Milat were arrested. Ivan's mother mortgaged her house to pay the bail money for Ivan, who paid her back by feigning suicide and skipping bail, hiding out in New Zealand.

He returned to Australia in mid-1972, and was arrested shortly after visiting his mother in hospital, Boris and Marilyn both claiming that the other had called the police. Naturally, bail was refused, but Milat was acquitted on the robbery charge, as there wasn't enough evidence to convict him; the evidence of his co-accused was worthless unless it was backed up independently.

The rape trial came a day later. The jury heard that both girls were receiving psychiatric treatment, and each gave conflicting accounts of what had happened. The girl who'd had sex with Ivan was by this time undergoing therapy in which she was pushed to take responsibility for her sexual actions, and told the court that no rape had occurred. Her friend's testimony that they had been threatened with knives and ropes was weakened when the court heard that she was taking Valium, and Milat was found not guilty of rape.

MARRIED TO THE MILATS

Ivan now seemed determined to go straight, taking a job as a truck driver and immersing himself in trucking culture. He started to see Karen Duck, the younger sister of one of his workmates. It didn't matter to him that Karen, then sixteen, was pregnant with the child of one of his cousins; and it didn't seem to matter to Karen that Ivan was sometimes rough with her, raping her early on in the relationship. She forgave him, and he would later treat her son, Jason, as his own.

Ivan left his job as a trucker and became a road worker. He was formidably strong and worked harder than anyone else, making good money with the overtime. He was promoted rapidly through the ranks and was respected by his workmates, although he didn't really fit in – he wouldn't drink with them and appeared to be teetotal, preferring to spend his time polishing his boots. He'd been living with Karen at her parents' house, but now moved with her to the Milat home.

While they were staying there Ivan told David's girlfriend, 'Toppy' Ambrose, that if anyone tried to mess with her she should turn them into a 'head on a stick', describing how to stick a knife through the top of a victim's spine to paralyse them. Ivan told 'Toppy' that he'd learned the trick from a Vietnam veteran, who'd told him that this was the best way to immobilise someone before having your way with them.

Ivan bought a house in Blackett, a western suburb of Sydney, and moved in with Karen. He kept a tight rein on his girlfriend – she had to pay for all the groceries herself on her single mother's pension, as Ivan wouldn't give her a thing. He was jealous of her as well, ordering her not to speak to any of the neighbours.

The cleanliness of the house became an obsession with him; she thought at first that it was due to Jason's chronic asthma, but there was more to it than that. He began to carry a gun all the time, and the trucking magazines were replaced by gun magazines, knives and military paraphernalia. At the same time he started to worry about security, engraving his name on to everything they owned and becoming leader of the local Neighbourhood Watch. He also started to beat her, and she would occasionally show her bruises to her neighbours.

Despite Ivan's increasingly erratic behaviour, Karen wanted the commitment and security marriage would bring, and the couple were married on 20 February 1983 in a no-frills registry office ceremony. Karen's single mother pension was now cut, and Ivan paid her $200 a fortnight for groceries and the upkeep of the house; she had to provide receipts for everything, and she wasn't allowed to buy herself any clothes.

On 23 April that year Ivan's father died of pneumonia, contracted during his treatment for bowel cancer. After the death Karen found Ivan even more aggressive. He raped her anally, and she was worried by his increasing obsession with guns. She had the impression that he'd done something wrong, something he wouldn't tell her about. But when they were out of the house Ivan seemed happier, and occasionally they visited Alex and went for drives around the nearby Belanglo State Forest, which Ivan appeared to know well.

Ivan's behaviour at work had become strange too – he started to take days off for no apparent reason, and was sometimes seen driving off after work away from his home. Nobody knew where he went – any stories he gave just didn't add up, but nobody wanted to challenge him – or why he took rolls of sash cord home from work when he didn't have a dog or a boat. His workmates kept their distance, especially when they noticed that Ivan's heavy blue bag, which he always carried around with him, was full of guns and knives.

Eventually Karen had had enough of living with Ivan, and left him. He'd driven her to a nervous breakdown with his behaviour, which seemed if anything to be worsening. Once he wasn't happy with a meal she'd cooked, so he smashed the plate down on the glass table, shattering it, then left the house to go to his mother's, telling her not to clean up any of the mess until his return. He'd also thrown a glass at her, and it only just missed Jason.

. She didn't want Ivan to know where she'd gone, but he drove to her parents' house and threatened to burn it down unless Mrs Duck told him where she was. Karen's mother refused to tell him anything, so Ivan returned later and set fire to their car, destroying it along with their garage.

Ivan moved back to his mother's house, illegally selling the house he owned with Karen by having her signature forged. Boris and Marilyn had split up by now, so Ivan started to see his former lover again. But Marilyn felt that Ivan had changed for the worse since she'd last seen him. He was obsessed with guns and shooting; he seemed to enjoy wounding animals more than actually killing them, and once grabbed her from behind, putting a large hunting knife to her throat and demonstrating how to kill someone without breaking the knife on bone.

She wasn't happy with the situation for other reasons too, as she wanted more commitment than Ivan was prepared to give. If he wouldn't marry her, she'd find someone who would. She left him, although later she would be convinced that this, coupled with Karen's desertion, had driven him off the rails.

Karen instigated divorce proceedings against Ivan, who left his job as a road worker when he was tipped off that his salary would be docked to pay for her maintenance; he worked for a while in a plasterboard factory. When his divorce finally went through in October 1989 he returned to work as a road worker, building the Mittagong/Berrima bypass. He was happy to be back, all the more so as they had a long Christmas break. Time to kill.

KILLER CHAT

On 6 January 1992 Ivan went to a panel-beater to have a bullet hole in the front passenger door of his car filled in. The panel-beater could see that the shot had been fired from the driver's seat, at an angle that would have passed through a passenger's hips. Ivan told him that he'd had an accident with his gun; it had gone off when he tried to pick it up. He told the same story to his friends, who thought it strange – surely Ivan was so careful with guns?

One night Phil Polglase, an old friend of David 'Bodge' Milat, was sleeping at Bodge's place. Ivan turned up at 5.30 one morning and woke Phil up. He was carrying guns and knives, including one large hunting knife on which the blood was still wet. When Phil asked him if he'd been killing goats, Ivan replied, 'That's human blood . . . I stabbed a bloke with it . . . stabbed him through the spine.' Polglase thought he was joking and didn't think much of it when Ivan offered him a German man's passport and showed him a couple of others, including one belonging to a blonde German girl.

Later that day Bodge drove Polglase to the Granville railway station nearby, and told him that Ivan had a few problems:

'Ivan's been doing something bad, years ago . . . We stopped him, but now we think he's doing it again.' When Polglase asked if it was armed robberies, Bodge told him that it was far worse than that.

Ivan's brother Richard was working at Boral, a plaster-works, under the assumed name Paul Miller. Paul Douglas, a workmate, hung out with him a bit and went shooting at Richard and Wally's property, although only once; the way they just got stoned and shot at everything freaked him out. 'Miller' once told Douglas that he knew someone who killed people 'just to see the shock on their faces'. He also told Douglas that 'Stabbing a woman is like cutting a loaf of bread', out of the blue, after they'd been discussing lenient jail sentences for rapists. At the time Douglas put it down as just more of his drugged ramblings, nothing to worry about.

When the discovery of the first bodies in Belanglo State Forest was discussed on 21 September 1992 'Miller' told his workmates that 'There's more bodies out there. They haven't found the two Germans yet.' He later stated that 'You could pick up anybody on that road and you'd never find them again. You'd never find out who did it either.'

'Miller' also boasted to another workmate, Des Butler, that 'I know who killed those Germans.' Butler had read about the missing Germans in the papers, but nothing about them being killed. Nobody wanted to challenge 'Miller', even about his bizarre habit of changing his appearance constantly, dying his hair, cutting it short, growing it long, growing a beard, shaving it off – it seemed to be an obsession with him.

Finally Des Butler and Paul Douglas decided to go to the police with what they knew about the Milats. Butler initially made an anonymous phone call, but his wife felt that he hadn't told the police everything he'd told her, and contacted them independently. Butler and Douglas were terrified of what might happen if 'Miller' knew that they'd told the police about him.

Similarly frightened was Phil Polglase, who'd been visited by Dick Milat. Dick had asked him if Phil remembered seeing Ivan at Bodge's place, the night he'd come back with a bloodstained knife, loaded with passports. Phil said that he couldn't remember a thing; but he later heard from mutual friends that Dick Milat was going around saying he planned to kill Phil.

CLOSING IN

When Detective Senior Constable Paul Gordon was given the file on the Milats, he thought it was worth checking out – Ivan and Richard's names had cropped up a few times so far in the investigation. He re-interviewed Des Butler and Paul Douglas, then checked the work records for Ivan and Richard. Richard appeared to be in the clear, having been at work for the period when Everist and Gordon had gone missing; but Ivan had been off work on every single crucial day.

Gordon delved further and found Ivan's quashed rape charge; when the details of it came in – involving hitch-hikers, knives and a length of rope – he knew he was on to something. But his supervisors refused to put a wiretap on Ivan; to them, Gordon's work was a little sloppy, and he appeared prejudiced against the Milats. He was told to find more evidence, to try to prove why Ivan *wasn't* responsible.

Gordon then found Onions's statement, and discovered that Ivan had been off work on the day of the robbery. He and other investigators began to question Ivan's workmates, although most of them refused to say much, out of a general dislike of the police and loyalty to their colleague. They found his former wife Karen a richer source of information, as she told them that Ivan was violent and had a strange obsession with control; she spoke of having been raped several times, at least once anally, and of going with him to the Belanglo State Forest, which Ivan seemed to know well.

Word that police had been asking questions about him got back to Ivan, and early in 1994 he asked Wally if he could stash some things at Wally's house; he said that he was worried that police would find some illegal guns if they searched his house. Wally parked his truck under a manhole in the roof of Ivan's garage, while Ivan passed everything down; by the time they were finished the truck was almost filled with guns, ammunition and backpacking gear.

Onions was asked to return to Australia; his flight and time off work would be paid for. He was taken back on the Hume Highway and identified where the robbery had taken place; he then picked Ivan Milat out of a video line-up as 'Bill', the man responsible for the robbery. The police now had enough evidence to arrest Ivan Milat and charge him with the armed robbery of Paul Onions, and possibly even attempted murder – but they didn't yet have enough evidence to link him to the backpacker murders.

They decided to raid the house Ivan shared with his sister Shirley, along with the homes of Richard, Wally, Bill and their mother. Forensic psychiatrist Dr Milton had assured Clive Small, who was then overseeing the investigation, that the killer would probably have kept mementoes from the murders, so that he could relive the crimes; it was a long shot, but Small hoped to find this kind of evidence in the raids. It was also hoped that Ivan might confess to the murders, as many serial killers were prone to do.

On the day before the raid, police visited Alex's house in Queensland, where they found a backpack that had been given to Alex and his wife by Ivan. The backpack was easily identifiable as having belonged to Simone Schmidl.

THE RAID

When the police negotiator called Ivan's phone in the early morning of 22 May 1994 and asked him to come out so that the house could be searched on armed robbery charges, Ivan told him that he and his girlfriend Chalinder Hughes would soon leave. But it took three more calls before he did, and in the meantime he was heard moving in and out of the garage. He was then handcuffed and had the initial charges read to him.

The plan was to keep Ivan on site while a general search was conducted, then to search the house more thoroughly once he was in custody. Police soon found money from New Zealand and Indonesia – countries visited by some of the backpackers before coming to Australia; gun parts from a Ruger 10/22, hidden in a bag in the garage roof; a homemade silencer; and a tent which was later shown to belong to Simone Schmidl. Milat professed not to recognise any of the items shown to him, and told investigators that there were no guns in his house. He was then taken into custody, and at the police station he played dumb, pretending not to understand the questions he was asked and generally being uncommunicative and obtrusive.

A more detailed search of the house revealed other hidden parts for a Ruger 10/22, including a magazine painted in camouflage colours; a photo of Chalinder Hughes in a Benetton top identical to one owned by Caroline Clarke – the top, which was never itself found, was of a type never sold in Australia; two sleeping bags, one belonging to Simone Schmidl and one to Deborah Everist; black electrical tape, sash cord and black plastic cable ties, all of which were identical to the materials used to make the leash found near the bodies of Neugebauer and Habschied; a camera of the same model as one that Caroline Clarke had carried, which was from a batch sold only in England; camping and cooking equipment belonging to Simone Schmidl; and a water bottle which had 'Simi' written on the side. They also found a number of guns, although they missed one buried in the garden until later. It would take some time to confirm the provenance of the material found at Ivan Milat's house, but investigators already felt that the gamble of the raid had paid off.

At Richard's house police found various items of camping equipment, including a blue tent given to Joanne Walters and Caroline Clarke by a fellow backpacker; Caroline Clarke's Karrimat bedroll; and sleeping bags belonging to Clarke and Walters. Richard said that he didn't know whom it all belonged to. In his car they found rope similar to that found near the bodies of the German couple; and in the garden was evidence of a recent fire, the ashes containing burnt buckles consistent with those from a rucksack. They also found a large number of guns.

At Wally's house 24 weapons were found, along with Simone Schmidl's blue knapsack. Ammunition from the same batch as that found by the German couple's corpses was also found, as were fourteen ounces of marijuana. Richard and Wally faced charges stemming from the unlicensed weapons and drugs found on their premises.

At Ivan's mother's house police found more guns and marijuana, along with a blue Next shirt that would eventually be shown to have belonged to Paul Onions. People who knew Ivan thought that for the police to find so much it had to be a fit-up; the police were clearly trying to frame him. Why would Ivan have kept so much booty from the crimes? Dr Milton felt that the killer was probably an intensely arrogant and egotistical man, who wouldn't have expected to get caught; he would also have enjoyed seeing his girlfriends wearing his victims' clothes. When he had sex with them, he could imagine having sex with the victims, reliving the experience.

On 10 April Ivan Milat was charged with the Onions robbery. While he was on remand police worked hard to link the items found in the searches to the backpacker murders. The ballistics expert had found that the breech bolt found hidden in Ivan's garage caused bullet marks consistent with those bullets found at the Clarke murder scene; and scratches on the casing of bullets found there linked that killing to the murder of the German couple.

DNA tests showed that blood found on one of the ropes taken from Ivan Milat's garage was 792,000 times more likely to have come from the Clarkes than anyone else. The police wanted to wait a little longer and gather more evidence, but an ill-advised newspaper interview with one of the investigation's leading detectives prompted them to charge Milat with the murders of the seven backpackers.

'CUT YOUR HEAD OFF WITH ONE BLOW'
Phil Polglase had been keeping an eye on the news and was convinced that he had information that was key to the investigation. He told the police what happened on the night Ivan had come back in the early morning with a bloodstained knife; he also told them that Bodge had once mentioned

seeing Ivan and Richard come home with a rifle and knife which were covered in blood. He knew how Richard idolised Ivan, and remembered that Richard had once told him that 'Ivan could cut your head off with one blow.'

The police were impressed – they had someone who knew the Milats well and was willing to help the investigation. Most of the other people they'd spoken to had clammed up. They offered to set Phil up in a witness protection programme, moving him to a new town and giving him a new identity, but his wife wouldn't hear of it and tried to persuade Phil to back out. But it was too late; he was now in too deep. Although he suspected that it wouldn't work, he allowed police to wire him up and listen in while he spoke to Dick.

Dick appeared to know right away that Phil was wearing a wire; Polglase was nervous, and he kept asking the same questions the police had asked, going back to the case again and again while Dick tried to steer the conversation away. Dick was convinced he was being bugged in any case, so he didn't give much away, apart from talking about serial killers in general:

> . . . if you decide today, when this cunt comes out in his four-wheel drive we'll get him today. We'll just go and shoot him, rape him, whatever we want to fucking do to the fucking prick, burn his car keep that car ourselves and drive round in it for six months. What, well, what'd you think in one month's time we're a bit sick of this, let's get another one . . . Where are we going to stop? Only when we get caught. You're not going to stop two years before. We're not going to stop because we think the police'll be hot on our trail. Once you get that sort of fucking thing in you, I figure it's just like having a beer.

He also revealed details of the Neugebauer and Onions cases that the police had withheld from the press; but it wasn't enough to charge him.

Dick told friends afterwards that Phil had been wearing a wire; and Phil knew that he knew, and he was scared.

Polglase was killed in a road accident a few weeks later. The police could find no evidence of suspicious circumstances, although members of Polglase's family were convinced that he'd been run off the road. His death rendered his statements inadmissible in court.

FAMILY TIES

The committal hearing took place five months after Milat's arrest. There was not enough evidence to charge Richard Milat with being a second killer, so Ivan Milat was to be tried alone for the eight charges on 19 June 1995. In fact the case was delayed for almost a year, as the defence team demanded more money from Legal Aid.

When it eventually began, the trial was presided over by Justice David Hunt; Mark Tedeschi was prosecuting for the Crown while Terry Martin conducted the defence. The defence used the ploy – unusual considering the family loyalty which had until then been a trademark of the Milats – of shifting blame for the killings on to Ivan's brothers, specifically Wally and Richard. Wally's motive for framing Ivan, it was argued, was revenge for the affair he allegedly imagined Ivan having with Maureen; no motive was given for Richard, although it was noted that Richard conformed better in a number of respects to Paul Onions's account of his assailant than Ivan. Ivan himself simply claimed that all of the evidence had been planted, and that somebody had tried to frame him, although he stopped short of accusing family members himself.

Martin, when summing up for the defence, had no such qualms:

> Whichever way you look at it, it is absolutely irrefutable that whoever has committed these eight offences must be either within the Milat family or so very closely associated with it, it does not much matter. The question is, who is it within the Milat family?

But the jurors were convinced that Ivan, even if he hadn't worked alone, was the driving force behind the murders. On

27 July 1996 they found him guilty of all eight charges. The judge, summing up before sentencing, said that in his opinion Milat had not worked alone; for the Onions attack Milat was given six years, and for each of the other charges a life sentence. When asked if he had any comment, Milat maintained that he was not guilty.

He was sent first to Maitland Maximum Security Prison, just north-west of Sydney. He has been involved in a number of escape attempts, since which he has had limited contact with other inmates. Early in 2001 he swallowed razor blades and other small metal objects in what was seen less as a suicide bid than an attempt to be transferred to hospital, where escape would be far easier. He has also conducted a hunger strike to get access to legal support for an appeal.

Despite the evidence against Milat, many of his family members and friends are convinced of his innocence, and a number of organisations are fighting to have him released, among them FIRM (Friends of Ivan Robert Milat) and Justice Action. Milat is now housed in a 'jail within a jail' at Goulburn, a 70-bed high-risk management unit considered to be one of the most secure jails in the world.

BODY-PIT BOASTS

Investigators strongly suspect that Milat is responsible for more murders than those for which he has been convicted. So do some members of his family. Boris is on record as saying that Ivan may have committed up to 28 murders: 'The things I can tell you are worse than what Ivan's meant to have done . . . Everywhere he's worked, people have disappeared.'

Nobody else has been charged with involvement in Ivan Milat's murders. Some of Ivan's workmates who spoke to police about him told journalists that they would leave Australia if Richard Milat were not arrested – they knew what the family was capable of.

In March 1998 a new task force was set up to re-investigate the disappearances of twelve women and three men in Ivan Milat's known hunting grounds between 1978 and 1993. Milat's past work movements demonstrated a possible link to three of the victims – Leanne Goodall, Robyn Hickie and Amanda Robinson – and there was evidence that Milat had boasted to an associate about body pits and graves scattered around the area. Bill Milat denounced the investigation, claiming that police and politicians were using Ivan as a scapegoat to improve their clear-up rate on backpacker disappearances across Australia.

But the 'lazy police work' at the time of the disappearances, as it was described in court in July 2002, treating the three women as runaways rather than potential homicide victims, meant that nobody has been charged with the suspected murders. Milat was one of a number of suspects to give evidence in court, surrounded by a large security presence, and told the court that 'I had nothing to do with whatever happened to their children. I can look at them people, right in the eye, and say, "I had absolutely nothing to do with your children going missing."'

MAKING OF A MURDERER
Did Ivan Milat act alone? The balance of probabilities is that he did not – the radically different MOs of certain killings, particularly those of Walters and Clarke, and the discovery of Habschied's body under a pile of logs it took three people to move, indicate the presence of another killer. If there is another killer, he has yet to be brought to justice – and as Richard Milat points out, if you enjoy killing, you won't stop until you're caught.

Any links between this case and the killings that have been taking place in recent years on the Queensland/New South Wales border are purely speculative, although prospective hitch-hikers would do well to seek alternative modes of transport – as the Australian Tourist Commission itself indicates, 'Hitch-hiking is strongly discouraged throughout Australia.'

As with most serial killers, Milat's problems seem to have started at home. The discipline meted out by his father was inconsistent, which corresponds to the findings of FBI investigators who have interviewed other sex killers: offenders often complain of inconsistent, abusive discipline during childhood.

There are also indications that Ivan Milat may have been sexually abused as a child. Marilyn Childs allegedly told her daughter Lynise that Ivan's murders were a form of unconscious revenge against his mother, who had allowed him to be abused by another woman when he was a boy. Journalists investigating the case were also told by a schoolfriend of Ivan's, known as 'Collar', that Ivan's father was responsible for making him a killer, although the friend refused to expand on the allegation.

Milat's choice of victims is telling – why did he progress from killing Australian backpackers to European ones? That Ivan Milat was consistently racist seems unlikely, as he had an Indian girlfriend, Chalinder Hughes, at the time of his arrest. The selection of backpackers seems perhaps more a case of pragmatism than anything else. Like prostitutes, hitch-hiking backpackers are easy to kill – they will enthusiastically get into a stranger's car and have rarely told other people exactly where they are. If they vanish, it can be some time before their families, especially if they are on the other side of the world, miss them.

This pragmatism might work on another level. It's conceivable that Milat felt a degree of guilt after the first known murders, those of two Australian backpackers; perhaps this led to his choosing people from other countries as his future victims. The fact that the head of Caroline Clarke was wrapped in red cloth before being shot at indicates a need to depersonalise the victims; and it's easier to depersonalise a foreigner than a fellow national, as wartime propaganda shows. We know from the attack on Paul Onions that the expression of racist sentiments immediately preceded the pulling of a gun; perhaps this is an instance of racism as an excuse, or justification, for violence whose true motivation comes from entirely different factors.

There is still a lot of fear surrounding the Milat case. Friends and colleagues are thought to know more than they are prepared to say – but they are just too scared to come forward. Where, for instance, is the head of Anja Habschied? A chilling picture forms of a network of people who are complicit in the serial murder of these hitch-hikers but will not – through fear of the Milats, the police and perhaps an admission of their own complicity – reveal any of the details.

The full story may never be known, but Milat's horrific legacy endures, with Australia back in the press with a series of tourist murders and other attacks in the late 1990s and the early years of the new millennium. Probably the best known of these is the mysterious disappearance of Peter Falconio, which we'll cover below.

BAD DAY AT BARROW CREEK

'The territory is full of mad mavericks with rifles. If you were to shake the whole of Australia all the misfits and scumbags would fall out in Alice Springs.'

Malcolm Brown, quoted in the *Guardian*,
28 July 2001

The area of the Northern Territory is almost exactly the same as that of France, Great Britain, Germany, Austria, Belgium and Hungary added together. It has 140,000 inhabitants – ten square kilometres of land for each person – and nearly half of the population live in Darwin, the state capital. That leaves a lot of room to hide a body.

27-year-old travel agent Joanne Lees and her 28-year-old boyfriend Peter Falconio, a building surveyor, were on the last leg of a dream holiday. The Huddersfield couple had been to Nepal, Cambodia and Thailand – their itinerary arranged by Lees – and just two days before his disappearance Falconio had phoned home to say that he was having the time of his life. Friends say that he had planned to propose to Joanne, his girlfriend of seven years, when they reached Hawaii.

On 14 July 2001 they'd been to the annual Camel Cup horse races in Alice Springs, and left at around four, driving north in their orange VW Kombi van. They stopped at Ti Tree, around 100 miles from Alice Springs, to refuel and watch a magnificent sunset. There they ate what was to be their last meal together.

At around seven they were heading north on the lonely Stuart Highway, just past the tiny settlement of Barrow Creek, surrounded by a vast expanse of flat, arid bushland. A white 4WD pick-up, its open back covered with a tarpaulin, pulled alongside and Falconio, who was driving, slowed down. The pick-up's driver, a man with long straggling hair and a droopy moustache, shouted to them that sparks were flying from their exhaust. Lees said later that she had felt uneasy about the encounter at the time, but Falconio stopped the car and got out.

He and the stranger walked to the back of the van to inspect the exhaust, and Peter asked Joanne to rev the motor. As soon as she did, she heard a loud bang, which she assumed at the time to come from the engine. The stranger reappeared, punched her in the face and tied her up at gunpoint, binding her hand and foot, her hands in front of her body, before bundling her into his pick-up.

When the gunman then left her, conceivably to deal with Falconio's body, Lees managed to wriggle to the back of the pick-up and out, stumbling past the stranger's dog and into the bush. She hid, petrified, not far from the road. It was blackest night. Using a torch and his dog, the stranger searched for but failed to find her, coming within a few yards before abandoning the search and vanishing into the night.

Lees remained in the freezing bush, wearing only shorts and a sleeveless vest, for the next five hours. Each time a car came past she cowered, fearing the gunman's return. Eventually she heard the approach of a truck and staggered into the road; the truck driver, Vincent Millar, saw her and screeched to a halt, convinced that he'd hit her. He got out to look around, then heard a small voice begging for help, and Lees stumbled into him. It wasn't until he moved her into the beam of his truck headlights that he got a good look at her – bound around both arms with heavy cable zip-ties, silver pipe tape around her neck and her feet scratched and bloodied from the spiny desert grass.

Lees frantically begged Millar to help her find her boy-friend, but when the truck driver saw the pool of blood – later identified as belonging to Falconio – by the roadside, and heard Lees's story of a gunman, he decided to take her to the Barrow Creek Roadhouse, where they could call the police. Joanne Lees's nightmare had only just begun.

When she arrived at the Roadhouse at around two in the morning, there were still a few people at the bar. Les Pilton, the owner, called the police in both Alice Springs and Tennant Creek, 180 miles north of Barrow Creek, and sat Joanne in front of a fire with a cup of tea.

Armed police in bulletproof vests arrived just after 5 a.m. Roadblocks were set up around the state, and the couple's Kombi van was soon found, abandoned 200 yards from where the attack had taken place. When police found the empty van, they warned Lees to expect the worst: Falconio was probably dead.

The day after the ambush, police asked Lees to return to Alice Springs for further questioning. It was intense, and began early every day; counselling for her bereavement wasn't offered until several days later. She received no legal advice and soon tired of the police asking the same questions over and over again. She also had a medical examination, although not for sexual assault; she hadn't been raped.

As if the police questions weren't bad enough, journalists from the world's media descended on Alice Springs *en masse*, all vying with each other to secure the scoop of an interview with the woman at the heart of the mystery. Lees was reportedly horrified at the large sums being offered by British tabloids and Australian TV channels, initially granting only one interview to the press, which was arranged by Pilton's girlfriend, Helen Jones. This was with a local newspaper, and was clearly a gruelling experience for Lees, who insisted that the most important thing was that the gunman should be stopped before he struck again.

As press speculation about Falconio's disappearance grew, the investigation foundered. During the first week of the manhunt 150 police searched the area, finding only Lees's sandals. Aboriginal trackers were then brought in, but found little beyond the police footprints.

An identikit picture of the suspect was circulated, along with a description of him as 'Caucasian, 40–45 years old with dark, shoulder-length hair with grey streaks, long thin face, droopy, grey moustache, medium build and an Australian accent'. As both the picture and the description matched a large number of itinerant workers in the area, many who sported the same look were picked up and questioned.

On 18 July Lees returned to Barrow Creek for a grim re-enactment of the ambush. She didn't appear in public for the next ten days, and while the police stated that they believed her story, which they'd found evidence to support, they refused to identify exactly what this evidence was, arguing that they needed to withhold some information to distinguish between genuine suspects and pathological attention-seekers who might confess falsely to the crime.

WHISPERS AND LIES

Rumour filled the void. Why hadn't Lees been seen for so long? Was she under house arrest? Had the couple had a bitter argument before leaving Alice Springs? Journalists speculated on the truthfulness of her story. Did she have a history of mental illness? Why hadn't the assailant's dog found her? On the face of it her story was barely credible: there was no body, no criminal, and an English girl had outwitted a bushman in his own territory. But the alternatives were no less unbelievable: if Lees had killed her boyfriend, how had she managed to dispose of the body? She would have had to have an accomplice to tie her up – why was there no evidence of this?

The rugged mystique of the outback was thought by some commentators to contribute to the welter of stories plugging the information gap. Les Pilton spoke to a British journalist about the outback: 'Life is in the raw here. You see death here. You can't expect a crime to be solved in a 30-minute TV show. Truth is always stranger than fiction.'

Lees was persuaded by Alice Springs police to hold a press conference to dispel the rumours; moreover, an emotional public appeal might jog some memories, or persuade those fearful of 'dobbing' someone in to speak up. It was not a success. Many wondered why it had taken her so long to appear publicly, and her demeanour during the conference – tearless and speaking with little emotion – was seen as inconsistent with what journalists expected from a grieving woman. Where were the tears? The anguish? Lees answered only three questions, all from one journalist and all regarding the press coverage of the case rather than the incident itself. Lees hit out at the press – although there had at this point been no explicit claims that she was a liar – stating that 'It is only the media that have questioned my story. Anyone that has spoken to me or been in contact with me, no one doubts me.'

Journalists sympathetic to Lees's case began to speak of her 'Lindification', referring to the similarities between her treatment and that of Lindy Chamberlain, the mother in the infamous 'dingo baby' case. In both cases a woman had been vilified for not displaying the 'appropriate' response to bereavement; in both cases nobody close to the women doubted their stories; and as both investigations progressed, with little new information appearing and an absence – the lack of a body – at their centres, journalists were encouraged by their editors to speculate, to fill the gap, as the public looked to them for answers.

The Northern Territory police did little to help Lees's case, bungling the handling of CCTV footage taken from the Alice Springs Shell truck stop on 22 July. The footage, taken just a few hours after the attack, shows a man and vehicle closely resembling Lees's description of her assailant; indeed, Lees told police that she believed this to be her attacker, and it was a crucial piece of evidence in support of her story. But the footage was not released publicly until three weeks later – it emerged that the police had made an analogue tape copy of the CCTV footage and sent this copy interstate to be digitally enhanced. In the meantime the original CCTV footage was lost.

Despite the discovery on Lees's clothes of DNA believed to belong to the gunman, the investigation grew ever more desperate. One theory rapidly followed another: that the gunman was a stalker obsessed with Lees, and had followed the couple from the Camel Cup; or that he was a fairground worker, travelling around Australia with country shows and races.

Police methodology became increasingly esoteric. Lees was hypnotised; a psychic was interviewed; and a water diviner claimed to sense that Falconio's body was at Renner Springs, 230 miles north of Barrow Creek, before complaining that a local farmer was blocking his psychic powers. The diviner then gave the police a lump of earth containing a blood-like substance, which they duly tested – to no avail. Nothing worked.

In mid-August Lees flew back to Sydney. The investigation appeared to be going nowhere. During the time that Lees had hidden in the bush, the gunman could easily have driven to another state to dispose of the body; and he would surely have gone to considerable lengths by now to change his appearance. Desperate for anonymity and a break from media and police interrogations, Lees returned to her job as a sales assistant at Dymocks bookshop in central Sydney, where she had worked for four months before setting off on the fateful trip.

But even in the bookshop she was routinely harassed by journalists and press photographers, as well as being approached by ghoulish autograph-hunters keen for a memento of the case. She grew increasingly despondent about the chances of Falconio ever being found alive, and returned to Britain in November, immediately going into hiding; she stayed with friends rather than her family, hoping that the press would not be able to track her down.

In January 2002 a team from Channel Four travelled to the Northern Territory to gather material for a documentary about the case. A company working for the British channel had approached Lees while she was still in Australia, hoping to interview her, but the request was turned down, along with all the others; they had hoped to interview her without offering money.

In February Lees accepted an offer of at least £30,000 from ITV to break her silence. She travelled to the Northern Territory to recreate the ambush for ITV1's *Tonight with Trevor McDonald*. Few who knew Lees have been critical of her decision, although her claim for compensation of around £18,000 from the Australian government was less well received.

PRIME SUSPECT

A year after Falconio's disappearance another tourist attack occurred, 700 miles from Barrow Creek and bearing striking similarities to the suspected murder. A German woman and her sixteen-year-old daughter, both from Nuremberg, were returning to their car at sunset after spending an afternoon swimming in the Litchfield National Park near Darwin, when they were approached by a man. He demanded money, and the mother gave him some – but that wasn't all he wanted. He led them into the bush at gunpoint, firing at least one warning shot to let them know he was serious, and hand-cuffed them to a tree. He then raped the daughter.

The women waited until he had left then struggled free, but only managed to find their way out of the park after another day had passed, when they flagged down a passing car. Police launched a manhunt. At first they didn't suspect the attacks to be related – this assailant was described as being larger and clean-shaven, with blond rather than dark hair and a beer belly – but the home-made handcuffs used in both attacks were very similar.

In August Bradley John Murdoch, a 44-year-old former farm handyman from Broome, Western Australia, was ar-rested in the South Australian town of Port Augusta on suspicion of having abducted the German women. When he was arrested, Northern Territory police realised that he looked a lot like the man described by Joanne Lees – and the man captured on the service station CCTV footage. They also realised that they had questioned him already, three months after Falconio's disappearance.

They requested a transfer of samples of genetic material from Murdoch, to be compared with a spot of blood found on Joanne Lees's shirt. South Australia police agreed, but Murdoch's lawyers appealed to have the transfer stopped. The appeal was overruled, and tests showed that the DNA matched – Murdoch was now the prime suspect in the Lees/Falconio case.

Northern Territory police are at the time of writing still building a case against Murdoch, who has to the dismay of the missing tourist's family said nothing about the Falconio case; they are anxious to recover his body. It may take some time before Murdoch faces trial over the suspected murder. He will probably stand trial in South Australia over charges relating to the abduction and rape of the German women first; if convicted, he could appeal against attempts to transfer him to the Northern Territory for a second trial until he has served his sentence – which would probably be around fifteen years.

DANGER DOWN UNDER

The Falconio case has sparked off at least one 'copycat' assault. On 25 March 2002 twenty-year-old Stephen Dixon attacked two tourists, a British man and an American woman, on the Stuart Highway, 70 kilometres south of Alice Springs, after they stopped to pick up a hitch-hiker.

Such cases are not isolated incidents in a country recently voted 'second safest in the world for tourists'. The past few years have seen a series of axe assaults on tourists in the Kings Cross region of Sydney, one of which resulted in the victim's death; the torching of a backpacker hostel in Childers, Queensland, in which fifteen people died; and the murder of a nineteen-year-old British backpacker, who was thrown to her death from a bridge in Bundaberg, near Brisbane.

Not everyone fits into the Brand Australia vision of a safe wilderness populated by bland suburbanites and folksy crocodile hunters. The country's reputation as a safe location, the easy option for those who want southern heat without the attendant risks, is in danger of being transformed into something quite different. As Australian tourism becomes ever glossier and more mediated, as the authentic experience is packed ever tighter into brochures and whirlwind tours, so the dark side of the Australian experience has grown.

8. LOVE YOU LONG TIME

SEX TOURISM IN THE DEVELOPING WORLD

Travel and sex. The intimate link between the two is assured, whether from our sexual vocabulary – comprising wandering hands and roving eyes, exploring, entering, coming, and going all the way – or from the technology enabling physical travel itself. Freud's comment on the 'compulsive link . . . between railway-travel and sexuality' reminds us of the erotic charge of travel, as providing both a site for sexual encounters – Erica Jong's 'zipless fuck' on a speeding train – and a facilitator of them. Much as the car, especially in 1950s USA, has allowed generations of teenagers an easy access to the privacy their parents had rarely known, so too modern jet travel provides the potential for a new realm of sexual experimentation.

The association has always been there. There are biological reasons for this – the genetic weaknesses resulting from an insular community have long led people to travel seeking mates – but the cultural reasons have traditionally seemed more important. Medieval diarists point to the sexual freedom encouraged by travel, and Chaucer's *Canterbury Tales* makes no mistake in depicting the Wife of Bath, the most experienced pilgrim of the group, as also the most sexually knowledgeable.

As we've mentioned earlier, contemporary tourism can be seen to have its roots in the 'Grand Tour', the popularity of which peaked in the eighteenth century. This became a cultural institution among the British aristocracy, whereby young men could travel around the Continent for a few years, educating themselves in the ways of the world. The ostensible purpose for such travel was given in *The Grand Tour*, Thomas Nugent's popular guidebook, published in 1749, as: '. . . to enrich the mind with knowledge, to rectify the judgement, to remove the prejudices of education, to compose the outward manners, and in a word to form the complete gentleman'.

But it was soon apparent that moral improvement was not a priority for many young travellers who, according to polemics of the day, were soon 'immers'd in all manner of Lewdness and Debauchery'. Those 'Grand Tourists' who kept frank diaries of their travels reinforce this view. Boswell, for example, described in his journals the permissive mores of other countries as a prime motivator for travel, arguing – much like the modern sex tourist – that foreign sexual mores both encouraged and justified the sampling of sexual product. When in Rome, he argued: 'I remembered the rakish deeds of Horace and other amorous Roman poets, and I thought that one might allow one's self indulgence in a city where there are prostitutes licensed by the Cardinal Vicar.'

Of all European countries of the time, Italy had the most iniquitous reputation, with the diarist revealing that 'My desire to know the world made me resolve to intrigue a little while in Italy, where the women are so debauched that they are hardly to be considered as moral agents, but as inferior beings.' Venice was estimated as possessing 20,000 courtesans in the early seventeenth century, leading to it being described as 'the best flesh-shambles in Italy' in an early guidebook.

Guidebooks to the prostitutes of a city or country were popular in the eighteenth century, with titles such as the *Filles du Palais Royale*, a frequently updated directory of Parisian whores which was intended for tourists, or Harris's *List of Covent Garden Ladies, or Men of Pleasure's Kalender*, which was updated annually between 1760 and 1793, and gave invaluable advice on where to find 'fine, bouncing, crummy wenches'; the tradition endures today, with contemporary information for the sex tourist ranging from glossy printed brochures or online guides devoted to providing up-to-the-minute information on prostitutes from Mayfair to Mombasa.

Other tour guides of the day revealed that the sexual enthusiasm of young Englishmen on the Continent often made them ripe targets for criminal predators, providing the basis for a fear of rip-offs and 'clip joints' that has never gone away.

But most tourists would feel, with their money and privilege, that they were in control – that they could dictate the terms of sexual contact. The amoral gaze, or sense of foreign society as spectacle, described in the second chapter, combined with economic power and sexual curiosity in some to encourage an element of sadism.

The narrator of the Victorian erotic novel *My Secret Life* described his experiences of Paris: '. . . where I ran a course of baudy house amusements, saw a big dog fuck a woman who turned her rump to it as if she were a bitch'; while Evelyn Waugh, also in Paris, attempted to arrange his own entertainment, as described in *Remote People*:

> . . . by which my boy should be enjoyed by a large negro who was there but at the last moment, after we had ascended to a squalid divan at the top of the house and he was lying waiting for the negro's advances, the price proved prohibitive . . .

The association of foreign countries with a degree of sexual freedom unavailable at home goes back to ancient Greek and Latin accounts of sexualised savages, which even then consisted of ideas of 'uncivilised' behaviour projected on to a 'barbaric' people. Later, the Enlightenment binary of nature and culture ensured that there was a strong demand in Europe for travelogues depicting the shocking yet titillating sexual liberty of 'primitive' or Oriental peoples.

Bougainville's Tahitian *Voyage* of 1771 was one of the most popular, partly because it explicitly described the 'native' female desire for the European male, an idea which was so well received that it endured long after the book was forgotten. Those taken with the idea at the time, actual travel to Tahiti being out of the question, had to make do with the tableaux based on Bougainville's descriptions offered in brothels in Paris and London.

This sexualisation of the exotic, primitive 'other' led in time to the image of the harem, associated with the Orient in general and Thailand in particular, with tales of the revered King Rama IV's 104 wives establishing the basis for the West's eventual interest in the country as a sex tourism destination. As European civilisation progressed, so too did the restraints on sexual freedom grow stronger; Freud's assertion that civilisation is paid for by the repression and sublimation of the sexual urge was amply supported by the sexual mores of nineteenth-century Europe in general, and Victorian England in particular. If sexual restraint was equated with civilisation, then sexual abandon was equated with primitivism or savagery: sexual vitality was racially determined. 'The primitive woman ... was always a prostitute,' wrote Cesare Lombroso in 1896, following a well-established pattern linking prostitutes – and sexual freedom – with primitives; fifty years before, Alphonse Esquiros's assertion that 'the black woman is naturally a prostitute' was taken as statement of fact rather than cause for controversy.

Naturally the idea of sexual abandon – the lure of the primitive – appealed to many, especially those who felt a growing distaste for the effects of industrialisation. Some Europeans indulged the appeal through a celebration of the wildness of nature, especially the untamed Mediterranean coast; others dreamed of a remote paradise island in the South Seas, where dusky maidens might attend their every whim. The tale of Gaugin, the French painter who left his stuffy European world behind to live in bliss in the South Seas, casts a long shadow over modern tourism, although 'primitive' beach huts now often come with air-conditioning and modern plumbing. The reality of Gaugin's retreat is rather less endearing than the legend, with the syphilitic Frenchman having to pay girls more and more money to ignore his running sores.

The tropes endure today. Many tourist destinations, and the women who inhabit them, are aligned with nature, receptivity and sexual allure. Whole countries are libidinised, with Thailand and the Philippines, among others, constructed as feminine in relation to Western nations: their landscape and people are there to be explored and penetrated, both literally – by tourists – and figuratively – by Western economies. Both scenery and women are primitive, exotic, mysterious, passively waiting for the foreign visitor to arrive.

'Prostitution', many tourists feel, does not exist in these nations as it does in the West. One sex tourist guide published in 1994, *Travel and the Single Male*, argues that Caribbean women are never prostitutes but rather 'nice' girls who want to have a good time. For many used to cold, mechanised encounters with prostitutes in their own countries, the warmth and naturalness they perceive with a prostitute in Thailand or the Dominican Republic confirms their assumptions about sexual contact being easier, more natural, in these countries. For some tourists the supposed naturalness of prostitution in the developing world even reassures them of their own racial and cultural superiority.

Guidebooks and advertisements for charter airlines and tour operators have been known to play on this equation of exotic other with sexual allure. Switzerland's Life Travel boasted of Thai girls that 'Slim, sunburnt and sweet, they love the white man in an erotic and devoted way. They are master of the art of making love by nature, an art that we Europeans do not know'; and an advertisement for a Frankfurt-based tour company stated that 'Asian women are without desire for emancipation, but full of warm sensuality and the softness of velvet.'

Without desire for emancipation. For many sex tourists this issue is key. Western women are seen as having usurped traditional male roles, and as having become both sexless and overbearing in the process; they are social, legal and economic equals, and are in a position to control themselves, to exercise choice over whether or not to meet a man's demands. Thai women are 'real' women because they are submissive. The prostitutes' malleability and apparent subservience, resulting principally from a lack of economic equality with their client, are recast in the tourist's mind as indicative of 'true' femininity, untainted by Western feminism, which is in turn usually conflated with individual subjectivity and assertiveness. A sexual relationship with a Thai woman – or a woman from many other developing world countries – re-establishes the natural order of things. This sense is reinforced for many Caucasian tourists by the way in which people of colour here serve them; they are not equals but rather subservient.

The dominance the tourist wants to express, for which he believes he may be censured at home, is here vindicated by local culture – acting in accordance with another country's cultural customs just happens to satisfy his own deepest desires. The videos of Dexter-Horn Productions, such as *The Erotic Women of Thailand* (1997), play on this vindication of masculinity abroad, explicitly appealing to men who are disillusioned with 'demanding, liberated North American women'. Even when Thai women write to tourists to ask for money, usually ostensibly to help an ill family member, this too can be construed as fitting the dynamic: the women are reliant on the Western tourists, a further indication of their submission.

This sense of returning to the proper order of things – where men are men and women are women, with a clear power differential at play – reminds us of an earlier age in European history. As anthropologist Claude Lévi-Strauss remarked, albeit in another context, 'The tropics are not so much exotic as out of date'; sex tourists buy the sexual privilege of a former age. In this sense the sex workers of the developing world replace the working-class women – servants, farm girls etc. – used for sex by well-heeled Victorians.

For most critics, this will be a clear example of male inadequacy – some modern men simply cannot cope with the emancipated modern Western woman. Others might argue: why should they? As the narrator of Michel Houllebecq's *Platform*, a rare literary voice in support of sex tourism, puts it:

Offering your body as an object of pleasure, giving pleasure unselfishly: that's what Westerners don't know how to do any more. They've completely lost the sense of giving. Try as they might, they no longer feel sex as something natural. Not only are they ashamed of their own bodies, which aren't up to porn standards, but for the same reasons they no longer feel truly attracted to the body of the other. It's impossible to make love without a certain abandon, without accepting, at least temporarily, the state of being in a state of dependency, of weakness. Sentimental adulation and sexual obsession have the same roots, both proceed from some degree of selflessness;

it's not a domain in which you can find fulfilment without losing yourself. We have become cold, rational, acutely conscious of our individual existence and our rights; more than anything, we want to avoid alienation and dependence; on top of that we're obsessed with health and hygiene: these are hardly ideal conditions in which to make love. The way things stand, the commercialisation of sexuality in the East has become inevitable.

Extract from *Platform*, by Michel Houellebecq, published by Heinemann. Used by permission of The Random House Group Ltd.

Many critics of sex tourism point out that prostitutes are commoditised, treated solely as objects, an argument which the behaviour of some sex tourists supports. American marines, for instance, refer to Filipino prostitutes as LBFMs – Little Brown Fucking Machines – and the view of the following German tourist in Thailand is not uncommon: 'My best time was being with a squad of deaf and dumb hookers who were really nice because they never got on your nerves with silly talk.'

Some sectors of the European tourist industry offering trips to Thailand have helped to encourage such a view. The German charter flight company Lauda Airlines promoted its services and destinations with a mock postcard depicting a topless young woman and a heart-shaped inscription – 'From Thailand With Love'. On the flipside the reader was told, 'Got to close now. The tarts in the Bangkok Baby Club are waiting for us'; the card was signed: 'Werner, Gunther, Fritzl, Moisel, and Joe'.

The way prostitutes are presented in some parts of the developing world helps to de-individualise and objectify them still further. Bangkok's live sex shows, demonstrating little but the pliability and functional range of a vagina, reinforce the idea of the girls as nothing but sex organs; the similar costumes worn in Bangkok go-go bars and brothels, the size of the girls and the length of their hair, all go to give a sense of a mass-produced, standardised commodity. That the girls are usually numbered, their eyes sometimes glazed over by heroin or amphetamines, further reduces their status as individual subjects. Such girls, sex with whom presents no danger of intimacy, will appeal to those tourists who abhor any whiff of emotion or dependency. That such objectification is common is clear from the obsession with price, and an attendant determination not to get ripped off, visible both in printed guidebooks and online sex guides.

Some tourists objectify locals in a different way, and will have sex with them in a conscious effort to get as close as possible to the host culture. This is often the case with young Caucasian visitors to the Caribbean or sub-Saharan Africa, who regard black culture as 'cool' but find black people in their own countries surly and stand-offish; here local poverty combined with the exigencies of tourist development ensure that they are surrounded by smiling, welcoming and sexually available black people.

What is penetrated or enveloped here is not an individual but a culture: the photographer Mirella Ricciardi, writing in the *Telegraph Magazine* (21 October 2000) of her affair with a black fisherman in Africa, claimed that 'At one with him, I was at one with Africa'. Nor is this urge for cultural immersion through sex confined to tourists from the developed world. One young Sudanese man commented of his experiences in Britain that 'One thing I noticed was that you can never understand a people well enough . . . until you are in bed with a woman.'

But for some this focus on sex as conferring or denoting authenticity, a truth about a people, derives from an obsession with sex that is, if not peculiarly Western, at least not shared throughout the world. Alaistair, a 50-year-old Australian, made the following points during an interview about sex tourism in Thailand:

In the end, you are not there as a person. You're just another shadow in their lives, one that coughs up the money. It is as though you do not reach them at all. What they are doing, they are doing with their bodies; certainly not their heart,

certainly not their mind and not their spirit. This means you
are involved with only a fraction of their being. I think there
is something about them that is inviolable; and that is why
they don't mind doing sex. It doesn't compromise the core of
them. They have a kind of purity, which I think only drives
Westerners more crazy because we can't understand it. I
think for us, sex has become the essence of life. That is a
Western error and we project it on to everybody else in the
world: if it's sex, it must be authentic; and that is not
necessarily true of sex in Thailand.

Projection – that's the secret of it. We see what we want to;
but we are not coming anywhere close to the reality of Thai
women; and that is both stimulating and, ultimately,
frustrating.

Many tourists, however, come to places like Thailand or the
Dominican Republic looking for love. A brothel may seem an
unlikely place to find it, but the tart with a heart is an
enduring image in Western culture – from Henry Miller's
Paris to Graham Greene's South America. Disillusioned by
relationships at home, these tourists may feel they have more
to offer a woman from a less affluent culture; and for all that
they may project racially determined fantasies on to the
women they meet, they also bring with them their culture's
norm of respect for the individual. Many will deny that what
they are indulging in is prostitution at all – they give gifts to
their girlfriend, as opposed to paying a stranger for sex – and
the girls play along, maintaining the tourist's sense of
reciprocity. Many keep a photographic record of past clients
with names and essential information, to ensure the satisfaction of a repeat customer.

Some see this as a projection of the fantasy of a relationship, a fantasy in which both tourists and sex workers play
their roles, on to what is a purely mercenary exchange. The
go-go bars, theatres designed specifically for the performance
of these roles, are simulacra, much like Disneyland – copies
of something for which no original exists. This is just one
example of the way tourist enclaves tend to fulfil tourist

fantasies rather than depicting any 'authentic', indigenous culture; unsurprisingly insofar as all brochures and marketing material concerning them are created in the West, rather than in the host countries. Travel guidebooks and tourist brochures are less about the cultures described than they are about the cultures that produce them. What is visited in most modern tourism is the Western idea of a country and its culture.

And yet some Western men claim to have made extremely successful matches in such environments. The working life of a bar girl is short – few find sex work in their thirties – and not all girls can become a madam, one of the few ways they can move within the industry; some *farangs* (foreigners) in Thailand maintain that they have met ex-bar girls in their thirties who have proved ideal partners.

But some tourists, who fear the kind of economic trap described in 'The Naked Eye', in which they are persuaded to invest in property which is then taken away from them, try to apply strict conditions to any longer-term relationships. The following comes from a letter written by an American to his prospective Thai wife:

> *You will do as I say and obey me. I do not want to take care of all your family. If you accept my conditions, you will have a nice house and a car and a good life. Send me some pictures of yourself, sexy ones, also some sexy pix of your sister.*

And some sex tourists marry Thai women who are then taken to Europe, Canada or the USA and put to work as prostitutes on the streets there.

If and when what seemed to the tourist like an ideal, loving relationship deteriorates – with repeated requests for money, with the realisation that he is expected to support a wider range of people – then the stereotype of the sensual Oriental is replaced by another, that of the scheming whore. The tourist – who has flown, perhaps, from Europe or the USA to take advantage of poor women's sexual availability – sees himself as a victim; he has been cheated.

We'll return to the broader issues of sex tourism – its ethics in the wider context of tourism and global development – later in the chapter, but before that we'll look at some distinct areas within sex tourism. Gay and lesbian sex tourism is conspicuous here by its absence; this is not because it does not exist – Egypt is well known as a popular destination for gay male sex tourists – but rather partly because of lack of space and partly because of lack of adequate research material.

Next will be a detailed look at sex tourism in Thailand, probably the world's most popular sex tourism destination; this will be followed by an overview of the hidden world of female sex tourists – and a focus on the depravities inflicted by jet-setting paedophiles.

ONE NIGHT IN BANGKOK

The following extract is taken from www.wsgforum.com:

Plan to go [to Bangkok's massage parlours] at 7 or 8 pm. Later, and the prettiest and most skilled girls are occupied. Earlier, and they haven't yet arrived. Closing time is universally 11 pm.

What happens when you go in? You'll find yourself with others like you, foreign and Thai, in a large, dimly-lit waiting area facing several plate-glass windows (one-way in some places), behind which sit, in ranks, up to 100 or more girls. They're in the establishment's uniform, usually a diaphanous thing, and all have a number pinned near their shoulder. They watch television, gossip, knit, read, or simply gaze. Very rarely, one will attempt to catch your eye.

You will immediately be approached by one of several 'managers', who will ask which girl you want. Don't allow yourself to be rushed; selection is part of the experience. Tell him you're in no hurry, and ask where you can get a beer (generally at a bar off the waiting room). Sit down or walk around, look at the girls, let your fantasies build, and RELAX. This can be intimidating the first time, and tension will detract from the experience.

If you have something specific in mind – anything at all that you can imagine – flag down a manager and tell him *exactly* what you want (a tiny bit awkward when the manager, as is sometimes the case, is a manageress). If you want the best blow job in the world, say so: he'll tell you which girls specialize in the field. If you want anal, say so. If you want to watch two or three girls making love to each other and then join in, say so. Be specific and graphic: they've heard it all before, and will steer you toward the right girl(s). Unlike the Patpong bars, here they're interested in the repeat business that customer satisfaction brings.

When you've settled on a girl or girls, it's time to talk price. The price per girl is usually around US$75, for two hours, though standard procedure is for them to hit you up for a nice, round $100. Bargaining is okay, but not to extremes. After all, if you're happy, $100 is not bad; and if you're not, $10 is too much. When you eventually agree to a price, do so reluctantly, and add that for that price you expect a VIP room. He'll know what you mean (even if you don't). VIP rooms are generally bigger than others, and often heavily mirrored.

The manager will call the girl(s) out through a microphone, and escort you to the cashier, where you'll pay up front and meet the girl. They all take credit cards, by the way. The cashier hands the room key to the girl, who will often remain silent until you address her. Smile, tell her your name, and try to refrain from asking particularly stupid questions out of nervousness.

She'll take you to the elevator, then to the room. You'll probably pass other men, with their particular fantasy-fulfillers, on their way in or out, who will usually not want to make eye contact. Your lady will pause to tell a floor worker the room number. Once in the room, she'll start water running in the tub, and ask what you want to drink. Say you want a beer, even if you don't, and get a drink for her.

In a moment the floor worker will knock and enter with a basket of oil, powder, soap, and some towels, and will take the drink order. Tip her well – she lives off your tips and those that the girl leaves when you vacate the room.

You'll start off with a bath and a body massage. The bath is self-explanatory; it also gives the girl a chance to check you out for visible sores or other indications that you might be her particular angel of death. You, unfortunately, proceed on faith. The body massage is done on a soaped air mattress next to the tub, and I'll leave its pleasures to you to discover. Later you'll dry off, move to the bed, and do whatever it was you paid to do. It's all very leisurely; you've got two hours to play.

Prostitution in Thailand is not a new phenomenon, and derives in part from Thai attitudes to men and women. The prevailing belief in Thai society is that men are naturally promiscuous and need sex, but that good women (normally meaning the better off) remain virgins until marriage. Prostitution traditionally satisfied this asymmetrical arrangement, allowing men to have sex and higher-class women to remain virtuous.

There is also a long history in Thailand (formerly Siam) of the objectification of women, with them being given as rewards for military achievement in the Ayutthaya period; until the twentieth century men could legally sell or give away their wives and daughters. Even now, with equal rights granted in 1974, polygamy is still rife – partly due to the country's low ratio of men to women – and laws concerning relationships, such as divorce laws, tend heavily to favour men.

Buddhist doctrine is said to favour this treatment of women, as to be born a woman is the result of imperfect karma; among other practices leading to such an inauspicious rebirth is sexual misconduct, and women are seen as a corrupting influence on otherwise virtuous men. The *dhamma* (moral principles) of Buddhism moreover expressly relate that it is the duty of children to support their parents, to work for the betterment of the family both financially and in terms of spiritual merit. This is easy for sons, who can simply become monks to ensure their parents' spiritual redemption; daughters have no such opportunity, and the sight of go-go girls making offerings at Buddhist shrines is common.

The industrialisation of prostitution, which reached its peak during the Vietnam War, began in the nineteenth century with the expansion of the rice export economy and the influx of male Chinese migrant workers. The ranks of available women swelled with the abolition of slavery in 1905, as many freed women had no means of subsistence outside prostitution.

The realities of Thai gender relations mixed with a correlation of the exotic with the erotic in the eyes of many in the West to distinguish Thailand as a sexual Shangri-La. Dutch traders returned to Europe with reports of Thai prostitution as early as 1604, but the idea of abundant, sexually pliant Thai women only became a European cultural archetype with the nineteenth-century popularity of harem tales such as Anna Leonowens's *The Romance of the Harem* (1891).

Leonowens's story, which percolated down into the musical *The King and I*, defined a Siam full of exotic, submissive women readily available to men in an atmosphere of sexual *laissez-faire*; although ostensibly an anti-slavery tract it played up the appeal of a sexualised Orient as one both popular with European audiences and one confirming what they already suspected.

The idea endured, helped by magazine features in Europe and the USA during the 1950s describing Thai women's beauty, the cheapness of the country and the socially sanctioned male polygamy, and novels such as Jack Reynolds's *A Woman of Bangkok* (1956), which contrasted a sexually repressed England with a liberated Thailand, to which the protagonist escapes after a disastrous relationship at home.

More recent examples include *Miss Saigon* and the Lloyd-Webber musical *Chess*, featuring Murray Head's song 'One Night in Bangkok', which replaced the Eagles' 'Hotel California' for a few years as the Thai bar anthem. By the 1970s Bangkok's reputation as a locus for sexual freedom and abundance meant that even the popular softcore icon *Emmanuelle* visited.

It was perhaps these ideas, along with the West-friendly Thai government's fervent pursuit of development which began in the 1950s – a military government slogan of the day was 'Work is money, money is happiness' – that persuaded the American government to arrange for Thailand to host 'rest and relaxation' (R&R) facilities for its servicemen stationed in the area during the Vietnam War. The arrangement proved as economically crucial for Thailand – by 1970 spending by US military personnel in the country exceeded twenty million dollars – as the functions served were crucial for the military. Commentators have pointed out that a sexualised 'R&R' period makes it far easier for the US military to send young men on long sea journeys and for protracted stays overseas; and that perhaps the idea of Asian women's compliant sexuality helps the soldiers maintain the sense of themselves as masculine enough to fight.

'R&R' arrangements in Thailand, along with similar set-ups for US military bases in countries such as the Philippines and South Korea, provided the basis for contemporary sex tourism: first, by maintaining and reinforcing indigenous gender relationships; second, by increasing the market value of sexual access to women by commodifying local women for foreign pleasure; and third, by creating economic structures and dependencies which would be filled by tourism in the wake of the military.

After the Vietnam War, as US servicemen pulled out of the area, early tourist development sought to capitalise on the accommodation and entertainment facilities which had been established for the military. In some countries this was done with the express intent of the government. The authoritarian governments of South Korea, from the 1970s to the late 1980s, not only encouraged but institutionalised *kisaeng* (prostitute) tourism. Prospective *kisaeng* were obliged to attend lectures given by university professors on the crucial role of tourism in the South Korean economy before being awarded licences for prostitution.

At the government 'orientation programmes' for *kisaeng* they were told that 'Your carnal conversations with foreign tourists do not prostitute either yourself or the nation, but express your heroic patriotism.' The South Korean Minister for Education during the early 1970s took it further: 'The sincerity of girls who have contributed with their cunts to their fatherland's economic development is indeed praiseworthy.'

But the promotion of sex tourism in Thailand after the Vietnam War stemmed not only from the country's government. In the early 1970s Indochina was politically unstable, and it was in the interests of the USA to bolster Thailand's economy, as the country was a friend both to US anti-Communist efforts and a more general drive for US-style development of the region. But without the US military personnel using the structures set up during the 'R&R' wartime period, which had provided a massive boost to the Thai economy, the country was in trouble.

In 1971 Robert McNamara, head of the World Bank, visited Bangkok and initiated a series of meetings whereby tourism was identified as a key component of the Thai economy – and not just any kind of tourism. With the cost of airfares at the time, families were unlikely to travel to Thailand; and if the single traveller with disposable income were targeted, then the 'R&R' structures already in place could continue to generate wealth. Given that McNamara had in 1967 been the US Secretary of Defence who oversaw the 'R&R' contracts, it's not difficult to believe that the World Bank and the Thai government agreed upon a cynical policy whereby it was inevitable that sex tourism would develop as the key sector of the industry.

In 1980 Booncha Rajanasthian, Thailand's Vice Premier, asked all provincial governments 'to consider . . . forms of entertainment that some of you might consider disgusting and shameful, because we have to consider the jobs that will be created'. Some critics maintain further that conditions of rural poverty were deliberately exacerbated – by weakening traditional patterns of land ownership, logging, manipulating water and irrigation policies, and by loaning money to subsistence farmers to encourage them to grow cash crops unsuited to the north-east's soil – to ensure a ready supply of young women from the rural north (which comprises over 80 per cent of the population) to supply the sex industry.

Traditional structures of culture and community have been further broken down by a drive to development which says that anything tending towards industrialisation and techno-logical achievement is good, and anything tending towards the archaic and traditional is bad – except where it can be reconstructed as tourist spectacle. The widespread availability of TV and popularity of soap operas among Bangkok's go-go girls and dancers will encourage them to embrace the ideas of wealth and power through economic progress and develop-ment commonly expressed through the medium.

The head of the Tourist Authority of Thailand (TAT) acknowledged the connection between tourism and prostitu-tion in 1976, but claimed that 'prostitution exists mainly because of the state of our economy, because everyone needs to earn their income. If we can create jobs, we can provide per capita income and do away with prostitution.' Yet it's difficult to see how an economic growth deriving from prostitution would eventually do away with prostitution; and most tourism in Thailand, which has provided the country's single largest source of foreign income, has traditionally been sex tourism – the vast majority of visitors are single men.

But if the head of the TAT could admit to a link between prostitution and tourism in the 1970s, his was a lone voice. A leading policeman during the 1980s asserted that there were no brothels in Thailand, an official denial stemming from the fact that prostitution is illegal in the country under the Prostitution Suppression Act of 1960, and the culture of official denial and unofficial encouragement – including the TAT use in brochures of images of Thai women in the kinds of string bikinis most Thai women would never wear – typified a kind of institutional mendacity that many Western tourists saw as giving them licence to do as they pleased.

It is not only sex tourism in which words and reality are at odds in Thailand; the same is true of pollution and working conditions. Issues are tackled by words, if at all, rather than action, and a wide space is provided by corruption on one hand and permissiveness on the part of authority on the other, as long as that authority is not challenged.

Things began to change in the early 1990s, with 1992 seeing a Women Visit Thailand Year, but it wasn't until 1995 that the Chuan administration admitted that prostitution was a serious national problem, and that steps would be taken to eradicate child prostitution. International pressure over child sex tourism, paired with fears about AIDS and its impact on tourism, and the murder of a young prostitute which made the national news during Chuan's term of office, all led to the abandonment of the policy of official denial.

And if the promotion of sex tourism seemed like a good idea in the 1970s, it doesn't any more. The Thai government realises that the country's image as a family destination for cultural tourism is tarnished by its association with sex tourism, and is alarmed by the growing number of visitors to nearby Malaysia and Singapore. But even new laws passed recently to suppress prostitution have had little effect on the Thai tourist industry – sex sells, and most people involved in the trade want to keep it that way.

It is impossible to establish how many women work in the sex trade in Thailand – official figures are unreliable, and other extrapolations vary wildly. Sex tourism accounts for a tiny portion of Thai prostitution, however, even while its visibility and the wealth associated with it help to legitimise local prostitution. The women who work in the tourist bars are at the higher end of the prostitute scale, as many are relatively free agents; in local brothels, by contrast, women are often chained to beds, and the Thai newspapers occasionally run chilling stories of charred skeletons still shackled to bed frames in fire-gutted buildings. Some women are bonded into prostitution – sold by their families to pimps or other organisations, a debt they are never able to pay off – and others are trafficked like cattle, the demands of the local industry seeing fresh women brought from hill tribespeople in Burma. Many of these women are sold into sex slavery and trafficked around the globe; but although such practices may be implicitly encouraged by sex tourism, most sex tourists neither know about nor intersect with them.

Who are the sex tourists? In terms of buying power the Japanese are the most important nationality, with North Americans, Western Europeans and the Australians following. Perhaps surprisingly, there has also traditionally been a contingent of tourists from the Middle East, Muslims keen to sample the fleshly delights proscribed at home. Some establishments, seeking to avoid blame for such religious infractions, post signs by their doors: 'We respect your religion. No Muslims allowed.' Their concern is not without foundation: Western residents of and visitors to Pattaya and Patpong, the country's most popular destinations for sex tourists, were recently asked to leave their names with their country's embassies, and were warned that rumours of a possible terrorist attack had been circulating. In the wake of the Bali nightclub bomb in October 2002, such an eventuality does not seem impossible.

The stereotype of the male sex tourist is that he is in his forties or fifties, often retired or recently divorced, and unattractive, whether through facial unsightliness or rank obesity. While some may well fit this description, the numbers of young sex tourists lacking such obvious hurdles in meeting partners at home shows that this is far from the whole story. Many simply seek relationships which are less complicated than those on offer in Europe or North America; and some may agree with Robert, one of the characters of Houllebecq's *Platform*, when he states categorically that you won't find a Western woman with a supple, muscular pussy any more.

Such a view is shared by some of the Thai sex workers too; when asked by a researcher why she thought Western men found her so attractive, one Bangkok bar girl revealed her assumptions about Western women: 'After married get fat', and 'have skin like frog ... hole is very big'. One correspondent assures me, however, that 'the Thai women have an "impish" sense of humour, and like twitting earnest interviewers. They frankly don't care why we like them, as long as the cash flows.'

Quite apart from vaginal dexterity, youth and availability, however, there is one trick used by Thai sex workers which rarely fails. It is to flatter the foreign tourist by homing in on his least physically attractive characteristic – where women in other countries might choose to avoid, not to look at, a bulging paunch or crooked nose, a Thai woman will say that she loves this, the most vulnerable part of a man, most.

Flattery is indulged in other ways too; many sex workers will tell Westerners that they are more generous, and better endowed, than the Thai men, and more gentle than the Japanese, about whom darkly sadistic stories circulate. Whatever the truth of these – the latter stories are often reiterated by Western tourists as justification of their own behaviour – they work: most sex tourists visiting Thailand return again and again, bewitched by the kingdom's most lucrative attraction.

GIRLS, CAN WE INTEREST YOU IN A PACKAGE HOLIDAY?

If I am going to walk down the road with a white woman then she must give me money. If I walk, I wear off some of my shoe's bottom. She must give me money to buy me a new pair of shoes.

Jamaican 'rent a dread'

Sex tourism as sleazy exploitation, sending a shudder down liberal spines, is a man's province. Women who travel to East Africa or the Caribbean to have sex with beach boys are considered 'romance' tourists; the exploitation and objectification indulged in by male sex tourists is here seen to be missing. There are a number of reasons for this. Male sex workers, whether working in pornographic movies or as gigolos, are rarely asked if they enjoy their work, or if they feel exploited; it is assumed that men are biologically hardwired to enjoy sex. Women, so the popular belief has it, are sexually passive and receptive; men, by contrast, are naturally indiscriminate and sexually voracious. The physical practicalities of the sex act, moreover, ensure that a man cannot be exploited sexually by a woman: he must be aroused for penetrative sex to take place, and then it is he who penetrates, who 'uses', the woman.

Male sex workers, whatever their relationship to their clients in terms of age, economic power or race, are thus believed to derive benefits from sex beyond the merely pecuniary – they want to have sex, especially if, as is often the case with beach boys, they are constructed in the client's mind as being highly potent sexually. The beach boys usually initiate proceedings, and the women often feel that they have been swept off their feet; and the system whereby beach boys are 'paid' in gifts and treats further confirms that this is a mutually beneficial, romantic relationship with nothing to do with prostitution.

The cultural references in the West to women who seek sex with locals on holiday reinforce this view of 'romance' tourism. In the film *Shirley Valentine* (1989) a middle-aged British woman locked in a dull marriage and life of domestic drudgery leaps at the opportunity to go on holiday without her husband to a Greek island. There she has a brief affair with the owner of a taverna, after which she is restored to her original, independent self; when the taverna owner quickly latches on to another holidaymaker Shirley does not mind – she is already liberated, and at the end of the film stays behind rather than returning to the UK. For her, sex on holiday has been an experience of emancipation, an expression of independence.

Independence is key here: single women travelling alone can test out ideas about liberated femininity, and can explore practices traditionally reserved for men. But just as male sex tourists project ideas about 'real' femininity on to bar girls in Thailand and the Dominican Republic, so too do female sex tourists project ideas about 'real' masculinity on to beach boys in Barbados or the Gambia.

Most female sex tourism involves white women seeking black men; such men will, for the women, represent a primitive masculine potency unavailable (or at least difficult to explore) at home. The techniques employed by beach boys and 'rent a dreads' demonstrate that they are aware of the role they are expected to fulfil and do their best to live up to it, marketing themselves along clearly defined lines: 'authentic' blackness will be signified by skin colour, dreadlocked hair and dance style; 'natural' passion and potency will be signified by singing softly in a tourist's ear during a slow dance and wearing tight-fitting beach shorts to show off their well-endowed proportions.

For the tourist, that she is publicly able to 'tame' this raw, highly sexed 'other' speaks volumes about her potent femininity – she is desired by a desirable man; she is a 'real' woman because she is desired by a 'real' man. This reassurance is especially keenly felt by some of the women targeted by the Caribbean beach boys: women who are not tanned (implying that they are recent arrivals) and who are perhaps a little overweight, so that they might not often attract men at home and will therefore be more susceptible to their charms. Some commentators have felt that these sex tourists are enacting a revenge on the white men at home who ignore them, by engaging sexually with the 'competition'; but such an idea is unconvincing considering that, like many male sex tourists, many female sex tourists are not unattractive.

For them the appeal seems more to do with control, with an affirmation of Western privilege; and with the ability to explore sexual practices unavailable at home, for whatever reason – from interracial sex to having many partners. Both the black men and the white women are aware of their stereotypes, and live up to them – whether the hypersexed, primitive black man or the promiscuous white woman who loves to suck cock. For some the stereotypes may ring true; female sex tourists characteristically refer to Caribbean men's lack of hang-ups about sex, their virility, their sense of fun. Perhaps, as Oscar Wilde once wrote, 'it is only shallow people who do not judge by appearances'.

Occasionally a relationship develops, and the women either stay at the holiday destination or bring the lover back to their home country. The former sometimes works well, with the establishment of stable, enduring relationships. In 1994 the *Sun* ran a series of features on British women who had set up home with Gambian men after meeting them on holiday, glossing one photo with the caption 'It's like a mix of *Shirley Valentine* and *Out of Africa* ... with more romance' and describing one woman as 'doing a Shirley-Valentine runner into the arms of a Gambian lover'. For both male and female sex tourists, evidently, true love can be found.

But taking the exotic partner back home often proves more problematic. For many beach boys, living in the north is too cold and restrictive; and the women are often surprised when their new husbands continue to conform to the stereotypes that had attracted them in the first place, expressing their primitive and potent sexuality through promiscuous behaviour. For men who bring their sexually dextrous partners home a similar phenomenon often occurs; as they say in Thailand, 'You can take the girl out of the bar, but you can't take the bar out of the girl', a point illustrated in the Australian film *Priscilla, Queen of the Desert*, in which a Thai wife escapes the clutches of her husband for an evening to perform tricks with ping-pong balls in a local bar.

Beach boys enjoy a position in Caribbean culture quite unlike that of female prostitutes. There is no stigma attached to their work; rather than being described as *putas* or whores they are beach boys or players. In an environment in which young men are often economically marginalised, expressions of sexual potency provide access to one of the few available socially respected power bases. This sexual potency is expressed through womanising, having affairs while married or fathering children by a variety of different women – poor man's riches.

A sexual relationship with a white woman, even while she may be the economically dominant partner, boosts this sense of worth in a way that a relationship with a local woman might not; apart from the status of having seduced a white woman, such a relationship does not threaten the beach boy's sense of masculinity, which demands on him by local women to act as a provider, a source of money, may well do.

But if the beach boys themselves are celebrated by their peers, the same cannot be said of many female sex tourists, who are often considered 'loose': the gendered stereotypes of stud and whore apply here as elsewhere. As one Jamaican man put it: 'Rassclat! That woman went with three different men last night. She act like a one-woman Oxfam shop.'

PLAYGROUND

> ... the heavy, mute spell of the wilderness – that seemed to draw him to its pitiless breast by the awakening of forgotten and brutal instincts, by the memory of gratified and monstrous passions. This alone ... had beguiled his unlawful soul beyond the bounds of permitted aspirations.
>
> Joseph Conrad, *Heart of Darkness*

The term 'paedophile' is a clinical description of an adult with a personality disorder involving a specific and focused sexual interest in children who have not reached puberty. The condition is extremely rare, and the term is often misused due to confusion over what constitutes a child. The UN defines as a child anyone who is under eighteen, and organisations set up to combat child sex tourism tend to concur with this definition, although the age of consent in some Western countries is as low as twelve. This makes it difficult to quantify the levels of paedophilia in child sex tourism; but that some exists is beyond question. Because very few countries feature large numbers of prostituted pre-pubertal children – Costa Rica, the Philippines, Cambodia and Vietnam today – those that do tend to attract the bulk of these abusers.

Most of what is termed 'child sex tourism' does not involve paedophilia but rather girls and boys in the young stages of puberty, and is as such not sold as niche prostitution to tourists with sexual pathologies, but rather as part of mainstream prostitution. There are many factors contributing towards the popularity of this phenomenon. Some tourists use racist stereotyping to argue that children grow up faster in these countries, and are sexually available at an earlier age:

Sex is a natural thing [in the Dominican Republic].
Everyone's at it, fathers do it with their daughters, brothers
do it with their sisters, they don't care. They'll do it with
anyone, they do it with everyone, they don't care who it is or
how old they are. They're like animals. That's the only way I
can explain it to you . . . By the time a girl is ten years old,
she's had more experience than . . . well, an American
woman or an Irish woman won't ever have that much
experience in her whole life . . . Girls learn it's the way to
keep a man happy. It's natural to them, it's a natural way to
please them.

American sex tourist, Dominican Republic

Some, put off by the growing commercialism of sex tourism
in their Shangri-La, favour younger and younger prostitutes:

The little girls, ten or twelve years old, I wouldn't describe
them as innocent, they're not innocent, but they're fresh. They
don't have the attitude of the older whores. The older whores
have gone downhill. They use foul language. They drink.
They're hardened. The little girls, they're not experienced.
They're not hardened, they want to please you, they don't
know what to expect, you get a better service from them.

German expatriate, South Africa

Some institutions play on such desires in the way they present
their prostitutes:

On one of my visits to a major Bangkok massage parlor, I
was comfortably sitting in the lobby and discussing with an
attendant the various attributes of the many girls behind the
glass wall. Picking out the best looker out of four or five in a
bar is easy. Picking out the best from over 80 gals arrayed for
your inspection is difficult.

Quietly, my helper suggested that perhaps I would be
interested in seeing what also was available in one of the
special bar areas. What he alluded to made my heart race
wildly. He said that in there they had some 'young ones'.

Seeing how most Thai women in their twenties look in their teens to me, this was something that I had to see!

Inside the other room off of the lobby, which actually was a small bar, sat about twelve little girls watching TV. As we entered, they were watching, playing grabass, and giggling! On a command from my attendant, they all sat back up on the couches and smiled at me, giving me their full attention. Before me sat the twelve, with the youngest at my guess about twelve. It was obvious that these young things had not yet matured into ladies . . . their giggles and squirming quickly gave them away. No dummies either, the establishment had made no attempts to dress them sexy, but rather clothed them in young girl outfits befitting their age.

I couldn't restrain myself! I had to have one of them.

www.wsgforum.com

For a number of tourists, virgins are the preferred sexual partner: if not for reasons of power – as proof or enhancement of virility – then because of fears of AIDS. Some 'virgins' are sold as such a number of times, elective anorexics fitted with ersatz hymens and put back on the street. The desire for younger and younger prostitutes in the belief that they will not be infected with HIV/AIDS – which has its horrific mirror in the baby rapes of sub-Saharan Africa, where sex with virgins is said to cure a man of AIDS – stems from a misconception about the way AIDS is transmitted. Transmission of the disease is in fact easier with barely pubescent or pre-pubescent sexual partners than with adult partners, as penetrative sex is more likely to involve organic damage.

Some tourists believe that they are not engaging in abuse, as the children approach them and offer them sex, and are often paid in gifts. The justification is used also in mainstream male and female sex tourism, in which the tourists, rather than exploiting an individual, feel that they are helping out those less privileged than themselves. But although child sex tourists are accused of not facing up to the truth about these transactions, such a gift-giving system can help a child in the developing world retain a sense of his or her integrity: the transaction is rationalised and pride taken in helping the family economically, while by contrast to be called a prostitute is invariably an insult. The denial works both ways.

Some men engage in the sexual abuse of girls in the full knowledge of what they are doing, as a form of revenge against women. The work of psychologist Robert Stoller identifies certain men as 'women-haters' who resent the control exercised over sexual access (to which they feel they have a biological right) by women. These men characteristically use, and often beat up, prostitutes, and have a marked propensity to abuse children. Their psychopathology, argues Stoller, is constructed from a triad of hostility: *rage* at being forced to give up the bliss of the womb and early identification with the mother, *fear* of not being able to escape the orbit of the mother's influence, and a need for *revenge* against her – and all women – for putting him in such a predicament.

For some the curiosity sparked off by being far from home and in a position of financial power leads to experimentation with young partners. As Sudarat Srisang, spokeswoman for the organisation FACE (Fight Against Child Exploitation), put it:

> . . . *industrial society gives people the idea that they have a right to spend, especially when they go somewhere else where all the social constraints are in abeyance. You see people dressed for the beach walking in Bangkok. It does not matter what you do on vacation in the 'Somewhere Else', it doesn't matter how badly you treat the people, how you violate their customs and social values. This is the malignancy of tourism. And when anything goes, it is not long before even the most vulnerable, the children, fall victim to the strange tastes that arise from this urge to try something new, taste the exotic. It is, above all, racist. Away from home, they are not Mr X or Mr Y, they won't be judged. At home, they may be a teacher, a professor, something respectable; but in a strange land, they can do anything, no one will know.*

That tourism can incorporate an exploration of transgression we saw in the first chapter; for some this transgression may act as a kind of revenge on forms of authority at home, a gleeful revelling in 'getting away with it' outside the jurisdiction of what are seen as repressive regimes.

Tourism is also in a sense a return to the world of childhood – a world in which desires can be sated instantaneously, in which the pressures of work or responsibilities of adulthood vanish temporarily. From one perspective, a key motivation for tourists is the search for Eden. The child appears to offer a forbidden route back to this prelapsarian world, but while this fantasy is deeply rooted in our culture, it is usually expressed only through a sentimental reverence for the innocence of children. Travel allows other interpretations to be explored – yet, rather than enabling a true return to innocence, this tourism destroys what it seeks, violates it in the consumption.

And the fantasy is deeply rooted in our culture. The recent hysteria over paedophilia in the UK and the USA needs to be seen in the context of the obsessive celebration of youth and sexuality in mainstream Western media; whether we look at the popularity of 'school disco' parties in which adult women dress as schoolgirls, the waif-like look characteristic of many fashion models, or the virgin/whore axis explored by Britney Spears, 'barely legal' seems to be the watchword for the sexual dysfunction of Western culture. In this context, it hardly seems surprising that the potential for exploring this potent nexus of desire – celebrated in fantasy but punished in reality in the West – is realised in practice by many sex tourists.

Who are the child sex tourists? All 240 sex tourists who were arrested for sexual offences involving children in Asia between 1989 and 1996 were men. As for their jobs, people in positions of trust towards children at home were massively over-represented, with the largest group being teachers, and doctors and clergy not far behind. In terms of age, 7 per cent were aged 20–30, 18 per cent 30–40, 33 per cent 40–50, 24 per cent 50–60, 15 per cent 60–70 and 3 per cent over 70. In at least two instances (Douglas Black and Brett Tyler), British paedophiles who have killed or been involved in killing children in Britain have either planned or practised sex tourism in Southeast Asia.

Not all child sex offenders are male. Recent studies have shown that female sexual abuse of children is probably far more common than is generally assumed, due to a widespread unwillingness to believe that women can be sexually abusive. There is anecdotal evidence of women using erection-inducing drugs on pre-pubertal children in Vietnam; quite apart from issues of abuse, the prolonged use of such drugs has a damaging effect on a child's health.

How do the child sex tourists know where to go? The Internet is routinely blamed as an enabler for child sex tourism nowadays, but is far from the only, or first, source of information. Magazines including *Mankoff's Lusty Europe* (published in 1973) and *The Discreet Gentleman's Guide to the Pleasures of Europe* (published in 1975) revealed where 'Lolita-eyed nymphets and ten-year-old prostitutes' could be found.

Expatriates have been known to run networks helping men satisfy similar tastes. North American Richard Casper moved to San Jose, Costa Rica, in the early 1990s, to set up a brothel called the BBC and an associated online escort service called 'Costa Rica Nights', which advertised itself as offering prostitutes aged eighteen or older. In November 2000 he was arrested for procuring schoolgirls aged between twelve and fourteen for sex sessions costing between $300 and $400; police also seized over 600 pornographic photos featuring underage girls that Casper was alleged to be distributing with Italian and Costa Rican business partners.

Briton Freddie Peats ran a boarding house for children in Goa, India, between 1984 and 1991. In 1996 he was found guilty of both abusing and prostituting them, which involved, according to the prosecution:

Photographing them in unnatural and obscene postures . . . transmitting obscene photographs abroad . . . having sexual intercourse . . . with the children . . . [procuring] children . . . for purposes of prostitution . . . sponsoring the boys under his care and control with those who called on him, especially foreigners, in order that they could abuse them sexually.

In 1996 British travel agent Michael Clarke was sentenced to sixteen years in jail in the Philippines, after being caught promoting child prostitution tours to the archipelago following an undercover operation conducted by Christian Aid. Clarke's brochure promised clients an 'Adult Disney World', admission to which would cost them just £600; they were encouraged to 'choose your mount' after taking 'a short Jeep ride into "Sin City" to a very special establishment, the OK Corral, where dozens of headstrong fillies are tethered!'

Clarke offered to arrange 'chickens' – child prostitutes – for a Christian Aid worker who posed as a potential customer. The undercover worker was told that to have sex with a twelve-year-old, 'You have to give her a nice time and treat her to, say, hamburger and chips, something she's probably never eaten before. Then she'll do what you ask her for.'

Until recently there has been very little legal risk for child sex tourists. Most child prostitutes are themselves children of prostitutes, or at least belong to the poorest sector of a community; there is often collusion between the guardians of a child and the abuser; if a foreign tourist is caught he can usually pay a bribe not to face charges; and sometimes the tourist's home country appears happy to put up with such abuse so long as it happens abroad – several European embassies have allegedly helped their nationals flee child sex abuse charges abroad. Other legal problems also contribute to the low level of risk to the tourist, as explained in a 1994 ECPAT [End Child Prostitution in Asian Tourism] newsletter:

> Most government officials are confused because of conflicts between the government's tourism promotion policy and child sexual abuse suppression policy . . . The staying periods in the host country of foreigners are usually short. Thus when offences become known the foreigner has already left the country. It is very difficult to locate the victimised children, who may be homeless or from broken homes, and to persuade them to testify in court. They do not want to be witnesses because they believe that they are guilty too.

Pressure during the 1990s from NGOs such as ECPAT and FACE forced Western countries to acknowledge the crimes their citizens were committing against children in the developing world. 'Extra-territorial legislation' was passed in the mid-to-late 1990s by most Western European countries, Australia and New Zealand, through which their citizens would be liable at home for child sex offences committed overseas.

The first Briton convicted in the UK under the new legislation (in Britain it was covered in part two of the Sex Offenders Act, passed in 1997) was Gerald Draper, a 64-year-old campsite owner who abused British children in France. In an unlikely twist on child sex tourism, the tourists were in this case the children being abused. Draper ran a campsite in Brittany, *Le Grand Motives* (sic), the land for which he'd bought in 1993. After failing to establish a nudist colony on the site, he built a campsite which was advertised in brochures as a family resort.

But only certain kinds of family were encouraged to apply. Draper turned away those families that would not include young children, and used a marker pen to highlight the ages of potential victims on requests for bookings. He was friendly with children, and soon won the trust of parents, after which he spent long hours playing with their children around the campsite – in the swimming pool, in the woods or on the swings. He assaulted young girls during babysitting and 'entertainment' sessions, telling them that it would be 'their little secret'.

It didn't stay secret for long. Some parents complained, and when police arrested Draper at his home in Exeter in January 2000, he told officers that he had a psychic rapport with children – 'They are good enough for Jesus, they are good enough for me.' He pleaded guilty to assaults on five girls aged from five to twelve, and was sentenced to three years in prison in the UK.

The difficulty in some countries of implementing the new legislation is demonstrated by the following case. Alexander Langenscheidt, a German engineer highly respected in his local Swiss community, was arrested in November 1995 in the Philippines after having been caught by police in a taxi with a twelve-year-old girl. A brief investigation into the engineer's activities on holiday revealed repeated abuse of underage girls and their appearance in pornographic films he produced and distributed.

He was released on bail of 200,000 pesos (£5,000), which he skipped after being issued with a new passport by the German embassy, fleeing first to Germany then to Switzerland.

Less than a year later Langenscheidt was arrested in the Czech Republic, which he'd visited many times during the 1990s. He was charged with unlawful sexual contact with at least nine girls aged between five and seventeen, some of whom he had deflowered, producing and distributing pornographic films featuring the girls, and drugging some of them into submission. Most of the victims were Romany girls – gypsies, the group most discriminated against in the Czech Republic.

This arrest followed a complaint to the police made by a girl prostitute who'd been offered to Langenscheidt and rejected. The girl complained to her uncle, who tried to make the engineer pay despite the fact that no sex had taken place. When Langenscheidt refused, the uncle took the girl to the police and laid charges against the engineer of rape and deprivation of liberty. When police visited Langenscheidt's hotel room they found him having sex with three girls aged between twelve and fifteen, which he was recording on video.

When his apartment in Zurich was searched, over a hundred videos were found depicting him in unlawful sex acts with girls, many of whom were Filipino. But because his crimes had been committed in many different countries, and because he was a German citizen living in Switzerland, the information shared between the countries, each of which held one piece of the criminal jigsaw, was minimal. He was finally charged in January 1998 of administering heroin, abducting minors and committing sexual acts with minors, and received a sentence of just two and a half years' hard labour.

The difficulty in implementing the new legislation enabling child sex tourists to be charged in their own countries is not its only flaw. Tellingly, it contains no provision for the care of the children abused. There is nothing in the way of follow-up counselling, and many children are so traumatised by the police attention and publicity given to their case that they leave whatever care they were in and usually end up homeless. The legislation is clearly not designed to protect these children, but rather to send a moral message to the countries' own voters, and to the world at large.

The zeal with which child sex tourism is damned again has little to do with actual sympathy with the children involved; it is, rather, indicative of the guilt felt by many Western nations at having created and maintained a situation in which such exploitation can occur. Child sex tourism is simply one detail in the wider picture of child exploitation in the developing world – once a child is seen as a potential source of revenue, it is not long before all avenues are explored. A consideration of the power differentials at play, and Western complicity in maintaining structures of gross inequality, are sidestepped by Western media and governments in favour of a focus on monstrous paedophiles and children sold into sex slavery.

The same phenomenon occurs in mainstream sex tourism. The economic exploitation that underpins sex tourism is a distillation rather than a perversion of the prevailing Western attitudes towards the developing world, in creating exploitative FTZs (Free Trade Zones) and insisting that their governments maintain non-unionised, cheap labour forces to feed Western profit. It is almost as though the structural adjustment programmes and tourist development policies pursued for poor nations by world financial institutions were expressly designed to encourage sex tourism – as indeed, in the case of Thailand, they may well have been. Global inequalities are exacerbated until all the inhabitants of certain poor nations have left to sell are their bodies.

Virtually any country in which sex tourism is popular supports this reading: Cuba, economically destroyed by US trade embargoes and the collapse of the Soviet bloc; the Dominican Republic, its currency devaluation mandated by the IMF to encourage export manufacturing in exploitative FTZs, with an attendant rise in prostitution; and Jamaica, where traditionally high unemployment levels were exacerbated by the Structural Adjustment Programs initiated in 1977 by the IMF and the World Bank. Tourism is promoted as a solution to Jamaica's woes, but has in fact led to the growth of enclaves of privilege that exclude most locals, extensive drug trafficking and prostitution, soaring prices and environmental degradation. For many Jamaicans tourism is the new sugar.

But sex tourism is treated as though it existed in a vacuum – the perverse tourist is foregrounded in media coverage, with no exploration of the wider issues enabling him to realise his desires. It has become a lightning rod for liberal guilt about Western exploitation of the developing world; sex tourists are for most in the West a monstrous 'other': they are not us, and they distract attention from our own complicity as consumers.

Yet sex tourism is in a sense indistinguishable from tourism in general. Tourism is a socially sanctioned escape route into fantasy: sex is another, and it's not unusual that the two should often merge. Are young Europeans travelling to Club 18–30 in Spain sex tourists? In a sense, yes. Being away from home, and being in a sultry climate, encourages sexual permissiveness – even the language used to describe temperature has sexual connotations, whether *caliente* or frigid. The holiday romance, or at least the hope of one, is a strong motivating force for tourism; and sometimes a holiday romance can end up being just as exploitative as paying for sex.

Holidays are routinely sold using images of scantily clad women, with brochures typically featuring an almost pornographic repetition of bikini, bottom and sun lounger. They also rely on selling the potential holidaymaker the idea of the exotic 'other', of the 'difference' available to them as a cultural consumer; as long as this is a key drive in tourism advertising, mainstream tourism will continue to promote sex tourism.

And is all sex tourism so bad? Certainly not in the wider context of exploitation. Sex work is often described as being both safer and better paid than working in sweatshops, or doing whatever other jobs are usually available. Sex tourists tend to pay local individuals directly, which is unusual in the context of modern tourism, in which tourist enclaves are often run by multi-national companies, leaving little money to return to the community. Some view working with sex tourists as an opportunity to escape – to leave the country, or at least the poverty line. The voice of sex workers in the developing world is rarely heard; perhaps, much as sex tourists project their own fantasies on to them, so too do Western researchers seeking insights into sex tourism.

Ultimately, although racist and imperialist assumptions are clearly made by sex tourists, and the context within which sex tourism operates is clearly exploitative, the pursuit of exotic sex also springs from a desire to penetrate, or be penetrated by, a foreign culture. Even though Westerners have had more opportunity to explore their exotic desires, those desires cut both ways – the drive to miscegenation is not confined to those in positions of power. The principal motivation of the first Tahitian who ever went to the West was for *les femmes blanches*.

Sex tourists and sex workers are individuals, with individual motivations and desires that may not fit any easy generalisation. By homogenising sex workers in poor countries as exploited victims of neo-colonial development, we also lose the sense of these women as subjects. Employment in the sex industry is just one facet of their lives – a job they do, usually just for a short time; they will not regard themselves simply as 'prostitutes' or 'sex workers'. Rather than seeing themselves in terms of the global sex traffic or as victims of the political economy, their work is put into context by issues of employment opportunities, family responsibilities and dreams of a better life.

Relations with foreign tourists are often seen as an opportunity for leaving the sex industry for good, and are thus seen in romantic or at least benign terms. In a country like Thailand, where householders are routinely jailed for raping, beating or killing maidservants, generous white men are a dream ticket for many girls.

And by homogenising sex tourists as grotesque, exploitative lechers in turn, we deny the possibility of mutual attraction, or a recognition of the vulnerability engendered for the sex tourist by an awareness that his masculinity is yoked to his wallet.

AFTERWORD: INTO THE BLACK

> *I think they ought to get the French police down here. The French are terribly good at things like this. But of course they can't. This is Italy.*
>
> Patricia Highsmith, *The Talented Mr Ripley.*

The archetypal tourist fear – of incompetence and corruption abroad, swarthy baggage-handlers rummaging through luggage or stony-faced policemen deaf to protestations of mugging or theft – is nowhere more justified than when tourists lose their lives.

A *mañana* mentality works both ways. What appeals about relaxed, *laissez-faire* attitudes – a loose interpretation of the law, or an endemic corruption that allows penalties for minor infractions to be paid off immediately – soon shocks when the tourist is a victim of crime. Many go abroad seeking an exotic yesteryear, a zone in which civilisation has not yet fixed its steely grip, where they can play at being pioneers on the world's final frontiers; but some find that this wildness is far more than they had bargained for.

In many of the cases listed in the previous chapters, parents of loved ones who have gone missing abroad have started to conduct their own investigation, in desperation at perceived failings on the part of foreign police. The families of those missing in Himachal Pradesh have formed their own task-force, convinced that the truth is out there; even in Australia the parents of Ivan Milat's victims hired private investigators, certain that their case was not being handled with the due attention.

And sometimes these fears are justified. Take for example Joanne Masheder, the British backpacker who was found raped and murdered by a Buddhist monk in a cave in Western Thailand. The Thai authorities initially refused to acknowledge even that she was missing, forcing her father to travel around the country in a desperate search to retrace her last steps.

This is the untold story of backpacker land – the posters, the notices in Internet cafés and guesthouses; the gaunt faces of those who have dedicated months or years to tracking down friends, partners, sons or daughters. Very few will help them. Most backpackers are too fixed on their own enjoyment to let the darkness of murder, the harrowing face of grief, distract them; enquiries are met with a blank face, minds already skipping ahead to the next beach party, the next casual fling.

Even the authorities in many countries prefer to ignore tourist murder. The Thai police during Charles Sobhraj's reign of terror buried his victims' bodies swiftly, in unmarked paupers' graves; coroners' reports were cursory, finding that these broken-necked tourists had drowned. Above all, other tourists must not be put off; waves must not be made. Some families who post notices and scour guesthouses for information find that after their departure posters are taken down, every trace of their investigation erased. Tourism is big business. Nobody likes it when people make trouble.

And in some instances it is the police themselves who are the criminals; a gang of rogue policemen in Thailand killed an average of two Chinese tourists a month over seven months during 1994, and tales of police planting drugs on tourists in order to force them to pay bribes are legion.

Sometimes the certainty desperately needed by parents and families – to know what happened, to have a line drawn under tragedy by the conviction of a killer – is denied them, its place taken by recriminations, rumour and incompetence. The murders of British tourists Julie Ward and Kirsty Jones, who lost their lives in Kenya and Thailand respectively, are still unsolved. In both cases rumours of cover-ups have circulated; in both cases their parents have vowed never to give up in the struggle to bring their killers to justice.

'NOTHING ADDED TO NOTHING MAKES NOTHING'

Julie Ward had been due to return to England in September 1988. She had fallen in love with Africa on her trip, which had lasted since February, and hoped to turn her new passion – wildlife photography – into a career. A week before the

28-year-old was due to take her flight home, she visited the Maasai Mara game reserve, in south-west Kenya, one last time.

This vast national reserve, at the northern tip of the Serengeti ecosystem, is one of the most popular tourist attractions in Kenya, visited by about a quarter of a million people each year. They come to see the wildlife – more than a million wildebeest, hundreds of thousands of zebra, gazelle and other antelope follow the seasonal rains every year, flanked by scavengers and hunters who prey on the weak; the big cats; the elephants, rhino and hippos – and the Maasai people themselves, visible in tourist villages in which they sell photo opportunities and handcrafted jewellery. It is not unusual today to see young Maasai men wearing Nike trainers.

It was the migration, one of nature's greatest spectacles and an unmissable experience, that drew Julie Ward. She set off with an Australian, Dr Glen Burns, but they were soon stranded in the reserve when their jeep broke down. They were near a reserve lodge, at which they spent the night, and Burns returned to Nairobi the next day to collect a spare he could send back to Julie.

But in his absence she managed to repair the jeep and headed to the Sand River campsite, where she spent the next night. According to reports at the time, she then ignored advice about the dangers of the drive and set off for Nairobi, nine hours away. She was last seen alive on 8 September 1988.

Burns soon found that Julie was no longer at the camp, and nor had she made it back to Nairobi. He alerted local police and Julie's father, who flew to Kenya and organised spotter planes to fly over the reserve. It didn't take long to find the jeep, SOS written in the dust on its roof. It was abandoned. A few hours later parts of her body were recovered by Simon Makallah, chief warden of the reserve; he said that he had followed vultures circling above the remains of a fire, by which he found part of a leg and part of a jaw, which had been sliced in half. Six weeks later her skull was found.

The Kenyan authorities denied that she had been murdered. They suggested that she had committed suicide – which prompted her father to comment, 'Yeah, she cut off her leg and jumped in the fire. Very likely' – or that she had been killed by wild animals. The official Kenyan post-mortem was doctored to state that her leg had been torn off, suggesting the work of a big cat; both an earlier version and a British autopsy by contrast reported that it had been cut cleanly off.

The suggestion that an animal had been responsible for a human murder recalled stories of 'leopard men'. These hired assassins had terrorised villages in East Africa during the first half of the twentieth century, wearing leopard skins on their backs and metal claws on their hands and feet; they used the claws to tear at their victims and left tracks which tricked people into thinking their murders were the work of animals.

John Ward conducted his own investigation, barely able to believe that the Kenyan authorities refused to launch a murder enquiry, and he hired private detectives to help him build a case. It was suggested that the Kenyan government was not only keen to do nothing to disturb the lucrative tourist trade, but also that they were reluctant to help their former colonial governors. They were independent now, and didn't take kindly to being told what to do, or to suggestions that they couldn't conduct a proper investigation themselves.

Ward deliberately courted publicity, hoping that the media glare would take its toll on Kenyan intransigence, and smuggled evidence out of the country. It took over a year for the Ward family to hear a Kenyan court state that Julie had been murdered.

Her father was convinced that the Sand River campsite held the key to the investigation – Julie's signature had been forged on signing-out forms, and he was sure that she had either been abducted from the site or murdered within it. The principal suspect, as far as he was concerned, was Makallah.

But Scotland Yard detectives, brought in after the intervention of the then UK Foreign Secretary Douglas Hurd, maintained that she had probably left the site willingly to drive to Nairobi, gone off-road and had been trapped when her jeep became stuck in a gully.

They believed that she was found by two rangers and kept captive by them for five days, during which time she was sexually assaulted, then murdered. They named Peter Kipeen and Jonah Migiroi as suspects in 1990, deaf to Ward's protestations that in his opinion his daughter had never left the campsite alive.

The rangers were acquitted due to a lack of evidence six months into a trial during 1992, and Ward made an official complaint to the British Police Complaints Authority that Scotland Yard had not conducted a thorough enquiry. According to him they had fallen victim to a conspiracy aimed at drawing attention away from the Sand River campsite.

The trial judge made the first public acknowledgement of corruption in the case, stating that there had been a cover-up to protect the country's tourist industry, at its peak Kenya's largest foreign-exchange earner. He insisted that police should investigate three other men in the reserve – Makallah, David Nchoko and Gerald Karori – but at the time nothing was done.

Over a year later, another story emerged. Valentine Kopido told Ward that Julie had been murdered after she stumbled on a smuggling operation involving a high-ranking politician and Israelis. It was a conspiracy story, but not the one Ward favoured; sceptical, he cross-checked the allegations and asked Scotland Yard detectives if they could find flaws in the story Kopido – who claimed to be privy to this information from his days as a government chauffeur – told. But Kopido's story held water until 1996, when he was exposed as a fraud after writing a letter to the Wards purporting to be a character reference from a Kenyan politician.

Finally, the embarrassment of having Ward keep interest in the case alive drove the Kenyan authorities to launch another investigation, offering him their complete co-operation. In 1997 they put an independent police team at his disposal. As a result of their investigation, Makallah was arrested and charged with the murder. But the warden was acquitted by the trial judge, who said that the prosecution offered only circumstantial evidence, and concluded that 'Nothing added to nothing makes nothing.'

Police in Britain began a fresh inquiry in November 2001, hoping that advances in forensic testing could help them resolve the case. Ward has spent over £500,000 pursuing his investigation – some of which has been paid by Kenyan authorities following a threat of legal action – and has visited the country over a hundred times. Despite the two unsuccessful murder trials, he has not given up hope of bringing his daughter's killer to justice.

'WE JUST KEEP ON FIGHTING'

Kirsty Jones, from Tredomen, near Brecon, South Wales, was taking some time off after having graduated from Liverpool University. She had been travelling around Thailand for three months on her way to Australia, and was staying at the £1-a-night Aree guesthouse in Chiang Mai, 420 miles north of Bangkok. The area is a typical backpacker zone, its streets lined with Internet cafés, cheap food stalls and second-hand bookshops, their shelves overflowing with yellowed Robert Ludlum and Wilbur Smith paperbacks. Many tourists stay there for months, reluctant to leave a situation in which drugs are cheap and easily available, and in which everybody minds their own business.

On 10 August 2000 she was raped and strangled to death in her room. She was 23. It's not even clear when her body was found, or exactly who found it. The maid, who initially told police she had found the body at 4 p.m., later retracted her statement, and revealed that she had been 'leant upon' to make it. Police theorised that Surin Chanpranet, a diminutive Thai man who ran a massage school in the upstairs half of the building, was the first person to find the body, some five hours earlier. Before police were called, many people had already been inside her room, including an entire Thai television crew.

Whether the delay in reporting the discovery of the body was the result of panic or a cover-up, it meant that the investigation floundered from the start. Police initially interviewed eight men – six foreigners and two Thai nationals – from the guesthouse, each of whom was considered a possible suspect.

Their descriptions read like a cross-section of the seamier end of the Thai backpacking world. Stuart Crichton, a 28-year-old Australian street-fighting enthusiast, who was held in custody after police allegedly found heroin and cannabis in his room; Glen, an American ex-Mormon, who also claimed to be an ex-CIA agent, and who had come to Thailand to recover from head injuries incurred in a car crash; Nathan Foley, a 27-year-old Australian, who had had dinner with Kirsty on the night of her murder, and who was initially interviewed by police for thirteen hours; and Steven Trigg, a 27-year-old bearded Briton who had been backpacking for four years.

It was Trigg who heard Kirsty scream, 'Leave me alone, leave me alone, get off me, get off me,' on the night of her murder. He and Chanpranet went to her room to investigate, but decided not to open her door, thinking that it was just a lovers' tiff. Thai police would later build on this assumption, surmising that Kirsty had not been raped at all, and that the strangulation – with a sarong – had been part of a consensual sex game that had gone horribly wrong. Her door had not been forced, indicating that she probably knew or trusted her killer. But her family was appalled by the suggestion that she had consented to being throttled during sex, and it was soon retracted, the Thai police then maintaining that she had been murdered.

The chief suspect in the early stages of the investigation was the guesthouse's British owner, 32-year-old Andy Gill. He had illegally bought the guesthouse after selling a house in Andorra (foreign nationals cannot by law own property in Thailand), and had been living off the rent since the previous November. He had been travelling to Thailand 'on and off' for twelve years and had a Thai wife. Police held him in custody for ten weeks before he was released due to insufficient evidence – he had maintained all along that he had been drinking in a bar at the time of the backpacker's murder. Less than a day later, he was again arrested, this time on immigration charges, as he had overstayed his visa by two years.

Rumours spread that Surin Chanpranet had allegedly attempted to frame Gill; the two were said to have had disagreements over the running of the guesthouse and Chanpranet's financial position, and it was thought that they would have been glad to see the back of each other. In the weeks leading up to Jones's murder, the hostility between Chanpranet and Gill was said to have reached ever higher levels, fuelled by the Thai's use of *ya-baa* and Gill's drinking. Both attempted to draw guests and colleagues into their circles, and pressure was mounting towards a confrontation. Then Kirsty Jones was killed.

An early news report in the British press claimed that it was 'only a matter of time before [the killer] is arrested, convicted and jailed'. Forensic tests on evidence left at the scene of the crime were thought to hold the key to the case, and plain-clothes detectives were assigned to shadow each suspect. But when the DNA tests failed to match any of the suspects, the investigation appeared to lose momentum.

While the British Embassy in Bangkok was keen not to criticise the police handling of the case, diplomatic officials privately admitted that it had been badly mishandled. The original chief investigator was taken off the case, and the regional chief in charge of the investigation retired shortly afterwards.

Leads were not followed up – the investigation's focus on Gill as their chief suspect was said to have blinded them to other possibilities; events on the street on the night in question, to which police were called, were not considered as a possible link; and reports that a Thai policeman, a good friend of Surin Chanpranet, had been hanging around the guesthouse that night were not acted upon until much later, when the Thai police, responding to rumours circulating around the country's ex-pat community, DNA-tested a number of their own officers. They refused to release the names of the suspects, and maintained that the tests exonerated them.

British police from the Dyfed Powys force flew to Thailand to help with 'specialist forensic matters', although they were at pains to point out that the case remained in Thai hands. Some sources speculated that the Thai authorities were unhappy about this involvement, which they considered patronising, and that they may have withheld certain items of evidence, including a four-page letter that Steven Trigg was alleged to have given to Thai police on leaving the country.

The Dyfed Powys police distanced themselves from claims that there had been a cover-up by their Thai counterparts, and from reports made in the British *Mail on Sunday* that a senior British police source had claimed that a group of Thai policemen were linked to the case as possible suspects. Wary of a diplomatic rift, spokesmen for the British force described the relationship between British and Thai police in terms of 'very good police to police co-operation'. The diplomatic stakes were raised when British Foreign Secretary Jack Straw brought up the issue of the murder with Thailand's foreign minister while discussing Thailand's involvement in the international peacekeeping force in Afghanistan.

The victim's parents were delighted that senior British police officers were to be involved in the investigation, considering it a 'breakthrough', especially as the Thai police were known to have been reluctant initially to work with them.

The British police officers returned to the UK with evidence believed to have included the sarong used to strangle Kirsty Jones, and then travelled back to Bangkok to present the results of DNA and forensic tests at the Thai national police headquarters.

The Thai police duly launched a new investigation based on the British evidence, DNA-testing six hill tribesmen related to a Chiang Mai farmer who was an early suspect in the case; his DNA was considered to be so close to that of the supposed killer that they were likely to be related. But the tests came back negative.

Thai police had just issued a report that they had 'a prime suspect, and soon the case will be completely solved, very soon', when local newspapers ran a story about two transvestites who had admitted to police that they had planted false DNA at the scene of the crime, allegedly at the instigation of Surin Chanpranet. While Thai police were initially quick to dismiss the stories as 'wild speculation', they did DNA-test a Pattaya transvestite sex worker whose sperm was said to have been placed at the site. Some commentators scoffed at the suggestion, maintaining that to involve *katoeys* – Thai 'lady-boys' or transvestites – in an investigation was characteristic of last-ditch attempts by Thai police to clear up unsolved crimes.

But in this case the news did anything but clear up the case. Faced with the possibility that crucial evidence had been destroyed before their arrival, and that misleading DNA evidence had been planted, Thai police admitted that they were now 'stuck'. The investigation had effectively come to the end, in the wake of accusations that Thai police had tortured suspects to make them confess, and uncertainty over whether the transvestites' story was to be trusted.

Two years after the murder of Kirsty Jones, her parents vowed to keep on fighting to have her killer brought to justice, releasing a statement in which they said:

> We have become increasingly frustrated by the misleading reports that seem to emerge from Thailand through the press. No sooner do we get our hopes of ever catching the killer raised than they are once again dashed. The one thing we want we cannot have, so we must continue to keep pushing to ensure that the guilty person is brought to justice. The correct person . . . Two years on and the missing and the hurt is no less, but we just hope that one day there will be a conviction. We just keep on fighting for Kirsty.

Her father went on, in an interview with BBC Radio Wales, to describe the Thai police enquiry as 'like something out of the 1930s – backward, slow, time-consuming, repetitive, with very few results'. He had earlier described Thailand as a beautiful country 'which has destroyed our lives'.

In the absence of any clear answer, speculation is rife as to what actually happened to Kirsty Jones. Some Internet postings refer darkly to the folk magic allegedly practised by Surin Chanpranet, who is said to have been ejected from the monkhood for sexual misadventure and a flirtation with the occult. Others agree with the initial Thai police statement that the murder resulted from a consensual sex act gone wrong. Whatever the case, it is unlikely now that the Thai police will ever solve the murder. As Kirsty Jones's father has pointed out, 'Somebody out there has taken our daughter, and he may do it again to someone else's.'

THE WORLD FOR SALE

MSN Expedia, Microsoft's travel branch, currently advertises its services with the slogan 'The World for Sale'. A similar message is conveyed in a recent Land Rover advertisement, in which an intrepid lone female tourist visits a primitive South American tribe to gather artefacts with which to decorate her apartment. The world is here portrayed as a series of experiences that are available for consumption for you, at least if you use the correct brands. Technology and privilege have made the world a giant theme park, its inhabitants on perpetual display.

But the world is not for sale. People live in 'paradise', and have lived there long before tourist development moved in. The individuals encountered on journeys to the exotic have a life beyond quaint photo opportunities, beyond acting merely as facilitators of tourist ease; they have their own needs and desires, too often sidelined in the gross inequities of the global economy.

For most tourists this is easy enough to ignore, whether by cultivating the negligent holiday mentality of package tourism or by surrounding themselves with other foreign tourists on longer journeys. Assumptions can be maintained, objectification encouraged: their hosts are uniformly friendly, or untrustworthy, or display some other uniform, determining characteristic.

For all this the tourist often desires to see the 'real' country, to have 'authentic' experiences; but such desires can be realised all too abruptly. Sometimes when the tourist bubble bursts, the 'real' country can seem far too close for comfort. In the face of real danger assumptions of Western privilege evaporate; fear reminds us of our common humanity, shrinking from the shadow of the greatest leveller of all.

Few holidaymakers will be as unfortunate as those described in these pages. But as tourism grows so too does its dark underbelly – with more people than ever on the trip of a lifetime, there are more than ever who seek to prey on them. Tread safely.

SELECT BIBLIOGRAPHY

Bishop, R. and Robinson, L. (1998) *Night Market*, Routledge, London.

Blackden, P. (2002) *Danger Down Under*, Virgin Books, London.

Buford, B. (1993) *Among the Thugs*, Secker & Warburg, London.

Fellows, W. (1998) *The Damage Done: Twelve Years of Hell in a Bangkok Prison*, Mainstream Books, Edinburgh.

Fromm, E. (1972) *The Anatomy of Human Destructiveness*, Penguin Books, London.

Garland, A. (1999) *The Beach*, Penguin Books, London.

Houllebecq, M. (2002) *Platform*, William Heinemann, London.

Littlewood, I. (2001) *Sultry Climates*, John Murray, London.

Milne, H. (1987) *Bhagwan: The God that Failed*, Sphere Books, London.

Neville, R. and Clarke, J. (1979) *Shadow of the Cobra*, Jonathan Cape, London.

Pelton, R.Y. (1998) *The World's Most Dangerous Places*, Fielding Worldwide, Redondo Beach, CA.

Seabrook, J. (1996) *Travels in the Skin Trade*, Pluto Press, London.

Thomson, T. (1981) *Serpentine*, Dell Publishing Co., New York, NY.

Whittaker, M. and Kennedy, L. (1998) *Sins of the Brother*, Pan MacMillan Australia, Sydney.